GODLESS NERDISTRY:
OR, HOW TO BE A BAG OF CHEMICALS AND STILL HAVE FUN

I0078877

By Dale DeBakcsy

Gentleman Scholars Publishing.
Castro Valley, CA.
2014.

Cover Design by Dario Sanchez-Kennedy.
Cover Art, *Onwards!*, by Count Dolby von Luckner.

Table of Contents

Part III: Good Reads, God Reads, and their Rare Intersection

Part IV: Science is the New Everything

THE LIGHTER SIDE OF
IMMINENT DESTRUCTION

Wednesday is, and has always been, my favorite day of the week. For on Wednesday, new comic books come out and we, the nerds, gather for breakfast, our pull lists clenched tightly in hand, to discuss our collective enthusiasms and disappointments, spending the hours until store opening in deliciously dorky speculation about the fate of Thor, the tragedy of Batwoman.

Every Wednesday, I wake up excited, eagerly awaiting what the greatest epic storytellers of our age (for such the current crop of comic writers are) have in store for me. Of course, it makes no sense to be excited. These comics, the minds that made them, and my eyes that will consume them, are all destined for absolute eradication. The universe will forget them, and in turn be forgotten itself in the vicious churn of cosmic evolution.

Getting nerdily excited about anything is a massive failure of perspective, a bit of presumptuous homocentrism that seems more at home in the thirteenth century than the twenty first. Every night, the facts of existence parade before me, screaming, "Whatever you're thinking about, it doesn't matter," as the stretch of time between now and my ultimate and complete erasing from the book of existence looms comically brief, no matter how I calculate it.

Every atheist, agnostic, and humanist knows these facts as well. But we keep on living and, by all accounts, have a grand time of it. How do we keep ourselves passionate about existence in the midst of such a gloomy destiny? How do we offer enjoyable lives to people who have left their own faith? My answer to that, as this collection of essays from 2012 to 2014 will show, is pure creative nerdistry – a passionate attachment to the passing whims of our collective experience on this planet, both those that have passed and those we are forging now. Getting as dopily enthusiastic about a Spider Man comic as a line of Tacitus, an elegant counterexample in mathematics as a piece of art featuring Abe Lincoln as a vaudeville lizard man.

So, come at me, universe. Do your worst. For, right now, I have a cat on my lap, a pile of comics and books about fops at my side, and a pesty but wonderful family to share them with. This moment is beautiful, and the next will be so too, and all of the terror of your gnashing entropy can't touch me here, in the lap of nerdistry, at the edge of unutterable oblivion.

Castro Valley,
October 20, 2014.

PART ONE:

Towards a Humanist Culture That Isn't Insufferably Smug.

WHEN ATHEISTS MOURN:
OR HOW I LEARNED TO STOP WORRYING AND LOVE CHEMISTRY

(Originally Published in Oct/Nov 2014 issue of *Free Inquiry*)

"So, what do you people feel at times like this?"

It was my grandfather's funeral, and in one version or another I was asked this question several times, *You People* being of course the polite way to say *Atheists*. My family members were genuinely curious whether a lack of belief in souls and gods made the process of grieving easier or harder to bear. I told them, and believe, that being an atheist makes no difference at all in what and how you feel, but all the difference in how recovery from tragedy unfolds. It is a tale written in chemistry, available to anybody willing to put some of their cherished self-conceptions aside, and offering some beautiful insights into how interconnected we truly are.

Why does the loss of a loved one, either through death or separation, hurt so much? The simple answer is that Other People Are Drugs. Of the best kind, mind you. Without them, our mind, quite literally, starts to disintegrate and everything that gives us a sense of meaning withers away. That's not just a flight of romantic excess, it is actually what happens on a biological level if we are removed from the mind-altering chemistries of sustained companionship.

Our parents set the pattern for how these systems of mutual chemical support work. When we are separated from our caretakers, a whole host of chemicals flood our brains, prompting us to cry out for our parents' return. In particular, the anterior cingulate, dorsomedial thalamus, and periaqueductal gray regions, all of which are tied to the processing and registering of pain, light up in a frenzy, making the absence of a loved one feel like physical pain. Even as adults, stimulation of the regions involved in this childhood separation response causes us to feel a sense of

8

indescribable loneliness and misery. For a child, it is only relieved with social interaction, with being touched and talked to and cared for.

When that happens, our brain is flooded with those endogenous opioids that our hardest of hard drugs work so hard to mimic. Crucially, however, simultaneously released oxytocin and brain prolactin dull the worst effects of those opioids, allowing us to take prolonged and deep satisfaction in human contact that can last a lifetime.

When we grow up, we still feel the quiet rush of oxytocin from physical contact, and the presence of loved ones still triggers those brain opioids that give a gathering of old friends its particular warm glow. But we develop other systems as well, anticipatory neural systems that allow us to experience pleasure from other people even when they aren't physically around. These systems and their unique chemical components are beautifully laid out in Jaak Panksepp and Lucy Biven's *The Archaeology of the Mind: Neuroevolutionary Origins of Human Emotion*, and their effects can be found in the pleasure we take in knitting a cap we know a friend will love or organizing twenty people to surprise a relative on their birthday. It's the same system that allows you pleasure just thinking about a refreshing glass of ice water on a hot day, regardless of if you have one at hand or not. These are the feelings that our body uses to motivate us towards the good things of the world, towards food and friends, laughter and sex. And there are few things that keep that system constantly humming like a relationship which inspires us to find ever new ways of pleasing others.

But what happens if we are cut off from this crucial source of social healing, if a trusted and beloved friend or lover is removed from our lives? The grief systems of separation kick in, just as they did when we were children, with the crucial difference that our caretaker isn't merely in another room, but is in fact gone forever. Robbed of the person who might make us feel whole again, stress sets in, and the dismal chemicals of that particular state start throwing their weight against us. Our hippocampus gets bathed in cortisol, which is all right for short periods of time, but if the stress lasts, if the mourning is deep, its presence starts killing off neurons and depleting our reserves of alternate happiness-inducing neural compounds. The hippocampus, source of our very memory, gradually erodes under the onslaught. We retreat into ourselves.

But chemistry isn't done with us yet, for those same pathways of grief slither into our anticipatory systems as well. The small daily pleasure of setting an extra place at lunch or calling our friend into the room to watch a funny YouTube bit is lost to us. There is nothing left to excitedly anticipate from that deceased person, and so a major dopamine-producing source of daily color and motivation is simply cut out from under us. The chemical resources that sustain our Get Up and Go motivational systems dry up under cortisol's withering attack, so not only are we miserable from the lack of those warm fuzzy chemicals of contentment which the other person's presence and touch gave us, but we can't even engage the systems that make us look for new ways to find beauty and satisfaction in the people we have left.

It takes a long time for this massive chemical structure to right itself, to accept our loss on a molecular level. Some people never recover – their loss too great, the other person's part in their day to day feeling of loving comfort too profound, to be overcome in months or years. We see the same thing in the children of negligent parents, whose lack of attention to their babies actually rewrites those children's brains on an epigenetic level, making it physically impossible for them to enjoy the fruits of a trusting and balanced relationship later in life. There is no greater testament to how much we touch each other's lives, how much we depend down to our very atoms on the presence of other people, than the cascade of chemical misery that their absence sets off.

There is deep and profound beauty in that fact which religious approaches to death can only ham-fistedly approximate. As atheists, we don't have to be ashamed about feeling fully the pain of loss, don't have to wonder if we are affronting God's plan by wishing with all our being for the return of those who have passed.

We don't have to stoically pretend that everything is all right and that our loved ones are in a better place.

Death is Not All Right.

Those we choose to love are our anchors to sanity itself – they are the preconditions of any happiness worth the name. "God has a plan" is the scantest of bandages on their loss, and evidence of the gravest underestimation of what we mean to each other. Better by far to recognize how much another person is wrapped up in us, their presence soaked into our cells, and let ourselves feel the full depths of disconnection as tribute to what was a life beautifully lived together than to paste over as quickly as possible their living memories with the Pollyannaism of Paradise.

And when we start at last recovering from our loss as new pathways of friendship and trust expand and thrive in our brain, perhaps we can take a look around at those people who live still, who love us, and know that we are inside of them, thoughts of us tapped into the source of their basic capacity to be happy. Maybe we shall be a little kinder to everybody we know as a result, aware of our stewardship of their joy and the capacity of passivity to do lasting harm.

This, then, is the comfort that we atheists have to offer others, as well as ourselves. A loved one is gone, to be seen and heard no more. But, that stomach-churning mourning that we feel from the moment that we open our eyes until we fitfully collapse into a restless sleep is our final testimony to their place in our lives, our assurance that we brought some good into their days. In a universe stacked absurdly against us, we found each other and built in each other's presence a small place to call home for a while, and no amount of sacred words spoken from a vain and attention-starved book can possibly match the beauty of that fact. We refuse to impose Jesus or any other celestial watchdog between us and the person we loved, forcing us to see that loved one as a ghostly shadow through some intervening theological construct. We want to see them fully as they stood in our lives, and feel the full force of our loss, and only then do we know that we are doing them and our shared time together justice.

And if, by observing how much a single human can penetrate into the inner world of another, we become a little less worried about our own demise in the process, well, that's not a bad thing either.

FURTHER READING:

Jaak Panksepp and Lucy Biven. *The Archaeology of Mind: Neuroevolutionary Origins of Human Emotion.* W.W. Norton and Company, 2012.
Sarah Blaffer Hrdy. *Mothers and Others: The Evolutionary Origins of Mutual Understanding.* Belknap Press, 2011.
Loretta Graziano Breuning. *Meet Your Happy Chemicals.* System Integrity Press, 2012.

SKEPTICAL ART:
WHY THE GREAT ATHEIST NOVEL
IS ALWAYS A DECADE AWAY

(Originally published in *The Freethinker*, July 2012)

Henry walked into a stationery store on a brisk bank holiday. The clerk asked him if he would like his receipt in the bag.
"It doesn't matter, I don't believe in God," Henry said.
The End.

Atheism always walks through the door in lead shoes. The fact that it is easier to smoothly introduce a character's love of medieval spoonware than his non-belief is the despair of those of us looking to craft balanced fictional representations of freethinkers. Civilization's long-standing collective horror of those who don't give themselves over to theological systems, our own veering between over-deferential timidity and unchecked bravado when put in the spotlight, and the structural complexity involved in making the *absence* of a belief system a driving force in a work of art have all conspired to keep the great atheist novel from surfacing.

There have been atheist writers - dozens and hundreds - conveying their life philosophy in works that are pro-science or anti-religion, and many of the greatest products of the human imagination belong to these. In grappling with the issue of representing atheists in fiction, however, these works all take it as given that the only way to make a story centering on a freethinking character interesting is to have him constantly engaging with the religious structures of the world until he is (often) crushed by them or (rarely) overcomes them in some generally implausible fashion.

The message is the same: atheists, by themselves in normal everyday life, are not the stuff of literature. We can let atheists get beaten to death by an angry mob of Christians for espousing evolution, but we cannot let them have a cup of coffee and read the morning paper. If a character is an atheist, that is more or less all they can be in the course of the story, their actions and comments all constantly referred to this one facet of their existence. This can be good fun - the surly side comments of Sinclair Lewis's roving peripheral atheists were the delight of my adolescent reading experiences - but attempts to build an entire fictional work around such characters have ended up as tedious as the characters in Christian fiction who cannot clean their cat's litter box without reflecting on God's glorious plans for the world. As long as this notion of atheists is the literary gold standard, both the public's perception of what freethinkers are, and our perception of ourselves, won't change appreciably from its current monotonality.

How do writers make the change from Atheist Heroes to Heroes Who Happen to be Atheists? There is not a tremendous amount of tradition to draw on. Prior to the twentieth century, when freethinkers showed up at all, they were as Cautionary Figures - Madness (Ivan Karamazov), Tragedy (the "grey men" of Dickens's post-1850 novels), and Intellectual Fraud (the Socrates of

Aristophanes) haunted their steps and twisted their lives. Even when portrayed sympathetically, they are doomed men, marching alone to destruction.

And so they had to be - to proclaim one's self an atheist or atheist sympathizer was, portions of mid-eighteenth century Europe excepted, the end of one's career and often one's life. The freethinker's right to Social Existence has only been conceded within the last century, and his ability to not only Exist, but Speak, is a development within living memory, with as yet unrealized issue in the creative realm.

We do not make it easy on ourselves. In the past decade and a half, freethinkers have crawled cautiously into the sun and found their voice, expounding without coming up for air millenia of pent up thoughts. All those Devastatingly Clever Things we'd been dying to say since the time of Constantine, and all the grievances that it would have been death to air centuries ago, are now flooding forth. And religion, with its sure instinct for self-dramatization, positively howls at the effrontery of this two percent of the population who unfairly wage war against the poor, defenseless ramparts of faith by callously bringing up things like Recorded History or the Suffering of Billions Under Religious Law. That characterization of freethinkers as unbalanced, bitter, arrogant Founts of Soul Venom has largely stuck (especially here in the United States), and we have responded to it with ever more clever articulations of our position, as if a surplus of Cleverness will eventually decide the day.

We are becoming who The Church wants us to be, defined by one of our beliefs, and driven back to egregiously limited tools of self-expression by that definition. It is devilishly hard to make compelling characters from such people, and this is why most attempts as of late to center stories on an atheist figure come across as cocky and self-satisfied to believers and rather uncomfortable to us. While making my own tale of non-belief, *The Vocate*, I agonized over these difficulties. Could I let go of history, both my own and that of the Church, and simply tell a positive story of people who are incidentally atheists, going about their lives? I sincerely tried, but in the end I had to resort to the practice of previous generations, and focused less on telling the story of non-belief and more on the conflicting, dangerous, and yet hilarious, nature of belief and beliefs. The humorous potential of world religion, and Voltaire's rallying cry of *Écrasez l'infâme!,* were too strong for me to resist. I am having tremendous fun telling this story, but I am under no illusions that this is the bold new step we need.

I rationalize this to myself by a comparison with that other long-suffering slice of society, the LGBT movement. There as well, the first generation that found its voice could not help but make Being Gay the touchstone of identity. The result in fiction was a lingering monodimensionality which has been steadily overcome as a new generation, more used to thinking of themselves and being thought of as individuals first, has manned the creative ramparts. Atheist creators are wrapped up in the same tendrils - still struggling with the balance of their identity, unable to prevent the burdens of centuries from speaking through their mouths - and all of this is good and as it should be, but perhaps it also means that our art must wait for us to hand over the reins of creativity before we can point to an atheist character in the fictional realm who is recognizable as a functioning and multi-faceted human being.

In the meantime, we can look to our children, and see in them the heroes that we often can't be, weighed down by historical baggage as we are - people who will say I'm An Agnostic with the same unconcerned matter-of-factness that they expound their preference for X-Box over Nintendo or cereal with marshmallows over that without. They will appreciate the work we have done, but they will have their own stories to tell. And what stories those will be - in about ten years.

GODLESS IN TIGHTS:
SIX GRAPHIC NOVELS EVERY HUMANIST SHOULD READ

(Originally Published at *The New Humanist*, April 2013)

For the last few months, atheist comic readers have had the delightfully guilty pleasure of cheering on a new character, Gorr, in the pages of Jason Aaron's *Thor: The God of Thunder*. Gorr's mission is simple – to free mortals from subservience and mental anguish by ridding the universe of all gods. His set speeches are Hitchens Gone Cosmic and, while he will almost inevitably be defeated by Thor in the end (the book *is* called Thor, not Gorr), his message that to believe in the gods is to poison the self is one that stands to have profound repercussions for how comics approach their more divine characters in the future.

Many reviews have treated this appearance of a largely sympathetic humanist anti-hero as something unprecedented in comics, but really it is more the full flowering of a process that began over three decades ago. While film and television were busy sensibly side-stepping the issue of atheism in media, the comic book industry took the initiative in producing a string of uncompromising narratives focusing on the problematics of divinity and the religious mindset. They make for powerful reading still. Here are six of my absolute favorites, with as few spoilers as I can possibly manage.

Preacher (1995, Garth Ennis). God's gone – ran off in 1994 and left a crew of too-righteous-to-be-bothered angels in charge of watching after Creation. And so it comes to pass that an unlikely trio consisting of a lapsed minister possessed by an angel-demon hybrid, his assassin ex-girlfriend, and a persistently foul-mouthed Irish vampire head off on a mission to find Jehovah and make him answer for his gross negligence. Deftly weaving between the barbarity of Christian theology and the camaraderie to be found in the very human pleasure of watching Laurel and Hardie with a good chum, Ennis turns the Bible inside out and lets its hidden twisted characters run wherever their fundamental natures dictate (the story of Jesus's last living descendent is so wrong it's delicious). In following those natures, he gives us often breath-taking insights into the tortured depths of theological creativity, and makes us wonder how such structures sprung from our collective fancy in the first place. Ultimately, he shows us that all of the forces of Heaven and Hell, the mammoth machinery of religious belief, are as nothing next to the bonds of friendship and dependence that link man to man. At turns hyper-violent and crushingly beautiful, thought-provoking and tea-spewingly hilarious, comics don't come much better than this.

There are also lots of boobs in it, so maybe not the best thing to read at work...

X-Men: God Loves, Man Kills (1982, Chris Claremont). The one that started it all? Claremont had already been writing *The Uncanny X-Men* for seven years when he penned this tale of the Reverend William Stryker and his evangelical crusade to rid the world of mutantkind. Its insights into the psychology of religious intolerance are things we have largely grown used to as they have been elaborated in decades of X-Men films and cartoons since, but there are scenes in this book that still have the power to chill. For me, the most visionary is a set of three pages in which Reverend Stryker is attempting to break Professor Xavier's will and convert him into a believer. The cycle of inflicting psychological agony and then proffering all-encompassing salvation is really the story of all religious conversion broken down to its brutal essence. The Church as a global scale case of Stockholm Syndrome. These themes have been revisited since in the X-Men titles (particularly in the current run of Uncanny Avengers), but there is an intensity and purpose to the original that has yet to be truly matched.

17

Archer and Armstrong (2012 and Ongoing, Fred van Lente). From the man who brought us *Action Philosophers* comes a tale of a ten thousand year old Epicurean fat man (Armstrong) who is well-nigh invulnerable and the Bible-Theme-Park-raised adolescent (Archer) who has been sent to kill him. The back and forth between Armstrong, who has seen a few world religions come and go in his day, and Archer, who believes with all the fervent righteousness of never having known differently, is consistently quick and clever, but what I love most is the scope of the narrative. By seeing the world through Armstrong's eyes, Christianity becomes the blip in history that it in fact is. There was life and purpose before Jesus, and there will be such after. And that's something that, particularly here in the United States, where Christianity is often seemingly omnipresent, we need to be reminded of from time to time.

Supergod (2011, Warren Ellis). Perhaps the most bleak but poignant sustained meditation on man's drive to craft deities even unto self-annihilation that has yet been published in comic form. It tells the tale of several nations' secret programs to create protector deities which instantiate various existential ideals. Once released, they act out to the fullest degree the consequences of the core beliefs that have been thrust into them, with chilling and disastrous effects for mankind. Ellis stares deep into the nihilistic, thoroughly anti-humanity core of our deity-smithing processes and forces us to confront the parts of ourselves that are so dependent upon these life-negating principles made divine. The great highlight for me is the confrontation between a British scientist and the god his team has developed. The god lays bare the grasping collective neurochemical dependence that forms the core of religious experience before defining the essence of the gods in the single sentence, "We are your STASH." That says almost everything that needs to be said.

Thor: Lord of Asgard (2002, Dan Jurgens). More Thor? Yes, more Thor. With over six hundred issues released since its inception in 1962, Thor is easily the comic of note when it comes to parsing the relationship between divinity and mortality. Many writers have used the platform as simply a stage for galactic-level fist fights. And those are fun, but every once in a while a writer comes along who sees the potential in Thor to tell a story that shines a light on something profound and disturbing in the order of the gods. Jason Aaron is doing it with devastating insight now, but a decade ago Dan Jurgens spun a story of such complexity that it's still difficult to craft a definite statement that captures all of the subtleties of his position. In this arc, which essentially starts in issue 553, Thor decides to stop serving humanity piecemeal and start devoting the full resources of Asgard to the betterment of life on Earth. Starvation, natural disaster, war – all are eliminated under the enlightened supervision of Asgard. The people, who find themselves no longer starving and oppressed, embrace the good work that is being done for them, particularly the creation of schools that allow them for the first time to learn the extent of their human rights and the nature of the world. Meanwhile, the heads of state and religion react savagely against the weakening of their power base, while religious zealots sabotage the new Asgardian clean energy plants and stage acts of martyrdom to discredit the new order. As you might have picked up, in these issues Jurgens is essentially retelling the trials of the Scientific Age. A new force arrives that heals you, makes your life easier and longer, connects the world in bonds of mutual interest, provides the sublime tyranny-defying mechanism of education, and calms the rage of the elements themselves. Science, though here it's called Asgard. Along the way, it makes a few old ideas seem awkward and unhelpful . By connecting people to each other, it works against the state's claim to absolute power and wisdom. By removing unnecessary suffering, it disarms the primary means of seduction by which religions gain followers. Their basic weapons taken from them, religion and government team up to undo the work of Asgard in a story that has been repeated again and again when science has threatened to give birth to new ways of thought.

By casting gods in the place of the usual forgers of Enlightenment and progress, Jurgens is able to tell stories about this recurring dynamic of progress and self-serving reaction to ears which would have rejected it in a more clearly positivist setting. In issue 557, when Thor addresses the UN for the first time, it is hard not to feel indignation at the wild accusations heaped upon Thor by petty tyrants. Such would not have been the case had it been, say, a lab-coated scientist on the podium. But the most brilliant stroke is yet to come, for this new Enlightenment IS being pushed forward by gods, gods who have not reckoned with the consequences of their own habitual lack of self-review (this is where Asgard most clearly parts ways with the scientific ideal) or with the impact their presence will have on a humanity given over all too easily to extremity in worship. How these oversights play out amongst the good intentions of the Asgardians makes for potent reading that is the perfect prelude to the extreme solution to the god problem that we see in the current story of Gorr, the God Butcher.

Silver Surfer: Parable (Stan Lee, 1988). The Silver Surfer has always had a special place in the legendary Stan Lee pantheon. While Lee used to employ the Fantastic Four to talk about issues of family and friendship, or Spider Man to plumb the depths of personal ethics, Silver Surfer was always the character he brought out to sound the biggest questions of mankind's goals and direction on the largest scale. In the first series, which ran for only eighteen issues in the late sixties, these questions tended to be resolved in a somewhat black and white manner. In issue three, for example, the Surfer faces off against Mephisto, who familiarly portrays himself as responsible for all the greed and suffering in the world. Not particularly nuanced. But then, two decades later, in 1988, Lee teamed up with the artist Moebius to write a two issue mini-series, *Silver Surfer: Parable,* in which the planet devouring force known as Galactus descends on the Earth. Having made a pact not to *directly* harm our planet, Galactus plans to use man's religious instincts to do the job for him. He lets the humans worship him and tear each other apart in their interpretations of his will. Central to the story is the character of Colton Candell, an evangelist who sees in Galactus the chance to become the greatest prophet of all time. Lee's conclusions about man's almost genetic need to worship resonate with those Ellis would express twenty three years later in *Supergod*, and the final pages express a pessimism about the human capacity for Enlightenment that all but smother the usual Lee ebullience. Within two years of *Parable*, the comic book industry threw itself into a Dark Age of foil holographic covers and style-over-story glitz that persisted for a half decade. But in those shimmering last moments of the old order of storytellers, a giant stood up, shook the dust from his pen, and poured forth the full measure of his concerns about the increasing sway of mass media based religion in public life. To many of us, it's the best story he ever told.

There are enough graphic novels, webcomics (I hear that The Vocate is *pretty* good... ahem), and single issue comics in a deeply humanist vein to fill out a list several dozen titles long, but in these six I see the germ of the several approaches that the medium has evolved since 1982. From the trust in humanity's ability to save itself through friendship that we find in Ennis, van Lente, and Claremont, to the dire skepticism born of man's chemical addiction to deities that Lee and Ellis evince, to the grand structural concerns of Jurgens and Aaron, the comic industry has given us a myriad of lenses through which we might observe the complexities of religion in a narrative context that makes you feel the weight of these issues in your very marrow. So, head out to your local comic store and pick up a couple of titles, then loan them to a moderately theistic friend when you're done. Because there are few gateways to humanism so reliable as a couple of beers and a good comic.

SOME TRICKS OF THE BRAIN: NEUROCHEMISTRY, THE WORLD OF WARCRAFT, AND THE END OF RELIGION.

(Originally Published in *American Atheist Magazine*, 4th Quarter, 2012.)

Every day over an intense period of a year and a half, I used to logon to the roleplaying game World of Warcraft and dither away anywhere from one to four hours there, picking virtual purple lotus flowers and joining up with old college chums to rid this virtual world of virtual evil. And it was great - I didn't think too closely about it at the time, but on a chemical level it was really doing everything necessary to trick my mind and body into believing that all of my primary biological imperatives were being fulfilled. Interestingly, day-to-day religion, as we'll come to see, does pretty much the same thing, just with thousands of years of added metaphysical and historical baggage. To answer, then, the oft-posed question, "If you get your way, what are you going to replace religion with to keep people happy and fulfilled?", an inspection of how Warcraft and similar games work on a neural level might well be in order.

But before we go there, let's look at the mind that is absorbing all of this adventure. The *Homo sapiens* brain has been in the business of keeping us alive in spite of ourselves for the better part of 200,000 years. It's done this by making us feel good about behaviors and items that increase our chances of passing on our DNA and wretched about things that don't. When we see a bit of food chock full of historically rare sugars and proteins, our brain pushes us at it by pumping us full of dopamine, and suddenly we feel very desirous of that food bit, and will exert ourselves to get it. Conversely, if our relationship of two years falls apart, our brain very sensibly decides that we are probably barking up the wrong reproductive tree, and lathers us in cortisol. This makes us feel terrible at the mere sight or thought of the lost loved one, shoving us along to the next mating partner, who will hopefully be rather less picky about our numerous personal, financial, and physical failings.

There are three things above all that our genes, through the mediation of our brain, want us to do: to pursue those resources that have done well for us in the past, to gather together in groups, and to climb to a position of authority in those groups. In other words, to keep our genes going, we need to eat, find the protection that communal living offers, and be so dazzlingly impressive that we have the pick of mating partners. Whenever we go along with this game plan, we're rewarded by our brains with shots of dopamine, oxytocin, and serotonin, respectively, and feel quite good for a while as a result. This is the real trinity that man has given himself over to since his inception, and it's one that World of Warcraft exploits to the fullest to keep us forking over $15 a month for the pleasure of mining imaginary ores.

In the game, there is always something that you are made to want - experience points, gold, honor points, faction points, armor, rare crafting components, skill levels - all entirely illusory, but so close to those reward systems that got us sugary candy and nice new bicycles in elementary school that our brain takes them for the same thing, and rewards us with dopamine shots for pursuing them. Surviving in a modern social system is so complex, and the needs so many, that our poor caveman brain is quite worn out keeping track of what we actually NEED, and has to make do with apportioning dopamine whenever we approach something that looks kinda sorta like something that once helped us out. By keeping us in constant anticipation of reward, the game keeps the chemicals flowing, and us playing.

Meanwhile, the social aspect of the game is perhaps even more compelling. With millions of players the globe over, Warcraft is teeming with other folks who need your help to achieve their in-game objectives, and thus do guilds form which have at their root the human interdependence that the brain decided long ago was a good strategy for survival. Being trusted and putting our trust in others to heal us when we are hurt, to jump in front of us when we are being attacked, and to craft the items that we can't make ourselves- all of this is close enough to the bonds of mutual dependency and trust that allowed us to successfully survive in days of yore that we are liberally rewarded with oxytocin for our efforts in spite of the fact that none of these people online can protect us from anything resembling an actual threat to our well-being. If a tiger walks into my study, it is going to eat me in spite of all of the frost spells my guild might summon.

And, oh, the opportunities for status seeking. There are entire websites devoted to ranking your armor, your achievements, your talent allocations, on a global scale, and these are a source of intense pride to many. Having the #4 hunter orc on the Zangarmarsh server makes you walk a little taller - people cower in your path and you are assiduously courted for guilds. From the brain's perspective, you have dominated your peers, which will surely make you a more attractive reproductive partner, and it rewards you with serotonin. In reality, that status cost you face time with actual potential mates, destroyed your physique through hours of sitting while drinking Mountain Dew and eating bags of Halloween candy, and dulled your social senses to the bare minimum required to communicate with your guild during a raid. But at that moment, when you are The Guy who can save the day, and you get the call to do what only your character can do, your brain thinks that you have hit reproductive gold, and you feel on top of the world.

Warcraft brilliantly manipulates, then, our brain's motivational system by offering substitutive virtual survival that we interpret on a chemical level as the real thing. In this, it is doing nothing new. Religion, after all, has been at it for thousands of years. It is a grand trick that we played on our own brains to get the drugs we like. In place of taxing displays of dominance, laborious achievement of real goals, and difficult forging of relationships, it substituted much more easily achievable, because entirely made up, paths to neurochemical happytown.

Why struggle to make yourself the head monkey when you can just kick back and believe the guy who says that, no matter how messed up you are, you are Jesus's best friend and have a seat at the celestial table waiting for you? Serotonin, check.

Why work on the real social issues that make forming a community difficult, or the real personality conflicts that make a relationship difficult, when everybody can submit to an imposed community based around repetition of a few stock phrases once a week that generates a rough feeling of togetherness? Oxytocin, check.

And why be tossed about on the back of your body's real physical needs and worldly goals, when you can spend a lifetime in delicious, constant anticipation of Heavenly reward? You don't even have to get out of bed for that! And so, dopamine, check.

This is the brilliance of religion, and also the road out of it. What thrived long past its time as a low-energy alternative to the reward chemicals of survival can be ended as such. We tend to think of religion as meeting deep spiritual needs that cannot possibly be answered by anything lacking the dominating edifice of metaphysical thought. And so we despair at what society might be like when it is removed. But that's just because we have believed the stories that religion has told about itself to obscure the fact that, in terms of its day to day pull on us, it has gotten by almost entirely on neural sleights of hand. Remove the chemical trickery, and what you've got left is the intellectual content of religion, consisting of a series of fumbling, foggily worded, and self-contradictory answers to ill-put questions of metaphysics. And that's just not enough to keep religion alive.

So, am I suggesting that we replace religion with video games? Not remotely. I started by saying that I played Warcraft intensely for a year and a half. Following that was about three years of once-a-week playing aimed more at drinking beer while chatting online with far flung friends than at actually doing the game justice, and then a year of paying fifteen bucks a month for the opportunity to play the game, if I should happen to want to, which I didn't. I found other things that fed me neurochemical happiness more effectively, though I was aided in that task by what I had learned about my head through years of having it batted about by the mad geniuses who design Warcraft.

Put simply, atheists need to combine the town hall with Azeroth - to connect actual, physical, oxytocin-inducing contact with other human beings with the constant dopamine and serotonin based reward mechanics that the online world has perfected. Frederick the Great noted long ago what men will do for a bit of ribbon and a title, and in our data-rich society, it shouldn't be too difficult to find a thousand ways of rewarding people for the things that they do as a matter of course, turning the mere act of living your life into a grand secular adventure all its own where your guild is the world itself.

The sanitation district says you just recycled your ten thousandth aluminum can - here's a badge for your jacket and the title of CanMan Supreme that you can display on your Facebook page. You've managed to go to work without calling in sick for 400 days - congratulations, Iron Horse, keep on doing what you do. If every act of yours works towards some bit of distinction, and all of that can be brought to a physical place where Everybody Knows Your Name, I think humans will have the chance to live happier lives than they ever dreamed possible, and that quaint chap people used to call religion will be just a thing we did for a while until we figured out what we wanted after all.

HERE BE NERDS:
A MODEST ACCOUNT OF SKEPTICON 6

(Originally Published at *The Twilight of Nearly Everything*)

Daleks. Picard v. Janeway. Super Soakers.

For the twenty-five hours I was stationed at my booth, these were the deep issues I and my fellow Skepticon attendees wrestled with – no First Cause arguments, no earnest discussions about The Future of The Movement, just a steady stream of entirely lovely people and our shared geekery.

How different it would be, if the world saw atheism more often from the vantage point offered by this humble foldable chair – the group huddled excitedly over a game of Settlers of Catan in the corner, another planning their big Karaoke Night Out, and right here, at this table, two strangers bonding over a shared love of The Wild Thornberrys.

Because that's what atheism is – getting ecstatically, unreasonably excited about the products of the human imagination, having the entire weft and warp of human fancy as your own private source of daily delight. That world of unhindered exploration is so tangibly yours for the having once you let fall the notion of the sacred and its shadowy Iago, Shame. The people I see have loosed the final fetter on their nerdishness, and it gives them this sort of radiance that it was my privilege to bask in for two days.

That's not to say we stop explaining and expounding and, yes, arguing, if need be, because there are terrible things happening in the world that must be pointed out, regardless of the opprobrium inevitably attached to the pointer. There is a hard-won heft to the notions of existence and purpose we have scratched from the often cold surface of reality, and we certainly do ourselves a disservice accounting it all as too austere or depressing for public consumption. But, as in all things, the key is balance.

Certainly, the last thing we want is the atheist equivalent of those sheepish Mormon ads that, in attempting to portray breadth and normalcy, come off portraying Mormons as, most likely, alien changelings. But a few glimpses of joyous humanity, here and there, could not hurt, to which end I offer the following Skepticon sketches in miniature of the people I met and conversed with over the last few days:

Steven Olsen is a strong proponent of Cookies For Dinner.

If you give Nicole Crenshaw a chance, she WILL wear your Victorian cape, and WILL twirl in it.

Rachel Berman has a sixth sense for knowing when somebody around her is starving, and a seventh sense for conjuring ways to feed them from the ether.

Amanda Brown will craft a captioned jpeg of you while you're not looking, just to make life that much more fun.

Lauren Lane's family can, within about ten minutes of conversation, fix all of your life's problems and will give you free beers while doing it.

K. Johnston is probably a ventriloquist, and more probably still is not aware of the fact.

Some small part of Ellen Lundgren is, even now, reenacting the Battle of Gettysburg.

When you're feeling a bit down, Sara Mayhew will draw a charming picture for you that suddenly makes everything better.

JT Eberhard never forgets a kindness, and is lusciously unashamed to wear the goofiest hat in the room.

And so many more who stopped and chatted, about Dungeons and Dragons version 2.5 and open-shirted William Ryker, Agent Coulson and those plastic jars of Real Ghostbusters ectoplasm that came with a ghost inside, and whose names my Convention-addled brain forgot to write down or who never left one, each a standing example against the popular conception of an atheist as a curious sub-species of human eternally gripping a Bertrand Russell text tightly in cold, unfeeling fingers. They are the future of humanism, and its great hope, and from where I sit, that future shimmers with promise and laughter.

Mixing Allah with Kal-El: The New Frontier of Islamic Superheroes

(Originally Published in *The Freethinker*, April 2014)

Strictly speaking, traditional religion in DC or Marvel comics makes no damn sense. We mere humans have some excuse for believing the dictates of Christianity or Islam because we don't have the ability to travel back to Jerusalem or Mecca to see what actually happened in the time of the messiahs, or forward to the end of the universe to see whether their great predictions come true. But in comic books, they can. They've seen and recorded the beginning of the world and also its end and know as a matter of observed fact that the proclamations of religion aren't true.

To introduce religious characters, then, is somewhat ridiculous. To believe that Jehovah is the one and only god, and humanity his one and only sentient creation when you have regular visitations by demigods and aliens is to be pigheaded to a degree that would render one unfit for normal society. But, of course, there's money and publicity in it, so regardless of whether it makes a lick of sense, first DC and then Marvel took their turns at unveiling Islamic superheroes with great pomp and spandex.

Leaving behind the palpable silliness of believing in the Koran when you can poke your head out a window and ask Galactus about his personal experience of the Big Bang, what we find are some interesting stories that disappointingly but inevitably soft-peddle the religious part of Islam, opting instead to tell cultural tales about being Muslim in America. DC started the trend with Simon Baz, who was introduced not only in one of their flagship titles, but square in the center of one of the most important arcs in DC history.

Without going too far into the nerdutiae of the matter, Green Lantern was a walking punchline for many years before Geoff Johns took the reins and crafted a consistent and compelling universe around this single neglected character. His run on Lantern is one of the great writer-character pairings of all time, and right in the midst of its titanic conclusion Simon Baz was introduced as the newest earthling to don the Lantern's ring.

Baz is a man racked by guilt. He challenged his brother-in-law to a drag race which ended in an accident which put said brother-in-law into a coma. To help pay the hospital bills, Baz turned to stealing cars and had the singular misfortune of nabbing a van with a live bomb in the back. To keep it from killing anybody, he crashed it into an abandoned building, it went boom, and he, as a man of Arabic descent from an Islamic family, was immediately arrested and brought to Guantanamo on charges of terrorism. Just before his waterboarding, however, a Lantern ring finds him and he is transformed into the next Green Lantern.

Simon himself says nothing about his religious beliefs throughout this arc, the only oblique reference being an arm tattoo which he mentions his father disapproving of for religious reasons. It is left to his family to provide a religious dimension, mentioning how they are not welcome at the mosque anymore because of the suspicion that Baz's actions have brought on their small, threatened community. His sister, in the meantime, is quietly told not to report to her job at the State Department until things have settled down, since her co-workers are no longer able to trust her.

And that's largely it. The word "mosque" once, the word "Allah" never, and Baz himself is quickly dwarfed by the galactic events Johns worked up for the end of his epic run. The depictions of everyday fear for people of Arabic descent living in America during the decade following 9/11 ring true and tragic. But that's where all dialogue ends. When Baz shows up again, as a member of the Justice League of America, he fills the role of the Rookie Who Doesn't Know How To Use His Powers Yet, and is again lost in the shuffle of the Trinity War.

One can't help but think of it all as a chance missed. Baz isn't terribly interesting – he's a carbon life form that events happen to more than an actual character, but his family is rich in possibility, and the one page spent on the sister and father is perhaps the best in his intro story. In all events, one gets the distinct impression that DC wanted the buzz of an Arabic superhero without the reaction that comes with actually saying something compelling about religion's status in the world.

Marvel, for its part, seems to have taken good notes in the crafting of its response character, an Islamic Ms. Marvel. Rather than introducing her in the middle of a titanic arc where she would necessarily get lost, they gave her a stand-alone title penned by G. Willow Wilson. That meant that they didn't need to rush character development, and so could avoid throwing Guantanamo at her to make her develop the semblance of a character quickly. No, the new Ms. Marvel is a slightly geeky kid named Kamala Khan who wants to be good but wants to be normal too. Her family is a bit heavy on the stereotypes, but at least they are willing to engage in a dinner table discussion about the merits of different degrees of religiosity. Her father is practical but firm, her brother a privileged ascetic, and her sister devout and stand-offish. They have character, they interact, and they have developed opinions, which is more than Boz's family were allowed to evince in their scant panels.

Kamala faces discrimination, but of that simmering everyday sort. Jocks and Barbies who say that she smells of curry and make fun of her social customs – stock characters from the Silver Age who we can only hope don't represent the last word on Islamic critique in the book. Still, though, in the character of Kamala Marvel has taken a decided leap over DC. She has interests and silly fantasies, normal problems and a quirky sense of self that will make her an interesting character to watch develop, as her beliefs come into contact with a wider world that includes Asgardian gods and Skrull shape-shifters. As I'm writing this, only the first issue has come out, but I have high hopes that here, at least, the tensions of religion in a modern world will have some purchase at last in a regular superhero comic from the Big Two.

In spite of how I began, I think religion can be done in comics, and well. Look at Lucifer or Preacher. They are filled with brilliant stories which grapple with the real meat of our twisted relations with our deities. But the world of superhero comics is, in many ways, the playground of all of our best instincts and ideals. Its heroes are champions of freedom, inquiry, science, and love in a way that is, at its best, timeless. It takes extreme sensitivity to motivation and psychology to make a religious family fit in such a world. But the potential for beautiful storytelling if the writers really let that gorgeous world of comics work its best on such characters is immense, and possibly very instructive for kids reading comics today, pondering the good and bad of how culture restricts and defines a person in a progressive world.

JEDI OR TREKKIE:
A HUMANIST DEBATE

(Originally published at *The Twilight of Nearly Everything*.)

The [Jedi] Order has long been about justifying its own existence, about acquiring and holding power… I know what I swore to do as a Jedi, and it didn't have anything to do with turning a blind eye to social evils because the Sith were a bigger evil. – Gotab (Bardan Jusik)

Your report describes how rational these people are. Millennia ago, they abandoned their belief in the supernatural. Now you are asking me to sabotage that achievement, to send them back into the Dark Ages of superstition and ignorance and fear. No! – Captain Jean Luc Picard

Ask any sensible 25 year old human which they prefer, Star Wars or Star Trek and, without missing a beat, they will reply Star Wars and proceed down the list of its clear advantages. It's more exciting. There's more action. The bad guys are cooler. It's grittier. It has women in leadership positions before 1990. The aliens aren't just people with face paint. There's magic. Light sabers, dude, light sabers.

And so forth.

Ask any 35 year old, and the answer just as inevitably comes back Star Trek, and especially from the people who most vociferously insisted Star Wars a decade prior. It's about bigger social issues. It's philosophically more subtle. The science is more interesting. The team dynamic is more compelling than the series of lone wolves that Star Wars has to offer.

And so on.

The implication seems to be that Star Wars is the stuff of idealistic, solipsistic adolescence, and Star Trek that of pragmatic, socially-oriented adulthood, but that is to do a disservice to the philosophies of power and social change present especially in the Star Wars expanded universe, and the sense of individual struggle to be found in Star Trek's most recent instantiation.

Starting with Star Wars, I won't attempt to instill the original films with more philosophical weight than they had. The movies were the defining experience of my childhood, and merchandise related to them continues to consume more of my personal income than I care to reveal. They are thoroughly rad, but they aren't particularly deep. They do, however, contain themes of astounding pregnancy which have been worked by others into fascinating ruminations about how change happens in civilization.

The best place to go to find this broader scope is undoubtedly the novels, of which there are hundreds, but the high point for me is definitely the nine-novel *Legacy of the Force* series, and particularly book eight, *Revelation*, by veteran Star Wars novelist Karen Traviss. The series centers upon the rise of Jacen Solo, son of Leia and Han, who possesses force abilities of untold power and flexibility, and seeks to use them in the service of a galaxy just rebuilding itself after disastrous invasion. It is hardly worth the hauling out of a Spoiler Alert placard to say that the Dark Side soon has him in its clutches. But what's interesting is that the Dark Side isn't some metaphysical notion of pure evil, but rather a philosophy about how you institute reform in a civilization. Presented with the self-serving inertia of those in power and comfort, how do you make life better for those actively but voicelessly suffering?

In grappling with this issue, the *Legacy* books are really looking at the structural flaws of Buddhist versus Christian practice. The Jedi, whose espousal of detachment allows flagrant injustice to continue in the galaxy so long as their precious monastery stays in power, are everything that's wrong with a classical Buddhist approach to society, and Jacen soon grows frustrated with their mysticism-laced unwillingness to get their hands dirty to help people. The Sith, full of absolute confidence in the righteousness of their own actions, gifted with the ability to take action in the name of galaxy-spanning goals regardless of consequence, are the Christians, drunk on their own supernatural power and convinced that anybody who opposes them opposes the universal order and therefore deserves death.

Jacen is tossed about on the horns of these polarities until the sheer need for resolute action in order to save the galaxy tosses him into the arms of the Dark Side. During one of his moments of introspection, he basically rewrites the original trilogy, showing that the Rebellion, in acting as it did, was far more Sith than Jedi in affiliation:

"Who would make the tough choices if they were hidebound by conventional law? Had anyone protested about Luke Skywalker bringing down Palpatine? The Rebellion broke every law in the book, and killed many people, but citizens were ready to accept that because *change was needed*. [Jacen] was only doing the same thing, and yet he was vilified for it. He was wounded by the blindness around him. Why could they not understand? He wasn't explaining it clearly enough, perhaps."

Ultimately, the fallout from all of this propels the Star Wars universe into *The Fate of the Jedi* series, which finds the Jedi in disgrace and the galaxy questioning whether or not we'd be better off after all without these self-appointed paladins of disinterested virtue in charge. These books make the original movies retroactively more profound, and are worth the reading by anybody wanting to expand their love of a galaxy far, far away into that stage of life that needs something more than the hiss of a light saber to capture its interest.

To Star Trek, then, and particularly to the most recent series, *Star Trek: Enterprise*. Responding to criticism that *The Next Generation*, *Deep Space Nine*, and *Voyager* were essentially tales of space bureaucracy incapable of bringing in a younger audience, *Enterprise* went back to the very beginning of humanity's interstellar program to catch us at a moment of cocky inexperience, before the Prime Directive, before the diplomatic concerns of negotiating borders with the Romulans. The crew, led by Captain Jonathan Archer, manifestly does not know what it is doing half the time, and in the space that protocol usually fills, they are left to suss things out for themselves as best they can.

And in that sense, this series is much closer to Star Wars than to the previous offerings of Star Trek. It is consistently about individual agency and power, and how that ought to be used to accomplish what you find to be the right task, precedent be damned. Whereas an episode of *Voyager* (incidentally, my favorite of the Trek series, though I realize I'm basically alone in that) will feature the crew agonizing over the application of Federation protocol to a particular instance, in *Enterprise* the issue Archer is constantly facing is what his power as a starship captain morally allows him to do, and what it *compels* him to do, which is a very Jedi/Sith kind of dilemma.

The framework, however, is still very Star Trek, in that Kantian philosophy and enlightened skepticism come to the rescue more often than not. The categorical imperative is the big machine that dictates how the episodes are going to turn out, while appeals to mystical explanations and vague religiosity, which cropped up from time to time in *Voyager*, are routinely squashed in favor of freedom of thought and the scientific method. It is entirely an amalgam of the personal drama of Star Wars and the larger concerns of Star Trek, with the occasional manifestly gratuitous Decontamination Room Scene by way of fan service.

The title of this essay implied a solution, that the weight of judgment would settle finally on one pole or the other of this, the most important question of our times. Certainly, looking at it casually, a humanist would be better rewarded investing their leisure hours in old Star Trek episodes than in repeat viewings of Star Wars, but that is to undervalue the richness of Lucas's original conception, one which set the stage for big questions to be asked, even if he didn't himself ask them. There is no need to hang up your Mandalorian armor upon reaching the august age of 30. Nor must you seek islands far from the Trek universe if you want to probe issues of individual psychology. The answer to Trekkie or Jedi is, simply, BOTH, or if you have utterly no sense of imaginative play, then NEITHER, but to alight on one side or the other exclusively is to do yourself a profound disservice.

Now, Marvel or DC, on the other hand…. That one's easy.

DID CLASSICAL MUSIC DIE WHEN GOD DID? THREE GODLESS COMPOSERS WHO STILL TUG AT OUR HEARTSTRINGS

(Originally published at *The Twilight of Everything*)

Among the various and manifold jackasseries nailed to the page by James R. Gaines in his Bach biography *Evening in the Palace of Reason* is the supremely unfair but wildly popular statement that, once God left classical music, so did its ability to say anything sublime or meaningful. To be fair, he said it while comparing the deeply religious music of Johann Sebastian Bach to the elegant and fluffily appealing court music of Johann Joachim Quantz, but that hasn't stopped the thought from being applied to the classical music of our own times.

The music written by modern, atheist composers, the argument runs, has an emotional spectrum running from "anxious" to "very anxious," and that's about it. Love, passion, and above all, sublimity, are entirely beyond these composers' capacity to portray with their shriveled, sarcastic hearts guiding merciless, ironic pens.

There are, let's be clear, composers for whom this is manifestly true. I mean, I love Iannis Xenakis, but I'm not going to say for a moment that I've ever felt an emotion beyond a sort of Vulcan creepy-cool mathematical appreciation when listening to his music. There are, however, atheist composers who have delivered unto us music of breathtaking scope and depth, and it's time to recognize that fact, starting

36

with the big three: Nikolai Rimsky-Korsakov (1844-1908), Béla Bartók (1881-1945), and Leoš Janáček (1854-1928).

"Holy shit, Rimsky-Korsakov was an atheist?!"

That was my reaction too when a copy of his memoirs first found its way onto my bookshelves bearing the categorical statement, "I took rather readily to the view that 'there is no God and it's all just invention.' However, this thought troubled me little... my piety, weak even before then, had completely evaporated, and I felt no spiritual hunger." And yet, religious music and the expression of religious sentiment is everywhere in Rimsky-Korsakov's music. How did he find it in him to write this music, and write it so very well?

A clue comes in his discussion of the opera *The Snow Maiden* (*Snegurochka*). "The melodies of ancient orthodox canticles, are they not of ancient pagan origin? Are not many rites and dogmas of like origin? The holidays of Easter, Trinity Sunday, etc., are not they adaptations of Christianity from the pagan sun cult?" Rimsky-Korsakov could continue to write music on Christian themes precisely because he took a larger view of what that religion was – a variation on ancient practices that were rooted in prehistoric people's awe of the world around them. By returning to that source, he could capture the naturalistic essence of religious wonder without groveling before the trappings of Christian specificity. It was religious writing more authentic than any particular religion could encompass, because at its center was not god, but humanity's perception of continuity and change.

Rimsky-Korsakov's love of fantasy and magic, of peasant melodies and pagan fairy tales, his intoxication with the sound of foreign lands and instruments, all combine in his operas and orchestral works to produce moments of ageless melancholy (take a listen to the death scene in *The Snow Maiden* or Lyubasha's aria in act I of *The Tsar's Bride*), sumptuous eroticism (take in that violin figure in *Scheherezade* and just try to not think about humping, I dare you), and, yes, old-fashioned haunting sublimity (his cantata *Song of Oleg the Wise* is crazy-good but largely unknown.)

So, fine, Rimsky-Korsakov got away with some degree of multi-dimensionality because he was a primarily 19th century composer of particularly broad interests. But Béla Bartók? The man who wrote such aggressively uncuddly music as the fourth string quartet and the student-twisting *Mikrokosmos*? It seems unlikely – the man had an awful life, full of disappointment and dislocation. Unable to believe in a higher power, to find success in his home nation, or to resist the allure of women waaaaaay younger than him, he coasted dissatisfied through decades of illness-bestrewn life before emigrating to an indifferent America one step ahead of the Nazis. It would have been the most forgivable thing ever if he just ground out Difficult compositions, one after the other, with a sort of "Screw all y'all" bitterness. But he didn't. The amazing thing about Bartók is that, even in the depths of isolation and misery, he was able to produce music of all hues, and indeed his most varied music comes from the low ebb of his fortunes, the years 1937-1945.

Starting at the end, his third piano concerto was the last piece of music he completed before passing away in a New York City hospital bed. The second movement of this piece is labelled *Adagio Religioso*, a reference to the musical idiom in which it was written, and is heart-rending throughout in a way that defies all popular conceptions about the rigorous inflexibility of Bartók's music. What I love most about it is the middle section, which is given over to Bartók's representation of the songs of various birds he heard while travelling through North Carolina. It's an amazing moment- one of the most challenging composers of the Twentieth Century, lying on his death bed, putting this beautiful music to paper and interspersing throughout it some bits of bird song that caught his ear in days past. That sense of vulnerable whimsy is so potent that my eyes welled up in tears the first time I heard it, and it impacts me forcefully still.

I sense you're still cynical. We've all watched *Amadeus*, we know that Writing Beautiful Things is just what composers do on their death beds. It's in the contract. So, let's go back a ways and see if we can catch Bartók being brazenly emotional any time other than when staring down the grim specter of death itself. It turns out that, when you start seeking out examples, they pop up all over the place. There is the madcap, almost drunken, abandon he allowed himself in the Finale of the *Concerto for Orchestra*, which is itself a spillover from the absurd fun he had in the third movement of his *Divertimento*.

Now there's a work for you, one which starts off at a mad tear and ends in a totally soused pizzicato dance punctuated by bleary hiccups. What makes both of these pieces of unchecked revelry all the more remarkable is that they were written in 1940 and 1939, respectively, during the first years of Bartók's exile from his homeland. A religious composer in those circumstances would easily have turned the Spiritual Escapism up to Eleven and offered the world yet another cantata on the subject of Jesus or Oedipus or some such thing. Bartók chose to laugh, to have himself a lark and take us along for the ride.

Going back to before his departure to America, we have waiting for us his 6th String Quartet, the last piece he wrote in Europe. You can choose pretty much any movement and be treated to a profound emotional experience, but the last movement is pure lyric tragedy, written just after the death of his mother, we hear in it Bartók pouring out every last ounce of his sadness and loss, and all the Ave Marias in the world can't match the power of its raw, wounded agony.

If Bartók is the closely guarded theorist who only lets the full color of his fancy out to play on special occasions, Leoš Janáček is the perpetually angst-ridden teenager whose passions are his curse and our blessing (if you'll pardon the use of the term). Many consider him the greatest operatic composer of the Twentieth Century, and it's hard not to at least put him in the top three. He was a man intoxicated by love and sound. Wherever he went, he would jot down the musicality of the everyday speech around him, its rhythm and flow, its characteristic pitches and melodic turns, compiling for himself a stockpile of thousands of utterances of everyday opera which then formed the basis for his tonal worlds, lending them a grounding in human expressivity rarely surpassed.

That alone was enough to make for some great music, but it might not have come to much had it not been for the fact that Janáček was a horn dog of the first order. One of the great guilty pleasure reads you can avail yourself of are the letters he wrote during the last decades of his life to Kamila Stosslova, a married woman whose increasingly alarming rotundity only stoked the fires of Janáček's passion further. What is both wonderful and terrible about these letters is how achingly reminiscent of high school they are – the words of a smart man who wants a girl not really that into him but who thinks that by displays of Importance and Learning he'll somehow impress her into loving him.

Or maybe that's just what high school was like for me....

In any case, what becomes abundantly clear is how, in his late sixties, the fire of passionate love was still burning him from the inside out, pushing him to write masterpiece after masterpiece as a substitutive act for the great love he couldn't have. Some of his most magnificent works are stoked on the fires of this passion, representing its different shades and flavors as the relationship waxed and waned. *Katya Kabanovna* is a more or less direct representation of his relations with Kamila, with Katya as the married woman seeking a passionate love to settle the deep longing she feels and which her business-traveling husband, Tichon (a substitute for her real husband, David, a generally decent bloke) is unable to provide.

It's Janáček's most intimate fantasy given sonic flesh. The exchanges between the character standing in for him (Boris) and Katya are filled with all of the unrealized desire of a man in the full grips of romantic delusion. At the conclusion of acts II and III, Janáček lets loose the reins of his fancy as Katya and Boris fall inevitably towards each other, igniting a love so intense it can only end in tragedy.

One would think that enough of a tribute to an infatuation, but Janáček kept drawing on different aspects of Kamila's characters for his other towering works of late life. He grasped her playfulness and sense of ease in *The Cunning Little Vixen* and her capacity for cold indifference in *Vec Makropulos*, the story of a three hundred year old woman who has fallen into complete apathy as regards love and life. There's hardly a nook of the emotional spectrum that he wasn't spurred to capture in sound by his overpowering love of the vaguely spherical Stosslova.

Is there modern music that rigidly denies itself any flavor of sentiment beyond anxiety-inducing orchestral noodling? Of course there is, and there are things to be said for it (some of the best of which were laid out by Milton Babbitt in his now-notorious 1958 article *Who Cares If You Listen?* and which are really worth a visit), however to lay all of that emotive monodimensionality at the foot of the rise of godlessness in music is a bit much. They don't come much more godless than the three gentlemen we've just spent some time with, and all three of them felt equally comfortable in portraying intensely personal moments of loss as towering themes of human transcendence. You don't lose your capacity for awe and sublimity just because you don't believe in superpowerful rules brokers. It is a case of there being more in our philosophy than is contained in our notions of Heaven and Earth, if only we are willing to look, and listen.

Let us LARP While We May

(Originally Published at *The Twilight of Nearly Everything*)

Nerds are destined to save secularism from itself. In our unreasonably, some might say disturbingly, passionate hearts lies the missing factor in the grand equation of a new age. A time when reason is married to a life worth the living.

That life is coming, and in the creation of it, we could learn a lot from a larp. Larping, once the dirty secret of the gaming community, is busting out in a big way. With documentaries like *Darkon*, feature films like *Unicorn City*, and books examining the past-time like Lizzie Stark's *Leaving Mundania*, larp has overcome its self-consciousness and is aimed straight at the hearts of a generation looking for a new sense of community. For those unfamiliar, larp stands for live action role play, and encompasses a robust variety of rich mystical escapism. At its most organized, it allows you to flee reality for a weekend and, dressed as a bard or goblin, live in a different universe for a while, playing your character in an elaborately crafted and exquisitely organized scenario with a couple hundred other similarly minded folk out in a forest or campground. In terms of immersive interpersonal experiences, there's really nothing comparable this side of, well, church.

It's a beautiful thing, really, the crossroads of so many skills that we don't get to exercise on a daily basis. Leadership and drama, costuming and music, set design and social networking, all meet in this one concentrated burst of creative output that I think anybody with the slightest historical or whimsical instinct can't hear about without secretly longing for. In every way, it is that realm of total human recreation that the 1950s thought we would have accomplished twenty years ago, but which our own misplaced sense of quietist dignity has prevented us from acting on.

41

People cannot do without people, and since we no longer particularly need each other on a day to day or community-wide basis, something must fill the void. Secularists, guided by their own lights, have come up with some notions, but the suspension of disbelief required to keep these secular "churches" afloat has been mighty, greater even than the relatively simple matter of believing that the forty two year old guy in a cat mask drinking Kool Aid across from you is, in fact, the King of Cats. We secularists place so much stock in our intellectual purity that we tend to instinctively eschew situations where we might come off as silly, but in the long run that's really only hurting ourselves.

Perhaps you don't have a weekend a month to spare. I certainly do not, and won't anytime within the next decade. You could still try a gaming convention near you, dip your toe in just for that brief bit of time and see what you end up doing when wearing a different face for a few hours. It might give you a notion of what sorts of interaction you are missing that perhaps you were unaware of, what you need psychologically but were not willing to admit out of dedication to your stoic self-conception. There are even purely online variations that attempt to capture the essence of the escapist-yet-somehow-more-psychologically-true-than-reality feel of live larping (or live-arping, as the case may be). Whatever your commitment level, there's some sliver of the experience available to you, and for creatures of a finite life-span, experience is the whole game.

Life is short. Imagine vigorously. Because if you don't feel just a bit embarrassed about your passion in mixed company, then it's hardly a proper passion, is it?

THE WAGNER WE DESERVE:
OPERA'S CHALLENGES IN THE NEW SECULAR AGE

(Originally Published at *The New Humanist*, May 2013)

Lamenting is something of the national sport for opera buffs. And of the many great laments that were raised by our people in the twentieth century, few were as plaintive and endearingly quaint as that against the disappearance of baroque and classical opera from live performance. A generation of producers and directors had made the decision that the mythological allegories and standard declamations were incompatible with modern audiences, and it took many years and much courage to drag, say, Mozart's *Agamemnon* back on the stage.

Just in time for the "modern" audience to change again. Here in the twenty-first century, we are positively ecstatic about anything featuring the faintest whiff of an Olympian. Mention Iphigenia in passing and we are, by and large, *there*, in our seats, waiting to be declaimed at. The fresh problem for the operatic producer, it turns out, isn't classicism, but the presentation of heavily religious operas to an increasingly secular audience. Operas that held the stage with an assured sense of righteous entitlement in the nineteenth and twentieth centuries tend to appear at best naïve and at worst positively shrill to humanist ears. This is a shame, as there is some beautiful music there, some of the most sublime ever written. Luckily, some dastardly clever directors have set about solving the problem of presenting these classics to a new generation of secularists.

One of the main dramatic conundrums centers on the portrayal of religious ecstasy. Deeply moving to believers, all of the lurching and renouncing and abject groveling come off as just plain creepy to a generation that has learned through bitter experience to see more of the emotionally abused terrorist-in-training in these surreal transports than the noble knight of purity. Think of

Marguerite in the marvelous trio at the end of Gounod's *Faust* singing

> Radiant angels above,
> take my soul to Heaven's breast.
> God of justice, I submit to Thy will.
> God of mercy, forgive me.
> Radiant angels above,
> take my soul to Heaven's breast.

The melody is glorious, but the dramatic effect is often that of a battered wife rapturously pleading with her abusive husband to be let back into the kitchen to make him his favorite dinner. The suffering she undergoes in the opera is entirely out of proportion to her vices, which amount to little more than credulity and a bit of vanity. She is a human caught and torn apart by the perverse logic of sin and retribution, and expires with a Stockholmish "Thank you sir, may I have another?"

Many directors trot out the full array of Heavenly Effects to realize this scene, with lighting and background imagery aiming at an overall conception of Marguerite as an innocent lamb of pure light and radiant goodness. In 2011, however, the Metropolitan Opera's production, which misfired on so very many conceptual levels (which I would *lament*, but simply *don't* have the time), tackled the issue of Marguerite's ecstasy in a rather bold way. Their take was simply, "We're going to turn the creepy up to 11." Marina Poplovskaya's Marguerite is a woman unhinged, and the more she turns to religious inspiration for guidance, the more wrecked she becomes. The production, as it read on the stage, implied that religion is where you go when everything else about you is broken, and that what it offers isn't so much salvation as a tainted morphine drip while dying. Faust doesn't kill Marguerite, nor Mephistopholes, but rather theology itself, and all it offers by way of consolation is a mad vision of tinsel angels while it finishes her off, covering its bloody tracks in a concluding chorus of gross self-congratulation.

Gounod's original intention? Almost certainly not, but in terms of uncovering layers of meaning for a fresh set of sensibilities, it was remarkably effective. It's certainly something that can be experimented with profitably in other scenes of variously goofy religious transport. At the end of Puccini's one act opera *Suor Angelica*, for example, the good sister falls into a mystical reverie that combines ruminations about the Virgin Mary, grace, suicide, damnation, purity, and a summons to Heaven from her dead son. It's a dense ten minutes which hardly gives one emotion a chance to breathe before throwing itself into another, resulting in the overall impression that the librettist, Forzano, was being paid by the job rather than the hour.

I know of one production that presented it as an over-the-top Italian melodrama (think of the "Mamma… mamma mia!" play from Godfather II), hoping to wring comedy from how utterly kitchen-sink Forzano's libretto is here. I had some laughs, because it expertly pushed precisely those moments that are on the verge of self-parody in the original completely over the edge.

It's clearly not a long-term solution, though, nor I think a generally workable one. Secular we may be, but I think the general tolerance for nun death-scene burlesque is probably not as high as my own. Really, the opera could benefit by approaching the problem through the same lens as Poplovskaya's Marguerite. This nun has had things done to her mind by the world and a religious order intent on exploiting the world's cruelty for its own gain, and there is true tragedy in that. It is a tragedy that is not beautifully resolved by her reunion with her dead son at the end, but is rather only deepened by the torture she puts herself through on the way to her final act of delusion. There is really nothing more moving that you could put on a stage than the misery of hope so glaringly unfulfilled. But you have to be willing to renounce the traditional role of religious ecstasy in opera, and that has been something slow in coming.

All of this, however, is detail work next to the real monumental task to be faced in the era of the stridently secular audience – squaring up to Wagner's big three Christian operas.

Tannhäuser, Lohengrin, Parsifal. I've heard radio advertisements for these that are positively apologetic in tenor. "This year – *Parsifal*.... But bear with us, and we'll do *Tristan* NEXT year!" You've heard them too, perhaps – lots of focus on the lush sets, shimmering orchestration, and featured performers, while the story gets shoved discretely out of the limelight like a murderer ever…so…casually pushing a bloody knife under the couch with his foot.

I understand. Take *Tannhäuser*, which was probably my favorite opera growing up. I love it, and even I have to admit it's dramatically tough to swallow if you're not massively predisposed to it through the greatness of the music. Here's the run-down: Tannhäuser is hanging out with Venus having way awesome sex all the time, but craves life on Earth, so he leaves, finds the beautiful Elizabeth, but makes the faux-pas of singing about Venus in front of her at a song contest, for which the assembled crowd threatens to slaughter him if he doesn't go to the Pope and slavishly abase himself. He goes. The Pope doesn't forgive him. Elizabeth decides to die because apparently then God *has* to forgive him… somehow. She dies. The Pope's staff sprouts leaves. It's a miracle! Tannhäuser is saved. The end.

Okay, that's flippant, but you see the central problems.

The opera demonizes human passion and lust which, if you know anything about Wagner the man, raises an eyebrow or two.

Nobody except Elizabeth seems to have any problem with executing Tannhäuser for SINGING AN ILL-CHOSEN SONG.

The Pope is kind of a dick.

And Wagner's theme of female self-sacrifice, which works to such stunning effect in The Ring and Tristan, makes absolutely no sense here unless you are locked into the Jesus trope, which as a society we increasingly aren't. Person A dying doesn't forgive the actions of person B. That's not how justice works anywhere except the twisted death cult reasoning of the Catholic Church. If that reasoning isn't compelling to you, the entire last act of the opera just seems cruel and arbitrary.

What is to be done? One of the tactics that seems successful to me is a shift of frame. Wagner's operas are populated with fascinating characters. For many operas, if the eponymous hero strikes you as something of an ineffectual dink, you don't really have anywhere else to turn to anchor your emotional investment. Not so with Wagner. In *Tannhäuser*, I think humanists gravitate instinctively to the character of Wolfram, the man who stays faithful to his friendship even as it costs him the love of his life, who believes strongly in companionship with humanity, and who struggles honestly with the contradiction between his faith and the tragedy he sees playing out before him by people crushed under the wheels of penance and salvation. He is us, and the more that character is brought to the foreground, the more that opera will resonate with modern audiences.

This frame-shift has paid off well in another Wagner religious opera, *Parsifal*. It features a central hero whom precisely nobody finds appealing. He has all of the negative aspects of Siegfried without the redeeming qualities of being helplessly in love or getting to fight awesome giants-turned-dragon. In the age of Big Dumb Christian He Men that was fine, but opera companies are rapidly figuring out that he's not quite the stuff intriguing radio spots are made of.

Which is why we see focus shifting more and more to the figure of Kundry. She is a creature of magic from times ancient who ever wishes to serve the noble warriors of her age, but who is treated scornfully by her latest charges, the Knights of the Grail. Worse still, she has recently fallen under the spell of the evil wizard Klingsor, and so is compelled to work against the very people her waking self suffers such agonies to protect. For those of us who could really care less whether the perpetually wailing head of the Grail Knights gets his mystical wound healed in the end by Parsifal or not, it is Kundry and her broken descent into emptiness that compels.

In the end, the revealing of the Grail forces her to fall to the ground, lifeless in some interpretations, though Wagner's libretto describes her state as "entseelt" which can be interpreted as alive, but de-souled. This is supposed to be a moment of redemptive purification, but played right, it could stand as a powerful instance of the mad quest for theological purity tearing apart those who are actually doing good in the world. The boys' club is reassembled, and the first order of business is to kill the witch who is too complicated for them to understand. It's a dark truth about how religion has functioned in the West since the fall of Astarte that only a dramatic genius on the order of Wagner could have set within the text so completely in spite of his own intentions.

I do love all of this music dearly, and I want to be able to see it all played on the stage many times more before I die. And not just these, but the other rich Christian-themed operas in the pantheon – Meyerbeer's *The Huguenots*, Poulenc's *Dialogue of the Carmelites* with its chilling mass execution scene finale, Wagner's *Lohengrin* with the delicious curse of the new Christian gods that falls from Ortrud's lips – there is shimmering beauty and fantastic drama to be had here. But I won't get to see any of it if opera companies chuck them all overboard as they did Baroque opera last century under the banner of "Modern audiences can't connect with this material." There is much that can be done to save these works for our secular age, to show that they have things to say beyond their veneer of unnecessary female sacrifice and ecstatic set pieces.

Because nobody knows how to portray the dark core of a religion so effectively as those who believe it free of darkness.

THE PRIMATE IMPERATIVE:
VEGETARIANISM, ANIMAL TESTING, AND HUMANISM

(Originally Published in *The New Humanist*, July 2013)

My first year as a teacher, I was shoved into my classroom by the Vice Principal and told, "You have three I Don't Knows that are going to have to last you to June, make 'em count." It was a slogan he'd developed after years of watching initially enthusiastic young teachers slowly devolve into instructors of the Read the Chapter the Night Before variety. The instant he said it, I knew precisely when I would need to use that small cache of professorial fallibility. It's the same thing I've been saying "I don't know" to myself about since sixth grade: animal testing.

There is no other problem out there that leaves me so intellectually flat-footed as how my humanism might shed light on my thoughts about medical animal research. When I became a vegetarian a decade ago, the decision took all of five minutes of sustained reflection. Meat is almost comically bad for my health, the meat industry is detrimental to the environment on a level that super villains would be envious of, and the cost is a living being raised as poorly and slaughtered as cheaply as possible. In exchange for all of that, all I get is that meat registers as delicious to the taste receptors on my tongue for a few seconds. Intellectually, it's an easy choice.

Animal testing, however, is a matter not so easily disposed of. At least, certain manifestations of it. I think we are all agreed as a civilization that, if it takes the poisoning of small mammals to produce the next line of mascara products, then we'll make do just fine with what we've got. It might only extend lashes by 115% instead of 122%, but somehow we'll muddle on as a species. By and large, we are very willing to pay an extra couple of dollars for cosmetics if they come with the peace of mind that nothing suffered agonies to make us look marginally better for our night on the town or shadow-bestrewn Skype date.

So, yes, cosmetic testing is a problem easily dealt with, but medical testing is an entirely different creature, breeding unreflective binarisms of the most trenchant sort. It is either never okay, or always okay, and in either case one searches in vain for a justification that ekes beyond metaphysical sloganeering. And that is all understandable, as a close inspection of the ethics of animal testing soon lands us in waters that call our very own existence as independent actors into question. Even those of us steeled in the fires of rigorous humanism find it a bleak and vertigo-inducing perspective from which to see ourselves, so it's hard to blame those who actually believe in gods and souls for stopping short of a thorough-going analysis of their own motivations and talking points.

But right here, right now, it is just you and I, so I am going to take you with me through the argument as far as I can and show you precisely where I think it breaks down and then, in fine and well established teacherly tradition, I'll hand the proof off to you to complete. Here are some of the ground assumptions I'm making which I think are necessary to honestly approach our relation to other life forms on our planet:

I do not believe in gods, souls, free will, or the afterlife. I consider myself in every way a machine with some interesting quirks and chemical properties that I'm entirely satisfied to spend a lifetime observing from the cheap seats that are my conscious brain (that sounds depressing, but if you don't make a habit of frequenting the cheap seats, then you don't know where the REAL party is). I'll do my best to stay alive and enjoy the relatively brief span during which this biochemical experiment currently wrapped in a Tears For Fears shirt will run its course. The decisions that emanate from me are the result of deterministic processes that, excepting some fundamental indeterminacy on the Planck level of space-time, I couldn't change if I wanted to.

There are two extremes one can take from this position. On one hand, you could see all life as just chemical reactions and conclude that all morality and ethics are meaningless afterthoughts, and so humans are entitled to do whatever they want to whatever they want. On the other, you could realize that there is nothing

50

qualitatively separating humanity from the other forms of life out there, and refuse to do so much as take medicine that could harm the bacteria seeking to eat you from the inside out. Both of these conclusions, however, leave out a crucial component – the mutual programmability of primatekind.

Determined my behavior might be, but it is determined in line with my primate inheritance, one which prejudices actions that favor social cohesion over those that do not. When others act out from their primate social instincts to pass judgment on the ethical rigor of my decisions, it programs me on a neurochemical level to make future decisions according to the best models and critiques I've been offered, and when I offer my opinions in turn, I help to program others. This mutual feedback system has pushed humanity into ever wider circles of inclusivity. We can't help it – we have been given a set of chemical reactions that reward a constant broadening of perspective, and are each other's watchmen in the advancing of this process.

We can modify each other's brains in ways unparalleled in most of the animal kingdom, for both good and ill. We police each other's biological imperative towards inclusivity, and that mutual reinforcement brings with it an expansion of our notion of responsibility that is just now extending towards the whole human race and will inevitably spread to other species as well. Eventually, we simply will not be able to bring ourselves to experiment on animals anymore – the self-reinforcing chemistry of that biological imperative will make it impossible to countenance animal testing as part of the ordinary course of civilization.

That's nice, but you can see where it's not an answer. As mammals, we have a biological need to include and program each other towards inclusivity, but a biological imperative is not a universal one. Sure, I'm acting in line with my basic biological drives when I treat animals better, but my biology is totally arbitrary, the result of an evolutionary process that made our species successful by stressing collaboration and interdependence. There is, however, no link between Successful Behavior Patterns and the universal imperative that we seem to crave. This is my problem with most people who come out with such strong opinions about animal testing – they behave as if there are universal principles to cleave to in this instance when there are merely interpretations and abstractions of various degrees of honesty.

The primate imperative cuts both ways, and that explains why the rhetoric seems so self-assured to members on both sides of the issue. Primates help each other even when it costs them resources, and so naturally the medical community feels itself to be acting in the best traditions of human nature when it bears the burden of sacrificing animal life to prolong and improve human life. Primates helping primates, even when it costs them peace of mind to do so. Research scientists are not evil charlatans who get off on inflicting harm on animals – they are men and women deeply connected to humanity and who sacrifice their time and happiness in pursuit of our benefit. They are caught up in our primate imperative in its human form.

Likewise, those unilaterally against animal testing have taken the line that any conscious act of will favoring one species at the expense of another is a betrayal of our best natures. Certainly, lines are always drawn and those lines are necessarily somewhat random (I don't know anybody who doesn't get inoculated, for example, out of sympathy for the viruses), but the general principle is there – don't hurt another species if it only helps your own. Here we have the primate imperative expanded to a kingdom-wide scale.

Ethics is the name we give to the rules extracted from our mutual chemical programming. In that sense, there is no deciding between the ethics of the research scientist and the PETA activist – they are both abstracted from the same source, the social imperatives that lie at the core of primate survival strategy, and are valid interpretations of the arbitrary evolutionary dictates of that source. There simply isn't any higher court to appeal to.

Lacking that, humans have to do what we have always done – cobble together a livable compromise that allows us to advance and extend our borders of inclusivity without sacrificing the well-being of our own suffering masses. It is a deeply unsatisfying answer for all involved, and leads quickly to absurdities of the Moral

Algebra type: "If one human is worth three bunnies, and an experiment that requires fourteen bunnies has a .5% chance of contributing to the cure for a disease that afflicts one quarter percent of the human population, is it ethical..." and so forth. The only comfort to take is that such a compromise is merely a bridge. Technology and our own biological imperatives are running a race to see which will shut down animal testing first. The only question is, will advanced computing and modeling techniques make animal testing impractical before our advancing definition of inclusion declares it unethical, or the other way around?

That will all probably take a good century to unfold, and in the meantime, there will be enough suffering on both sides of the species divide to call forth sympathy and action. There will be experiments that go positively nowhere at the cost of hundreds and thousands of animal lives, just as there will be breakthroughs that save millions of people from disease, and we will know that the latter does not make up for the former, nor does the former invalidate the worth of the latter. We are at that terribly awkward stage of species adolescence when our intelligence and the tools crafted therefrom don't quite match up to the most faithful and general realization of our civilizational principles. It is a stage to be grown out of, not regressed away from. The only way out is forward, as much as that road is filled with things we would really rather not face.

A society polarized into the Yes, Always and No, Never camps only assures that this adolescent phase will be as gruesome and lengthy as possible. The unwillingness to seek a minimally destructive compromise through a renouncing of ethical absolutes can only keep us in a self-imposed immaturity both unnecessary and cruel. This is where humanists can make themselves useful – by highlighting humankind's role as the shaper of its ethical world independent of god and eternity, we offer the metaphysically neutral ground where compromise can grow and even flourish. In the swirl and clamor of polarized invective, we can make humanist philosophical reduction the stable foundation from which to build a path to the adult phase of our species, and that will work wonders not only for us, but for the growing family of life forms we include within our familial embrace.

With that, I pass the chalk to you, and wish you the best of luck.

The Atheist Classifieds: Who We Need, Who We've Got.

(Originally Published in *The Freethinker*, May 2014)

Twenty Five years ago, there were basically two jobs open to the public atheist: you either became a professional arguer, or a person who facilitated professional arguing. It was our punk era, a brash, underground stirring that had a rushing sense of its own vitality and zero tolerance for flabby ideas or expression. We strutted around like West Side Story Jets, looking for a rumble, armed to the teeth with a glistening array of philosophical constructs and wicked argumentative gambits.

There was a subversive sexiness to that style of atheism that still allures after so many decades and so much evolution within atheist circles. We try and recapture it every time we invite a big-name pastor to a debate or head into a crowd of protestors and throw down the gauntlet in challenge.

But you can't go back, unfortunately. The things we did a quarter century ago (and, yes, I am infinitely depressed to report, 1989 WAS a quarter century ago) which had a mystical allure coming from our position as underdogs have a very different flavor to them now that secular humanism is such a dominant and established line of discourse.

As a movement, then, we've become top-heavy on arguers and ludicrously understaffed for every other job position. The shame of it is that there are atheists with precisely the skills we need right now, who are kept from making their own crucial contributions by the perception that, if you're not a thuggish debater, we don't require you. I modestly present, then, some Atheist Classifieds for the sorts of positions we need to be fostering to keep atheism from swallowing its own tail in the decades to come:

Education Volunteers: *Especially* in low income areas. You don't need to be an educational genius, you just need to be someone of patience and persistence. Some time ago, I started working with adults who, for one reason or another, weren't able to get their high school diploma, and who very nobly sacrifice time out of their three-minimum-wage-paying-jobs workweek to try and get an equivalent certification. And the stories I hear are appalling with regard to how these people have been taught to think of themselves and their minds. Some think they can't learn because God made them a certain way. Others were told by teachers at a young age that they were wasting the public's money and time. It is a truly rewarding and I think important experience to be able to take these people and say, "No, here's how learning works on a purely neural level, and here's how we're going to use that knowledge to get you where you need to go." Using a non-metaphysical outlook to give people a renewed sense of potential is one of the best things atheism has to offer, and we usually only offer it to people of a certain minimum social class just because our weapons have historically been so thoroughly bourgeois. That's something we need to change, and something that anybody with a couple spare hours a week can help us with.

Shopkeepers: Atheism is building up its base of local organizations and meet-up groups and all of that is entirely excellent, but hasn't it struck you how, for such a geeky, books-and-board-games crew, there are so few shops that act as friendly gathering places that can also serve as aggregation points for humanist events? A place that stocks a good selection of interesting science, psychology, and philosophy books and magazines, and also perhaps a fair amount of those games and puzzles that we devour in groups by way of oblique social interaction. An informal rally point where good conversation can be had, a place for our burgeoning artists to display their works and our musicians to perform, and a place to sell coffee at an outrageous mark-up to a civilization that has been carefully trained to find it normal. Ten years ago, such a venture would smack of fateful hubris, but there are numbers now to make it financially doable, and it is certainly something that we need by way of day-to-day community interaction.

Social Workers: An increasingly atheist/humanist population brings with it a radically different set of emotional issues in need of support. Right now, we have a bulging sack of people telling the world *why* they should be atheists, but relatively few telling them *how* to live with the consequences of that decision. A new generation of social workers, therapists, and psychologists will need to bring not only the traditional tools of their trade, but an understanding of what lack of belief does to one's sense of societal integration and self. "A psychologist can't help me, because they're too caught up in their metaphysics to hear and understand what I'm saying," is a sentence I've heard too often preventing people from getting help they need.

Lifestyle Bloggers: We're pretty good for blogs that jump on William Lane Craig's every logical slip, or that repost stories about terrible things happening in the world at the hands of organized religion. That's covered. But what is in somewhat precious supply are people just demonstrating the nuts and bolts of what a life without gods is like. What gives you satisfaction? How do you think about the relationships around you? What are your doubts and hopes? A simple accounting, without spending every other post attempting to prove how You Are Right, of the manifold decisions and discovered joys of life minus afterlife. Others would then be able to see how, ninety eight percent of the time, we're doing the same mundane stuff as everybody else, but that in the remaining two, some warm, personal, and lovely things tend to happen that grow naturally from a secular foundation, but have nothing to do with waging war on behalf of secularism. By being manifestly normal, you could do more for humanism than the most eloquent and clever members of our current pantheon.

And on. Anything you can do to bring out the secret moments of warmth that we atheists experience regularly but never talk about out of fear of being thought *superficial*, or to help other humans understand themselves a little bit better, gives atheism as a body of ideas something slightly more societally substantial to rest upon than, "Our logic is The Best Logic." We need to keep arguing, by all means, but we need to stop evaluating the work of the rest of the atheist community based on how well it supports our arguers, however sexy they may be. Our snarl and snap youth is behind us; it's time to start our less glorious, but more community integrated, adulthood, and to learn to enjoy the constructive pleasures and opportunities it has to offer.

ATHEI-ETIQUETTE:
WHY YOU DON'T NEED
TO GIVE UP IMPECCABLE MANNERS
WHEN YOU COME OUT AS AN ATHEIST.

(Originally Published in *American Atheist Magazine*,
3rd Quarter, 2014)

Rule of etiquette the first – which hundreds of others merely paraphrase or explain or elaborate – is: Never do anything that is unpleasant to others.
- Emily Post, *Etiquette*.

There seem few things more at cross-purposes than public atheism and etiquette. If Emily is right (and I think she is) about good manners consisting primarily in doing everything you can to make life more pleasant for those around you, then merely *being* an atheist in the first place is a shocking breach of decorum. What could make life more immediately unpleasant for your fellow man than steadfastly refusing to acknowledge the possibility of his theological whims? Is the choice, then, between being well-mannered but silent or uncouth but true-to-self? Put more bluntly, must atheists always appear as clumsy, ill-bred bullies?

Of course not, though *some* of us seem to rather delight in our reputation for coarse disregard, consciously cultivating a punk-sneer to shock the bourgeoisie out of their inertia-sustained religiosity. And that's absolutely necessary, and I'm supremely glad that we have people who are doing it, but I admit to never being comfortable in that role. So, I've set about, with the great minds of historical etiquette to lean on, trying to craft an atheism that is able to express itself while still obeying Emily's First Law.

My basic principle is this: *Never initiate a religiously contentious moment. If somebody else should drag you into one, you deserve to assert your existence as an atheist, but always in proper proportion to the intimacy you have with that party.* Let's see how that plays out:

Situation 1: The Clerk.

You are at a store, and the clerk wishes you "Merry Christmas" as he hands you the receipt. This is the most trifling of religious assumptions, and most of us are entirely fine with letting it pass, but let's say you can't. You just can't. You've been wished Merry Christmas ninety-nine times that day, and you are DONE with being bombarded with Jesus in the Manger.

The important thing to keep in mind is that this person is an entire stranger to you, and your response should therefore be of minimum complexity and zero tendentiousness. "Happy Holidays" is fine, but generic, and doesn't really assert much of anything. My stand-by is, "Ah, and a happy season to you!" The "Ah" expresses a recognition that they have gone out of their way to wish you well, and that you appreciate it, and the remainder of the message expresses returned good will, but with the slightest whiff of secular suggestion. The important thing is, it's distinctive without being accusatory. If the clerk is particularly perceptive, you've done something towards making them realize that there are entirely decent, understated people out there who aren't Christian. And if he's not, well, you did what you could within the realm of pleasantness, and that's all that can be asked.

Situation 2: The Door To Door Proselytizer.

Be they Jehovah's Witness, Mormons, or something else utterly, there is no doubt that they have come asking to start a religious conversation. You will not change their mind with a virtuosic display of logic or a burst of vitriolic indignation, but you may give them pause with some honest pleasantness. "I'm terribly sorry, but I am an atheist, you see, so I don't think we have much common ground as to religious discussion. But would you like to come in for a bit and have some tea (if it's cold out) or ice water (if it's hot) before moving on to the rest of the neighborhood?" usually works rather well. The offer is generally rejected, but the unexpected civility noted.

With those who actually take me up, given the understanding that we won't talk about pesky religious things, I chat about everyday life, learn something of their troubles and hopes, and they some of mine, and we part quite cordially, never to meet again. From a crass tactical standpoint, they see that one can be an atheist and still remain quite considerate and generally well-adjusted, and that always works out well for us.

Situation 3: The Internet.

Amazingly, most of the etiquette book guides to Large Dinner Gathering Manners work pretty well here. In the face of unpleasantness, a person of manners realizes that an unpleasant response, while personally gratifying, makes one's guests uncomfortable, and is therefore a failure of hosting. The fact is that, for every one person who eggs you on in making a discussion inelegant, there are fifty quietly hoping that you'll find your better instincts.

A proper response to unjust and insulting online criticism is silence. Politeness *will* be deliberately misconstrued as hauteur, and anything less is beneath the dignity of a responsible human being.

If the criticism has a nugget of merit, however coarsely stated, it deserves a response. If their point is one you want to follow up on, then do get into the formal details, always placing a request for elaboration in place of an accusation of incompetence: "I have to admit to finding this step rather worrisome. Could you perhaps flesh it out a bit for us?"

If the point isn't one you terribly much want to go into, a subtle diversion is in order. I like books, so that's usually where I go: "I notice you mention X. What are your favorite reads on the subject?" expresses the appropriate amount of recognition and good intent while at the same time effectively ending the discussion before it gets tedious.

Situation 4: Well Meant Praise.

You are volunteering, and somebody you just helped fulsomely praises you with, "Bless you for your time" or "It's been a real Blessing to have you" or more embarrassingly still, "May God bless you for what you've done here." Their eyes beam with genuine warmth and human regard that you can't help but feel moved by. You have to choose whether to thank them in return and move on, or find a gentle way of expressing your own perspective.

You probably have some acquaintance with these people, so your response can be rather more elaborate than in situation 1, where no future contact is assumed. Again, there is nothing wrong with taking the praise and letting it be. I think it's what most of us actually do in this situation out of pure empathy and humanity. But there is also no reason

60

why you can't be honest while still being pleasant and gracious: "Well, thank you very much, and as a grizzled old atheist, I can tell you, I don't get blessed NEARLY enough, so I certainly appreciate it!" There is a bit of self-deprecation, a sliver of a joke, and never the slightest suggestion that you don't deeply appreciate their sentiment.

I have to say, I never liked, "Thank you, although to tell the truth, I'm an atheist" which has been touted as a good stock response. It ends too abruptly, and doesn't offer a path back to normal conversation that all awkward but necessary comments *must* have. Also, just in general, the words "but" and "although" should simply never be used in an expression of thanks, no matter what follows them.

Situation 5: Grace, the Pledge of Allegiance, and Other Unavoidable Religious Ceremonies.

You have been asked to lead grace at a family event, perhaps by a family member who doesn't yet know that you're an atheist or by one who does and likes watching you squirm uncomfortably.

I can think of no condition, short of it being your dying grandmother's last wish, under which acceptance is the right course of action. Decline politely and indicate somebody who would do better in your stead. "Thank you all terribly much. I think Grace would mean so much more coming from somebody SLIGHTLY religious. Plus, we all agree that we haven't heard nearly enough from Ted this evening. Go on, Ted!"

During the grace, the same rule holds as for all religious ceremonies you find yourself present at: You *need* not participate, but you *must* not interfere.

I don't care how ridiculous or disgusting the event is, if you have been invited to it, your behavior reflects upon your host, so you will keep your grimaces, eye-rolls, and mutterings to yourself. If you have invited yourself to the event, then you are your own host, and so should be doubly courteous. At the same time, you should feel no compulsion to join the rituals. No good host would invite you if such a lack of participation would reflect badly upon him or herself, nor any friend expect you to betray your principles to make up for their own lack of invitational foresight.

And while we're on the subject, a word about hats in Church. I am a hat wearer. I admit it. I wear them more or less everywhere, and only feel compelled to remove them at funerals, at events where their bulk blocks the view of people behind me, and during the National

Anthem of countries I like. As such, I regularly wear them in churches, and occasionally get scolded for it. I usually respond with some variation of, "Mistrust all organizations that attempt to remove you from your headwear, especially when it is the only thing interesting about you," which is received as a benign statement of foppishness rather than an act of irreligious contempt, and the bomb is defused. If you need to err, err on the side that makes yourself look a little vain and silly rather than on that of righteous pride, and you can't go wrong.

This will all doubtless seem incredibly wishy-washy to a significant portion of the atheist world. Those who relish going out and finding debates with hapless but cocky rubes might think I am criticizing their approach to atheism, but that is not my intention. I aim to find a livable compromise for the rest of us, less meteoric, types. We want to exist, and be recognized for what we are, without making of that existence a standing accusation against the world. And it can be done, if you are willing to be understated where you could be indignant, and self-effacing where you could be caustic. Certainly, after millennia of persecution, we have earned caustic indignation as our hard-won due, but sometimes a prize rejected brings rewards greater still, and the lessening of the overall unpleasantness of man towards man certainly counts as one such.

PART II:

Religion and Spirituality

THE DARK SIDE OF BUDDHISM

(Originally Published in *The New Humanist*, February 2013)

On paper, Buddhism looks pretty good. It has a philosophical subtlety married to a stated devotion to tolerance that makes it stand out amongst the world religions as uniquely not awful. Even Friedrich Nietzsche, not known for pulling punches when it came to religious analysis, only said of Buddhism that it was "nihilistic", but still "a hundred times more realistic than Christianity." And we in the 21st Century have largely followed his lead in sensing something a bit depressing about Buddhism, but nothing more sinister than that. But if we start looking a bit closer, at the ramifications of Buddhist belief in practice, there is a lurking darkness there, quietly stated and eloquently crafted, but every bit as profound as the Hellfires of Christianity or the rhetoric of jihad.

For nine years, I worked as a science and math teacher at a small private Buddhist school in the United States. And it was a wonderful job working with largely wonderful people. The administration, monks, and students knew that I was an atheist and had absolutely no problem with it as long as I didn't actively proselytize (try and find a Catholic school that would hire a moderate agnostic, let alone a fully out-of-the-closet atheist). Our students were incredibly sensitive and community-conscious individuals, and are my dear friends to this day.

However.

I have no doubt that Buddhist religious belief, as it was practiced at the school, did a great deal of harm. Nowhere was this more in evidence than in the ramifications of the belief in karma. At first glance, karma is a lovely idea which encourages people to be good even when nobody is watching for the sake of happiness in a future life. It's a bit carrot-and-stickish, but so are a lot of the ways that we get people to not routinely beat us up and take our stuff. Where it gets insidious is in the pall that it casts over our failures in this life. I remember one student who was having problems memorizing material for tests. Distraught, she went to the monks who explained to her that she was having such trouble now because, in a past life, she was a murderous dictator who burned books, and so now, in this life, she is doomed to forever be learning challenged.

Not "Oh, let's look at changing your study habits" but rather "Oh, well, that's because you have the soul of a book-burning murderer."

To our ears, this sounds so over the top that it is almost amusing, but to a kid who earnestly believes that these monks have hidden knowledge of the karmic cycle, it is devastating. She was convinced that her soul was polluted and irretrievably flawed, and that nothing she could do would allow her to ever learn like the people around her. And this is the dark side of karma - instead of misfortunes in life being bad things that happen *to* you, they are manifestations of a deep and fundamental wrongness *within* you. Children have a hard enough time keeping up their self-esteem as it is without every botched homework being a sign of lurking inner evil.

As crippling as the weight of one's past lives can be, however, it is nothing compared to the horrors of the here and now. Buddhism's inheritance from Hinduism is the notion of existence as a painful continuous failure to negate itself. The wheel of reincarnation rumbles ruthlessly over us all, forcing us to live again and again in this horrid world until we get it right and learn to not exist. I remember one of the higher monks at the school giving a speech in which she described coming back from a near-death experience as comparable to having to "return to a sewer where you do nothing but subsist on human excrement." Life is suffering. It is something to be Finally Escaped.

Now, there are legitimate philosophical reasons for holding to this view. Viewed from a certain perspective, the destruction of everything you've ever cared about is inevitable, and when it's being experienced, the pain of loss does not seem recompensed by the joy of attachment that preceded it. And that yawning stretch of impermanence outside, so the argument goes, is mirrored by the fundamental non-existence of the self inside. Meditation, properly done, allows you to strip away, one by one, all of your merely personal traits and achieve insight into the basic nothingness, the attributeless primal nature, of your existence. Those are all interesting philosophical and psychological insights, and good can come of them. Being hyper-sensitive to suffering and injustice is a good gateway to being helpful to your fellow man and in general making the world a better place.

However.

There is something dreadfully tragic about believing yourself to have somehow failed your calling whenever joy manages to creep into your life. It is in our biology, in the fabric of us, to connect to other human beings, and anything which tries to insert shame and doubt into that instinct is bound to always twist us ever so slightly. If the thought, "I am happy right now," can never occur without an accompanying, "And I am just delaying my ultimate fulfillment in being so," then what, essentially, has life become? I've seen it in action - people reaching out for connection, and then pulling back reflexively, forever caught in a life of half-gestures that can't ever quite settle down to pure contemplation or gain a moment of genuine absolute enjoyment.

The usual response that I've gotten to these concerns is, "You're sacrificing truth and wisdom for the sake of feeling good. That's just what you criticize Christianity for, isn't it?" This would be a pretty damn good argument if I were convinced that the conclusions of Buddhist belief were as ironclad as their usually serene-unto-finality presentation makes them seem. There are two central claims here: that our own fundamental essence is non-existence, and that the nature of the outer world is impermanence.

The idea of the void-essence of self is one arrived at through meditation, through exercises in reflection dictated by centuries of tradition. That's enough to give us pause right there - it's not really a process of self-discovery if you're told the method, the steps, and the only acceptable conclusion before you've even begun. Here's the fourteenth Dalai Lama on how to start a meditation:

"First, look to your posture: arrange the legs in the most comfortable position; set the backbone as straight as an arrow. Place your hands in the position of meditative equipoise, four finger widths below the navel, with the left hand on the bottom, right hand on top, and your thumbs touching to form a triangle. This placement of the hands has connection with the place inside the body where inner heat is generated."

This is already an unpromising start - if you aren't even allowed variation in the number of sub-navel fingerwidths for hand placement, how can we hope to be allowed to even slightly differ on the supposed object of inner contemplation? And the text bears this out. When speaking of meditating on the mind, the Dalai Lama maneuvers his audience into a position where his conclusion seems inevitable:

"Try to leave your mind vividly in a natural state... Where does it seem that your consciousness is? Is it with the eyes or where is it? Most likely you have a sense that it is associated with the eyes since we derive most of our awareness of the world through vision.... However, the existence of a separate mental consciousness can be ascertained; for example, when attention is diverted by sound, that which appears to the eye consciousness is not noticed... with persistent practice, consciousness may eventually be perceived or felt as an entity of mere luminosity or knowing, to which anything is capable of appearing... as long as the mind does not encounter the external circumstances of conceptuality, it will abide empty without anything appearing in it."

If this reminds you more than a little of *Meno*, where Socrates leads a slave boy into "rediscovering" the truths of geometry through a combination of leading questions and implied conclusions, you're not alone. Notice the artful vagueness of the phrase "may eventually be perceived or felt as an entity of mere luminosity" - the subtle pressure that, if you don't perceive consciousness that way at first, you must keep trying until something in you falls into line and you end up with the "right" answer to meditative practice. Or take into consideration the construction of the questions - how the second question immediately shuts down any actual consideration of the first, and how the answer to that second question leads to a single special case open to multiple interpretations which are again immediately declared to be explicable by only one single answer. As it turns out, you have as much freedom of inquiry as you had freedom in hand placement. In a curious twist unique to Buddhism, rigidity of method has infected the structure of belief, ossifying potential explanations of existence into dogmatic assertions mechanically arrived at.

The impermanence of the outer world seems more solidly founded. Five billion years hence, I'm pretty sure that this novelty shot glass next to me is not going to exist in any sort of recognizable novelty shot glass form. Nothing in this room will functionally persist as long as you only admit my Use Perspective as the only relevant lens of observation. The matter and energy will both still exist, but they won't exist in the configuration which I am accustomed to. And that, apparently, is supposed to fill me with a sense of existential dread. But it doesn't - at all - and this is the weakness of the conclusions that Buddhism draws from an impermanence theory of the external world. It supposes that I cannot hold in my mind at the same time both an appreciation and attachment to an object or a person as they stand in front of me right now AND a recognition that my use of a particular configuration of matter and energy at the moment doesn't determine how it will exist for all time. Buddhism's approach to use-based impermanence attempts to force us into a false binarism where we must either be the slaves of attachment *or* the cold observers of transience, and that only one of these offers us a way out of suffering. Compelled by the forced logic of its myopic perspective on self-analysis that we saw above, it opts for the latter, and presents that choice as an inevitable philosophical conclusion.

So, it's not really a choice between Feeling Good and Truth. It's a choice between being able to unambiguously enjoy companionship and a system of thought which uses an ossified methodology bordering on catechism to support a falsely binary approach to our relations with the outside world.

At the end of the day, it's still true that, in many respects, Buddhism maintains its moral edge over Christianity or Islam handily. That instinct for proselytizing unto war which has made both of these religions such distinctly harmful forces in the story of mankind is nowhere present. But, the drive to infect individuals with an inability to appreciate life except through a filter of regret and shame is perhaps even more dangerous in Buddhism for being so very much more subtle. Squeezed between the implications of inherited evil instincts and a monolithic conception of what counts as a right answer to the question of one's own personal existence, a young person entering a Buddhist community today is every bit as much under the theological gun as a student at a Catholic school, but because society has such a cheery picture of Buddhist practice, she has far fewer resources for resistance than her Catholic counterpart. And that allows sad things to happen. I would urge, then, that as fulfilling as it is to point out and work to correct the gross excesses of Christianity (and, let's face it, fun too), we can't let the darkness of Buddhist practice go by unremarked just because it works more subtly and its victims suffer more quietly.

RAPE: THE CHRISTIAN TRADITION

(Originally Published in *The Freethinker*, February 2013)

One of the most surreal aspects of our 2012 political season here in the US was the sight of not one, but two, highly placed Republican officials waxing philosophical about rape. Shortly after Representative Todd Akin offered us his distinction between legitimate and illegitimate rape, Indiana State Treasurer Richard Mourdock opined that rape is all part of God's larger and benevolent plan. Many found these statements outrageous, but I find it odd that we were all so shocked. Akin and Mourdock, as we shall see, are precisely in line with mainstream, orthodox Biblical thinking on the subject of rape and women's duties in preventing it. The Bible is very explicit in its views about women as property and man's authority over them, and subsequent theology has done little to ameliorate those original sentiments.

The Old Testament places an interesting and horrifying dual burden upon women. Firstly, they are property, owned originally by their father and then bartered to their husband. If a woman displeases her husband, he need only write out a bill of divorce and send her on her way, to make do as best she can (Deuteronomy 24:1-4). The only time when he loses this right is if he rapes an unengaged virgin, after which he must pay 50 shekels of silver to the father and marry his victim, the marriage being then indissoluble (Deut. 22:28-29). This is the ancient equivalent of "You Break It, You Buy It." The daughter is no longer saleable goods to the father, and so he is monetarily compensated for his loss, while the new husband has leave to legally rape his victim in perpetuity. Virginity is a commodity under this system, and both Judaic law, and the Christian theology that sprung from it, are positively frantic about guarding it.

But it is the second burden that is particularly cruel. Not content to reduce women to property, the ancient Israelites then charged them with being their own subjugators. Women must not merely accept their role passively, but must actively fight to maintain it, and if they don't, they are to be exposed to the full measure of punishment the law can mete out. This is the great legacy of Biblical thinking on the subject of rape: that the responsibility for a woman's rape only rests fully on her rapist's shoulders if every other alternate explanation has been eliminated first. It is worth quoting the relevant passage of Deuteronomy in full:

In the case of a virgin who is engaged to a man - if a man comes upon her in town and lies with her, you shall take the two of them out to the gate of that town and stone them to death: the girl because she did not cry for help in the town, and the man because he violated another man's wife.... But if the man comes upon the engaged girl in the open country, and the man lies with her by force, only the man who lay with her shall die, but you shall do nothing to the girl... He came upon her in the open; though the engaged girl cried for help, there was no one to save her. (Deuteronomy 22:23-27)

This is the germ of Todd Akin's worldview. If a woman is raped anywhere in the city, she bears the blame of it for not having tried hard enough to rouse her neighbors to her protection, and deserves to die for her failure, and the man to die for having ruined another man's property. Only if she is far removed from all possible help, so far that her loudest scream couldn't be heard, is she allowed to live. The former is an *illegitimate* rape - she could have fought harder against it, but didn't, and the latter is a *legitimate* rape. Akin maintained precisely the same structure, but just added a biological sugar coating to it when he said, "If it's a legitimate rape, the female body has ways to try to shut that whole thing down." If the woman's internal organs do not fight the invader's sperm hard enough, then the rape was not legitimate - her biology somehow *wanted* it to happen. The woman merits consideration and pity only if she is successful in internally repelling the semen of her attacker. For a Christian to express horror at Akin but not at identical sentiments in his own central spiritual text is a maneuver in double-think that can only be excused by the fact that Deuteronomy is a book more often skimmed than read.

But perhaps our horrified Christian has indeed read these lines, and responds with the usual, "But that stuff is in the *Old* Testament - the *New* Testament does away with all of that barbarism." *Does* it now? After all, you don't have to look particularly far to find the rape mentality of the New Testament. Jesus is, quite explicitly, the product of a rape. Mark and John, in their accounts of Jesus's life, pass over the topic of his birth entirely. Matthew is, typically, more concerned with detailing the bartering

71

between god and Joseph over the affront to his property than with Mary's story (Matthew 1:18-25, in which god pays his 50 shekels by promising fame and glory as recompense, as long as Joseph agrees to keep the girl.) Luke, however, in his telling of Jesus's birth, wrote a positive text-book for "authority" rape. Susan Brownmiller, in her genre-defining *Against Our Will: Men, Women, and Rape* describes this mode of violation as follows:

"Rapists may operate within an emotional setting or within a dependent relationship that provides a hierarchical, authoritarian structure of its own that weakens a victim's resistance, distorts her perspective and confounds her will." (p. 256)

And such is the rape carried out by Jehovah against Mary in Luke's account. It makes for chilling reading, particularly in view of the thousands of years of priests and teachers that have used it as a primer for their own debauches:

Gabriel appeared to her and said, "Congratulations, favored lady! The Lord is with you!"
Confused and disturbed, Mary tried to think what the angel could mean.
"Don't be frightened, Mary," the angel told her, "for God has decided to wonderfully bless you! Very soon now, you will become pregnant and have a baby boy, and you are to name him Jesus. He shall be very great and shall be called the Son of God."
Mary asked the angel, "But how can I have a baby? I am a virgin."
The angel replied, "The Holy Spirit shall come upon you, and the power of God shall overshadow you..."
Mary said, "I am the Lord's servant, and I am willing to do whatever he wants." (Luke 1: 28-38)

In summary, one of god's lieutenants shows up, tells Mary how it's going to be, how she's going to be impregnated, what to name the child, and how she should be glad about being done the

72

honor. She is told, not asked. And she submits in the manner of so many women since presented by the authoritative command of a figure they trust and respect. But this isn't enough for Luke - in a positive orgy of male domination fantasy, he puts a long, panting speech into Mary's mouth after the act, glorifying her rapist's power, and rhapsodizing over the favor done her:

"How I rejoice in God my Savior! For he took notice of his lowly servant girl, and now generation after generation forever shall call me blest of God. For he, the mighty Holy One, has done great things to me... How powerful is his mighty arm! How he scatters the proud and haughty ones! He has torn princes from their thrones and exalted the lowly." (Luke 1:47-53)

This is every wretched stereotype about rape writ divine. Women want to be overpowered. They want to be shown who's boss. They consider it an honor to bear the seed of powerful men. They view being taken as something great done TO them. Even when they seem afraid that's just a sign of how much they actually want to be violated. Mary is every girl or boy who has ever been taken in by a priest with soft, glorious words and the promise that they are doing the Lord's Work. She is a submissive breeding vessel who worships her defiler, and that trope has been part of the Christian mindset, and the rapist's ready vocabulary, ever since.

The years that separate the Bible from modern times have seen variations upon these themes, but little in the way of improvement. St. Augustine notoriously added to woman's double burden a third: not only must she be property, and not only must she fight to protect her status as property, but if that fight fails and she is raped, she must accept the fact in chaste humility, taking it all as a fruitful lesson about the dangers of being too proud. She is not to be stoned to death, granted, but her emotional life after the event is to be dictated by the men around her who would really rather she just get over the whole incident and get back to normal life.

This enforced stoicism is, in effect, her punishment for not having had the good sense to die during her rapist's attack. For there is nothing that medieval Christianity (and not just medieval, as it turns out) loved so much as a virgin who dies at the hand of her rapist. In 1975, Brownmiller ferreted out no less than five medieval saints who were noted for nothing more than dying to protect the commodity of their virginity: Agnes, Agatha, Lucia, Philomena, and Susanna. The interpreters of the New Testament, for all their obscure talk about not casting stones at prostitutes, still plainly expected of women that they protect their status as property to the death, awarding them with sainthood if they succeeded, and punishing them with a code of silent humility if they survived.

In this context, Mourdock's opinion of rape makes complete sense. In his view, "Life is that gift from God that I think even if life begins in that horrible situation of rape, that it is something that God intended to happen." In other words, if the woman were really the stuff of a saint, she would have followed St. Agnes and died during the rape, but given that she didn't, she must suffer in silence and bow to the wisdom of god. In Mourdock, and in the tens of thousands who rushed to his defense, Augustine walks again, and women, after decades of struggle to be recognized as independent entities, are to be reduced to the watchdogs of their own virtue, and given sympathy only in so far as they match up to that standard.

Akin and Mourdock are not the archaic examples of a worldview gone by that the religious establishment rushed to characterize them as. They are rather the faithful interpreters of two thousand years of theological tradition in a country still overwhelmingly steeped in that tradition. They present the thoughts in their original essence, as they stood then, and as to thousands of American Christians they still stand now in various diluted forms. Women as self-guarding property form the basis of the Judaic conception of family and our modern expectations of women's duties during their own rape, just as rape as a zealous surrender to a superior being inform both the birth of Jesus and the fraternity mentality that has plastered modern headlines with cases of gang rape on American campuses. Dealing with the modern incarnations of rape requires grappling honestly with the root sources, something that can't be done so long as we see Akin and his ilk as aberrations rather than faithful representatives of their religion.

Thrashing for Jesus, Rapping For Science: The Evolution of Christian Metalcore and Humanist Hip Hop

(Originally Published at *The New Humanist*, April 2013)

Every Living Thing
Will bow down at his feet,
And every enemy
Will suffer their defeat.
Our deliverer has come.
This is WAR.
-For Today, *From Zion* (2013)

Like most of you I was indoctrinated with religion
at a time when I was much too young to make decisions
dragged by the hand without permission
lacked the cognitive ability to see the contradictions and the superstitions
I know my mother really thought that she was doing right
cause after all this wasn't a war that she was taught to fight.

-Tombstone da Deadman, *Ballad of a Non Believer* (2012)

For decades, the words "Christian Music" evoked little more than swirling recollections of late Elvis, twangy Louvin Brothers revival songs, and a mass of innocuous fluff on the order of Amy Grant or Carman. Meanwhile, the term "Humanist Music" drew mostly blank stares with the occasional, "Yeah, 'Dear God' is a pretty good song." The last fifteen years, however, has wrought some rather titanic shifts for religion (and anti-religion) in music. On one end of the spectrum are the growling, pounding sermons in thrash by Christian Metalcore bands like For Today. Though different in instrumentation and use of melody, they all share that heady potpourri of violent *ressentiment*, savior guilt, and low self-esteem that has been the bread and butter of Christianity since Saint Paul first hung out his Faith Before Works shingle.

About as far from Christcore as you can get, a community of humanist rappers has been slowly congregating since the early 2000s. These performers wield the lyrical deftness of the rap medium to do everything from recounting their personal experiences of a youth laden with imposed religion to correcting misconceptions about scientific theory and practice.

It is a fascinating battle to observe, the Christcore contingent in possession of all the massive psychological machinery of Christian imagery and rhetoric, while the humanist rappers carry into the fray little more than a wagonload of textbooks and the fearless irreverence of the historical underdog. In the back and forth between these camps there is much that we as humanists can learn, not only from how our rap champions are infusing philosophy and science into a living art form, but also what day-to-day psychological needs the Christcore musicians are fulfilling that will always keep us coming up short with their fanbase and the large slice of humanity they represent, no matter how clever or creative we are.

To delve deeper into the strengths and tools of the genres, I'm going to limit myself to two sets of representative work, the EP *Prevailer* by For Today released just this month, and a set of tracks from the rap collective Grand Unified featuring the work of Tombstone da Deadman and Greydon Square. *Prevailer* begins with the call to arms that I began this article with, and just gets creepier from there. It is a straight out military order to rise up under the command of Jesus and destroy this world of sinners. As if the opening declaration of war were too mild and understated, the song continues

Rise up, rise up.
Never again do we fight alone.
The promised One has come to set His people free.
From the ashes came our greatest victory.

This mystery has been revealed to the discerning:
The Lamb was slain; the Blood was shed; let death pass over us.
The sacrifice was made for sinners, undeserving.
Now we stand set apart to storm the gates of hell.

As extreme a rhetoric of ecstatic genocide as all of this is, it's not atypical for the genre. "Wages of Sin" by War of Ages, "The Call" by In The Midst of Lions, and "Condemned" by Impending Doom are all more or less interchangeable songs that glorify holy war by dehumanizing the unfaithful. No, where For Today really pushes the envelope is in the inclusion of a concluding mass chant of "Rise Up! We are the Resistance!" that has a certain whiff, well more than a whiff – a positive SCENT, of Nuremberg to it.

For the suburban kid playing Call of Duty at three in the morning, unnoticed by his peers in the present and nothing more grand than a managerial position at Quick Burger to look forward to, this call to glory could easily be an attractive thing. The danger, of course, is that if that guy ever feels more than halfway decent about himself, the call will lose its luster and start to appear more like the grotesquely shambling farce it is.   That's where the rest of the songs come in. Track two, "Crown of Thorns", seems at first like the usual "Crucifixion is really quite unpleasant" song that we've been hearing since televangelism first made mass market thorns-

and-nails fetishism a thing back in the eighties. Where it starts to turn is with the tear-soaked lament-scream of

It should have been me,
With the nails through my hands and feet,
Facing the wrath of God.
It should have been me,
Left to pay for my sin, forsaken.
But in the blood, I stand here.

Is there anything more diabolically well suited to keep somebody enlisted in the warrior mindset than thrusting upon them a world-historical level of survivor's guilt? (Though, come to think of it, if one would define Christianity generally as Survivor's Guilt Gone Galactic one wouldn't err over-much.) You will stay, and you will fight, because this perfect man died when it should have been YOU. And so, by track four, after several more exercises in declaring one's own personal worthlessness and being assured that the rest of the world despises you as you are, we are set for the rousing terrorist in training conclusion that

I walk the narrow road,
And follow the one that can set me free.
I never have to walk alone.
This is my destiny.
I've found something worth dying for.

End album. I'm not saying that the musicians of For Today are master manipulators of mass psychology. For the most part, they can barely be compelled to play their guitars outside of The Box let alone craft a master plan for building an army of disaffected youths. What they are are six guys who were so utterly overtaken by a tradition of imagery and linguistic feints that they can't help but reproduce that process of subjugation in their work. In *Prevailer* what we see is men re-enacting their own emotional execution at the same time as they perpetuate it. That's a powerful thing when you've got nothing going for you. It carries an intensity that fills voids which humanism, and particularly atheism, has been justifiably reluctant to engage with.

Or rather, had been. Enter Grand Unified, a collective of around twenty humanist musicians formed in 2011. The collective is the brain child of rapper Greydon Square, a veteran of the war in Iraq and committed atheist whose 2007 album *The Compton Effect* stands as one of the foundational works of humanist rap. What makes the album work so well, and has also served as a template for the larger success of the Grand Unified project, is its willingness to add personal narrative to the usual atheist repertoire of clever argumentation and snark.

Don't get me wrong – there is enough of both of those in the average Square song to keep an old school atheist happy. "A Rational Response" faces off against Pascal's Wager and clarifies the finer points of Argon dating. "Squared" quotes Stephen F Roberts and Carl Sagan while delving into the theological issue of God's benevolence. It's fun and clever, and turns the fine-honed smack talking skills of the rap battle tradition firmly at a target fully worthy of their devastating deployment. But if it were just fun and clever games of logic and science, humanism would be where it has always been – that kid in the class who knows the answers but whom nobody can identify with and therefore nobody wants to emulate.

No, Square and Grand Unified offer something more – a biographical approach to the atheist story, a humanizing of humanism that anybody can relate to and sympathize with. In "Molotov", Square raps about what it was like to be a soldier in a United States Army that was overwhelmingly suspicious of atheism and atheists:

> God Bless the troops, that's kinda odd
> America only blesses you as a troop if you
> believe in their Gods
> So where does that leave me?
> They tell me to leave G

But at the same time they tell me America
needs me.

In those five lines, Square captures an entire way of life – a desperate and confused hiding in the shadows not for something that you've done, but for something you don't personally believe. There's not a person in the world who hasn't had to deal with the dull ache and fear of carrying convictions that aren't those of one's peer group or colleagues, and for those people, should they hear this song, humanism becomes less The Practice Of Insufferable Smart Alecks and more A Hard Fought Path Against Far Odds.

Tombstone da Deadman, another member of Grand Unified, continues this mixture of emotional investigation and rigorous positivism to great effect in "Ballad of the Non-Believer", the first lines of which I quoted at the outset. Leading up to the first chorus, Tombstone ruminates on his upbringing, on being a kid thrust into a belief system not of his choosing. What makes it such a uniquely powerful piece of music is that he is honestly concerned with parsing the experience in its fullness, rather than simply raging against lost innocence and ignorant parenting, as many of us are wont to do. He peels back the layers of emotional significance in search of what that type of upbringing offered, why it felt so natural for so long, and how easy it would be just to rest in the comfortable place it provided. It's one of the few pieces of humanist music that I can play for theists that they don't instantly reject out of hand, just because they sense how earnestly Tombstone is working to understand what was done to him and where it all tends when stretched to the global scale.

Of course, that indulgence usually vaporizes with the second verse, where Tombstone rises to attack the hypocrisy of defaming science and villainizing scientists while benefitting massively and directly from both, while the third is a full-on rap battle call out, a throwing down of the gauntlet in the grand style. Each verse could form the backbone for a whole song, and those songs would be enjoyable, but fused together they represent a sort of living document of a new approach to positivist artistic expression –

uncompromising in fundamental principle, fearless in its championing of science and human freedom, but with an emotional sophistication that was often lacking in the "And here is a forty-SEVENTH argument against the Ontological Proof of God's existence" brand of atheism that I grew up with.

Even at their most inflammatory, in those songs dripping with frustration and disappointment that so much of the structure of daily life is ordered on religious principles of dubious provenance, Grand Unified keep on their message of education and discussion, a devotion which keeps them from the excesses of the Christcore camp. Instead of calling lonely and hopeless individuals to rise up and destroy the enemies of their wrongfully executed savior, Grand Unified urge them to demand the right to think, and offer up their own stories of struggle and hardship to light the way out of the dark.

If we could do that more often, laying aside our love of debate and conflict in favor of the simple connection found in creatively sharing our stories of adversity overcome (and not yet overcome), perhaps we could finally work our way as humanists out of the tightening circle that the logic of over-cleverness often demands. Taking notes on human frailty from Christcore and on ourselves from Grand Unified, perhaps humanism can craft for itself a face to go with its brain.

Wouldn't that be something?

STUMBLING TOWARDS PROPHECY:
A BRISK ROMP THROUGH
THE LIFE OF MUHAMMAD

(Originally Published in *The Freethinker*, November 2012)

It has happened to perhaps every atheist: you start to talk about your problems with religion, when somebody says, "Well, yes, certain of the beliefs are flawed and the practitioners misguided, but the founders of these religions are still moral examples to be studied, followed, and revered." This is the Believe In Christianity Because Jesus Was a Great Guy brand of religion, and it is a tenacious fellow. We realized a while ago that the slavery-loving, baby-killing ways of Moses aren't *quite* the stuff of moral legend (take a gander at Numbers 31 for something truly heinous), and are coming around to the idea that Jesus, with his tendency for throwing people into realms of eternal torment for the crime of disagreeing with him, isn't so hot either. But we seem to be rather stuck on Muhammad.

For centuries during the Middle Ages, he was Evil Incarnate, and with the recent meteoric rise of Islamic Radicalism that unbalanced conception has been revived, most notably in the works of Robert Spencer . As against this trend, those who have attempted a measure of objectivity, like Karen Armstrong and Yahiya Emerick, have let their anger at Spencerian exaggerations get the better of their scholarship, and the Muhammad that has emerged from their portraits is several shades Too Good - somehow the prophet of peace even when planning unprovoked war, the brilliant politician even when forced to resort to Revelation to explain away his most recent failed venture. What is wanting in all of this is the less dramatic truth that in Muhammad we have a man with initially good ideas slowly but entirely corrupted by his belief in the divinity of his message.

It is fair to say that, for the first fifty or so years of his life, Muhammad was as decent a human as could be expected in his surroundings. At a time when you could be killed with impunity, your life literally worthless, so long as you weren't under the protection of a clan, Muhammad made a case that it was the duty of all to care for the community's downtrodden. His goal was to make people reflect on the consequences of the new Cult of Wealth that had sprung up in Mecca since the Quraysh people had made the transition from nomads to merchants, and this was a good and noble thing.

Such ideas naturally attracted people on the fringes of society - sons of the major clans who were kicking their heels waiting for their turn at power, and prominent members of the lesser clans who were facing extinction at the hands of the great merchants, not to mention scores of servants and slaves with nothing to lose. So many people dedicated so thoroughly to the undermining of the material and traditional structure of Mecca naturally brought a good deal of pressure down on Muhammad, whose (eventual) steadfast refusal to rescind any of his beliefs got him drummed out of Mecca, a death sentence on his head if he should return. Had he died at this point in life, we would find little to object to and less to remember about him.

It is with his retreat to Medina that Muhammad was taken over by something more than zeal to profess his religion, something which made him act in ways that are questionable not only by our lofty modern standards, but even by those of his own day. His position in Mecca seemed hopeless until a collection of Arab and Jewish settlements based around Medina offered protection for him and his followers if he would agree to be an impartial judge of their disputes. The offer came at a hefty personal risk to them, as they had to cancel many of their old alliances in order to extend their protection to the wanted man. But they took the chance, and Muhammad, rescued from sure destruction, joined their community.

And immediately did everything he could to bring disaster on their heads.

Within a year of his pilgrimage, he began ordering raids against the Meccan caravans, knowing full well that this would direct the wrath of the most powerful force in the region, the Quraysh, against his protectors. Muhammad's apologists point out that caravan raiding was a normal part of life for the bedouin tribes but, having failed several times to pull off a successful raid, the prophet concocted plans that went far beyond anything that had been done before. In one instance, he had his operatives disguise themselves as pilgrims, join the Meccan caravans, and kill the guards in a surprise attack. What's worse, this was timed to coincide with the Arab holy months, when violence was forbidden so as to allow pilgrims safe passage to their places of worship. When many of his followers reacted with horror to these new tactics, he had a convenient revelation which said, in effect, "Yes, killing during the holy month is bad, but they were really mean to us a few years ago, so Al'lah is entirely fine with it." The poet Ka'b ibn al-Ashraf dared to compose lyrics against these increasingly erratic policies, and was assassinated at the Prophet's command. So did the notion of the limited raid evolve into that of the ji'had, a war in which any violence done was justifiable so long as the victim was in some way related to someone who once said something bad about Muhammad.

From 623 to 632, Medina saw itself thrown again and again into entirely unnecessary conflict with Mecca at the hands of Muhammad's need to humble his former antagonists. During that decade, the solution to every problem was to strike at Mecca, no matter who died in the process, no matter what the consequences might be to the people who had housed him and his followers, no matter what violence he had to do to the purity of his original revelations to keep his people towing the line. Alternate solutions, whether engaging in trade with their Abysinnian connections, engaging in agriculture on the readily available arable land, reverting to a traditional nomadic form of life, swallowing their pride and letting their hosts continue to provide for them as they had been, or even carrying out raids against non-Meccan caravans, were simply not considered.

One by one, the Jewish tribes of Medina found themselves disagreeing with their new leader's path, and just as quickly being expelled from their own homes that the prophet might continue his antagonistic policy of tactical revenge. The culmination came with the mass beheading of all 700 male members of the Qurayzah tribe after Muhammad won the Battle of the Trench (two guesses as to how he won it - if your guess is "by digging a trench," you're on the right track!). At the same time as his Qu'ran revelations stressed the importance of gratitude for the things of the Earth, Muhammad's consistent ingratitude and indifference to the suffering that his vendettas visited upon people who had given him a home when he had nothing must strike the moral sense of any age as reprehensible.

Unfortunately, it doesn't stop there. Having expelled or slaughtered everybody in Medina who was a threat to his status as prophet, and puffed up by the success of his ditch strategy in holding off a Meccan siege, he thought himself an unstoppable force and declared that he was taking his followers on a pilgrimage to Mecca, sure that the Meccans couldn't possibly resist him after his mighty victory. As it turned out, they did, and he and his followers were stuck outside of the city. To save face, Muhammad grasped at a peace treaty that ended the war and allowed him to try the pilgrimage again in a year. His vision and sense of invincibility having been brought up so glaringly short, he returned to Medina, mumbling along the way yet another opportune revelation that said, in effect, "That's totally what God *meant me* to do."

This degradation of his revelations from statements of religious purpose to covering devices used in times of failure is, interestingly, something that Muhammad shares with Mormon prophet Joseph Smith. Both men started off with a body of revelation that was almost entirely devoted to laying out overall principles of the nature of God and life and, as the pressures of leadership fell upon their shoulders, increasingly employed their gifts to simply Get Things Done. When Smith needed a hotel built in 1841, he received a revelation from God not only telling the faithful to build it, but laying out the precise compensatory stock options plan that the All Mighty would prefer. Similarly, Muhammad's messages of God moved from the really rather beautiful

> We showered the water in showers,
> Then fissured the earth in fissures,
> And cause to grow in it grain,
> And grapes and clover,
> And olives and palms,
> And orchards dense,
> And fruits and pastures.

of Sura 80 (among the earliest chronologically) to the rather more pragmatic revelations granting him dispensation for marrying Zaynab bint Jahsh against common practice, for clearing his favorite wife of public accusations of loose morality, and for getting the Prophet's party guests to leave in a timely manner. When you are using revelations from God to tell people to go home, you really have to question how much of it is divinity speaking through you and how much is just wanting to go to bed.

Returning to the timeline, the treaty that brought his first pilgrimage to an end called for a cessation of violence and raiding and, inevitably, as soon as he was back in Medina, Muhammad sent one of his more unbalanced followers, Abu Basir, out to form a private raiding gang and resume hostilities against Mecca. His plan was simple - to strangle the economy of Mecca to the point that they would have no choice but to take him as their leader if they wanted to survive economically, while at the same time expanding his sphere of influence to the borders of the Byzantine Empire. He failed spectacularly at the latter when he attempted it with an army of 3,000 men, but was entirely successful in the former. In 630, he returned to Mecca and assumed control, sending his men out to the local shrines to smash the idols that his ancestors had worshipped. Of course, this provoked a desperate last attempt by the Meccans to protect their old way of life. The Hawazin tribe rallied to the defense of the al-Lat shrine, and were cut down. The Muslims prevailed, with seventy Hawazin dying and six thousand women and children taken prisoner as the cost of Muhammad's impatience to impose the full extent of his new power immediately upon grasping it.

"I have spent so long in the revenge business, now that it's over, I don't know what to do."

The rest comes as something of an anti-climax, with Muhammad returning to Medina and living out the last few years of his life in increasing ill health, his spiritual role filled by others. He had spent a decade bending his own life and those of everyone around him to the end of humbling his detractors, and finally met his own end in 632, while his head rested in the lap of his young wife Aisha, the girl who would come to be a force all to herself in shaping Islam over the next century.

Jesus had it easy. He never had to be a leader, to provide for a horde of followers in the midst of a harsh and unforgiving climate. Muhammad did, and many of the unquestionably awful things that he did from 622 to 632 stemmed at least partly from the unique necessities of Arabian leadership. But those necessities don't explain everything away. There was a seed of vengefulness in Muhammad after his Meccan exile that over-rode all matters of pragmatism and obligation to those who had protected and believed in him. He was a man looking for a fight, poking the Quraysh dragon until he got one, and turning back savagely on any of his own people who had the audacity to suggest that he had somehow lost his way. Anything was permitted against anyone in the name of this one great goal, and time and again it nearly cost him everything. Only the supreme lack of cohesion and initiative in his enemy and the steadfast devotion born of desperation in his followers allowed him to survive each disaster long enough to throw his resources into the creation of the next near-disaster. The reformer of such initial promise became twisted by his visions of revenge, and as much as we ought to give credit to the benevolent impulses that drove that young man to argue against even the most powerful of his society, we can't let those efforts, or our distaste for the venomous and vulgar caricatures offered up by his later detractors, prevent us from saying quite plainly, "Muhammad was not, in the final analysis, a good man, and if his goodness is in any way decisive for your faith in his message, you have quite some thinking to do."

How Europe Got Its Aristotle Back: The Life and Philosophy of Ibn Rushd (Averroes)

(Originally Published at *The Humanist*, July 2014)

In an era when anybody can call up the sum total of human knowledge from any of half a dozen devices within an arm's reach, it's often hard to wrap one's head around the historical fragility of information. And not just via the grand conflagrations – the burning of the Great Library of Alexandria, the closing of the School of Athens – but through that slow, imperceptible vanishing that passes unremarked until what was once the wisdom of a civilization exists only as whispers and rumor, leaving us to wonder how we casually let so much of our cultural past slip through our fingers.

The great example is the West's seven-century-long amnesia as to its classical legacy. From roughly 500 to 1220 CE, Aristotle and Plato lay almost entirely forgotten, the entirety of their formidable knowledge reduced to one translated volume of the former, and a fragment of the latter. The regaining of their intellectual legacy is, among historians of philosophy, almost universally considered the great turning point in Western Civilization, and the man most responsible for it was a Spanish Muslim philosopher who stands as perhaps the only figure in world history to have an equally towering influence in the development of Islamic, Christian, *and* humanist thought.

His name was Ibn Rushd (1126-1198), though we know him as Averroes, or simply *The Commentator*. He came of age during the great flowering of Andalusian thought under the Almohades caliphate. Until that time, Baghdad was the intellectual center of the world, and it was there that the rationalists of the Islamic tradition waged their philosophical war with the traditionalists, armed with the inherited wisdom of the Greeks. In the Western part of the Islamic Empire, however, the traditionalists, those who could not countenance the use of reason in the realm of theology, held sway until Ibn Tumart founded the Almohades Dynasty and encouraged the importation of the ancient classics.

Within a half century, Cordoba's intellectual influence was second only to that of Baghdad, and towered over a Parisian academic climate that was just finding its feet. Ibn Rushd was born to a family of celebrated jurists during a time when the rationalist camp had been forced into a corner by the fundamentalist vigor of Al-Ghazali's *Incoherence of the Philosophers*, a work which labeled as heretics all who attempted to philosophically probe the content of Islam. He was the reigning titan of Islamic theology, and in four decades none had stepped forward to contest his vision of strict scriptural obedience.

And then came Ibn Rushd, a man who seemed to master anything he put his mind to. He studied law and medicine, astronomy and philosophy, with some of the greatest minds of Cordoban society, and could have made a full career out of any of them, so easily did proficiency come to him. However, though given the distinguished position of Judge of Seville in 1160, it wasn't until 1169 that he stumbled into his true calling.

The story goes that his friend brought him one day to see Abu Ya'qub Yusuf, the second caliph of the Almohades dynasty. Yusuf asked Ibn Rushd if he believed the sky had existed for all time, or if it had been created at some point. The question seems innocuous and speculative to us, but it was in fact one of the most dangerous things Yusuf could have inquired about. The Muslim community was fiercely split on the issue of the eternity of the world, and the wrong answer could have destroyed Ibn Rushd's career. Quick on his feet, he protested ignorance of the topic, whereupon Yusuf began talking freely of the opinions of the Greeks and other philosophical traditions, putting the rationalist-leaning Averroes at ease.

The two fell into easy conversation, and Yusuf suggested that Ibn Rushd should write a full set of Aristotelian commentaries. It was an immense task, but that's precisely what Ibn Rushd committed his life to achieving. Displaying a mastery for synthesis, he wrote summaries of all the Aristotelian works then known, and severely criticized the shortcomings of previous Arabic interpretations of The Philosopher. Beyond that, using Aristotle as his firm base, he struck out against the prevailing anti-philosophical bent of Islamic theology, aiming his scorn directly at its most intimidating work, the *Incoherence of the Philosophers*. With a boldness in the face of superior power almost unfathomable today, he wrote a work whose title set the tone for all that was to be found within: *The Incoherence of the Incoherence.*

It was a thorough and merciless attack on Al-Ghazali and everything the fundamentalists had wrongly imputed to the Islamic philosophical movement. Where Al-Ghazali had said, in an attempt to preserve the existence of miracles, that there was no natural order and in fact that God is directly intervening anytime *anything* happens, Ibn Rushd argued that this elaborate attempt to discredit the power of causality was unnecessary, unsound, and admitted of no possible knowledge of the workings of the universe, rendering all science void. Where Al-Ghazali stuck firmly by the Judaeo-Christian-Islamic account of the beginning of the universe, Ibn Rushd declared that all three religions were mistaken in their shared tradition, and that the idea of creation out of nothing was scientifically and philosophically abhorrent. And where the traditionalists maintained steadfastly their exact knowledge of the attributes of God, Ibn Rushd countered with the impossibility of accurately employing nature-derived vocabulary in the description of super-natural capacities.

But the most impressive thing about the book is its pragmatic approach to religion itself. Following Plato's *Republic*, on which he wrote a commentary, Ibn Rushd gives pride of place to philosophy as a way of investigating the world and its truths, and of explaining how a good and happy life is to be achieved, but he recognizes that it is entirely too subtle and intricate for most people to follow. He holds it to be the job of religion, then, to provide laws and enticements to improve the common people's lives. Whichever religion has the best laws at a given time is, by his account, the best religion, and it is to be entirely expected that, no matter how good a religion is now, it will be eventually superseded by something that practically does the job of inspiring the masses better.

On these and many other points, what Ibn Rushd consistently fought for was the right to use reason to illuminate theology and life. It was the responsibility of humans to reach their full intellectual potential by considering the causes of what they saw around them, and with each discovery to climb to higher levels of intellectual clarity. To an Islamic establishment that called for full and unquestioning subservience, and accused of infidelity all who dared question the content of religion, Ibn Rushd responded that the true infidelity was disobeying God's command to investigate reality, to be given a divine instrument like the brain and then not use it to its fullest.

His works were understandably controversial in Islamic circles, and towards the end of his life, during a moment when the caliphate needed to appease the orthodox elements of the Empire, he was sent into exile and his books burned, though he was called back once the political situation had simmered. Roundly condemned by most, his influence as the greatest expositor of Islamic rationalism nevertheless survived as a strand of Islamic thought down to the present day, a constant reminder of Another Way for those oppressed by the strictures of Islamic belief.

That he was a massive figure in the history of Islamic thought (and I haven't even touched upon his definitive contribution to Islamic jurisprudence) there is no doubt, but for those of us in the West, his contribution to our intellectual life is if anything *more* pronounced than his domestic legacy. His works were taken up with an unabashed zeal by the Spanish Jewish community, and translated with an astonishing rapidity by a culture that found in his treatment of Aristotle and Plato a whole new world of intellectual possibility. From Spain, his works passed to Europe via the translations of Michael the Scott, William de Luna, and everybody's favorite medieval translator, Hermann the German. (You just snickered, didn't you? *So* immature.)

To a Europe that had known only a book and change of the entire Platonic-Aristotelian tradition, the arrival of Ibn Rushd's complete commentaries on all known works of Aristotle was a thunderbolt. While Aristotle came to be known by medieval scholars as *The Philosopher*, Ibn Rushd became simply *The Commentator*. He was a hero to Siger of Brabant and Boetius of Dacia and, even when arguing against him, the influence of Averroes is very much present in the Aristotelianism of Thomas Aquinas. Aristotle's teleological approach to investigating the cosmos became, as a result of Ibn Rushd's masterful expositions, the dominant intellectual force for the next four centuries of European thought.

More than that, he has often been credited as well with the founding of modern skeptical philosophy, centuries before Descartes. His rational approach to theology inspired the Averroist movement, which was eventually condemned by the Church as being tantamount to atheism, and which served as the source for luminaries like Dante Alighieri in arguing for the separation of Church and State, and other philosophers to argue that if investigation and reason deemed something to be true, then religious tradition *had* to give way. Regardless of whether Ibn Rushd would have condoned the conclusions that people derived from his work, the fact that his thought was so rich as to inspire internal changes to Islam and Christianity, as well as providing the raw material for a philosophical school a good four hundred years ahead of its time, speaks to the breadth of his philosophical project.

Now, there's one of you out there who has been very patient while dying to ask a question. Now is your chance.

"But isn't Aristotelianism *bad*? Didn't scientific progress come to a dead stop until we broke away from teleological explanations of nature? Why are we celebrating this dude, then, for bringing us a set of works that delayed for centuries our intellectual progress?"

That's a very fair question. If Plato was the Bad Greek of late nineteenth century philosophy, Aristotle was that of the twentieth, as historians of science pieced together what made our scientific revolution possible, and came to the conclusion that it was when Aristotelian *why*-type explanations were replaced by

93

Newtonian *how*-type ones.   And that's a very important observation, but let's not forget what Aristotle improved upon. Faced with the Platonic conception of a world of Forms that exist outside of their physical instantiations, Aristotle called foul and said that the way we know things is by abstracting from the real. Intellectual inquiry for Aristotle is not a matter of positing metaphysical absolutes behind mere reality, but is rather an investigation of how things came to be the way they are.

That was a hugely important adjustment to make – it put the focus back on the world as it is, and if his successors became so wrapped up in the potential of this cause-and-goal way of looking at the world, to the point that it took them centuries to do for Aristotelian thought what he had done to Platonic belief, it's because of the raw power of his notion of causality.   It got people thinking about mechanisms of change and motion, and that was all for the ultimate good. Had it been Plato's works, and not those of Aristotle, that Ibn Rushd concentrated on explaining, the Scientific Revolution would likely have taken even longer, and had he not existed, leaving the more modest accountings of Avicenna and other Arabic commentators to do their work, the delay would have been longer still.

All roads lead from Ibn Rushd.   In him, the three great religious traditions of the West met with a full accounting of the wisdom of antiquity and found a synthesis that would define the Western intellectual project for centuries to come, and a tension that would set the stage for the great rationalist turn that we are still enjoying. In the near millennium since his death, the only figure of remotely comparable stature in terms of philosophical impact on the structure of world thought is Karl Marx, and yet a stroll down Berkeley's Telegraph Ave. will net one very few Ibn Rushd-inspired tee-shirts.   He's the world historical intellectual figure we've decided to forget about. And that's rather too bad.

FURTHER READING:

If you don't read Arabic, your options are pretty limited in terms of works concentrating solely on Ibn Rushd. I think Majid Fakhry's *Averroes: His Life, Works, and Influence* is a nice, brief introduction that highlights the revolutionary aspects of Ibn Rushd's thought without overlooking the areas in which he was more of a compiler than an innovator. If you read French, the godfather of Western sources for Averroes is the great Ernest Renan's 1852 *Averroes et l'Averoissme*, which is pretty easy to flag down in print-on-demand form. The works of Averroes were made available in Latin in the 60s in an eleven volume edition, but for English your starting point is probably the Simon van den Bergh translation of *Incoherence*.

A Murder for All Seasons: The Odd Intersection of Blood Sports and Christianity

(Originally Published in *The Freethinker*, February 2014)

Just when you think that American Christianity can't be any less self-aware, along comes a movement of such brilliant and crass vapidity as to make all the vile evangelic excesses that came before seem somehow reasonable and under-stated. The new trend here is a vigorous application of Christian principles to a spirited defense of hunting. Between the gore soaked ramblings of the Duck Commander and a steady flow of Gun Sport Devotionals, we are told to believe that the wholesale murder of innocent creatures by massively over-equipped and under-contemplative white males is precisely what Jesus always had in mind for the human race.

And perhaps these writers are correct, as their works throw more light on the twisted psychology of Christianity than the more PR-minded works of traditional theology. All of the sweaty-palmed fetishism of religious practice, the idolatry of blood and suffering, are writ with unabashed pride by these authors too far lost to their death-and-Jesus kink to dissimulate.

I spent some time that I'll never get back ploughing through the NINETY CHAPTERS of Steve Scott's *Faith Afield: A Sportsman's Devotional* recently. Structurally, it's a hard book to take. Each of those chapters has the exact same build – take an object related to hunting, explain it in a couple of paragraphs, and then spend the next three paragraphs trying to justify how Christian Living Is Like That Thing. Chapter 68, for example, starts off talking about scent eliminating products and how they affect your need to be aware of the direction of the wind, before lunging desperately at a segue with, "I believe we Christians sometimes forget the wind in our lives too. The Holy Spirit is described as "wind" in the New Testament..."

Each chapter is therefore a game of Six Degrees, where you start off with a bit of hunting vocabulary and have to leapfrog it through obliquely selected bits of scripture to a standard message about Christian Life. The sheer devotion with which Scott sticks to this construct through ninety almost identical iterations is phenomenal but not surprising for a book that takes George W. Bush's "Stay the Course" as its inspirational leitmotif.

Yes, it's tedious. Yes, it has nothing to say in its Life Advice that hasn't been said in tens of thousands of other pot-boiler devotionals on the shelves. But that's not why we're reading it. We're reading it to see how a man convinces himself that he has the right to take the life of something that never did him any harm. Scott slips up every so often, and lets some tantalizing bits of psychology through which have as much to say about the Christian mindset as about the hunter's doublethink-mortared lifestyle.

The best comes in a masochistically-fraught passage detailing the rules of the chase. After a fantastically dishonest section detailing the high ethics of hunting practice ("There are no fences, no unfair advantages, and no guarantees – just passion and pursuit") he moves on to the real story. "Our god is a god of fair chase. He views us as a trophy worthy of pursuit. He is passionate about his hunt, and our love, affection, and obedience are his most prized trophy.... God is relentless in his pursuit of us."

Amazing, isn't it? Here, Scott is turning his tawdry need to destroy life into something holy by simultaneously playing the role both of hunter and prey, exhilarating in the notion that he is being stalked by God just as he stalks the deer, which of course means that, just as he Wants to be captured by God, so does the deer really Want to be taken by him. It is a grand moment of imaginative sado-masochism in which a man, in a single moment, gets to experience the thrill of killing and surrendering. That's potent stuff, and it's understandable that it becomes addictive to the point of over-riding all other evaluative processes.

Take for example the few parts in this book where Scott honestly attempts to grapple with the horror of what he is doing. It's a classic moment of Scripturing taking the place of Thinking at precisely the moment where Thinking might fail to give you the result you want:

"All sportsmen must grapple with the issue of killing. Without killing there is no authentic hunting. How is it that we can love wildlife yet be able to pull the trigger or loose the arrow knowing that a life will be taken? There is no easy answer, and the role of hunting is not for everyone."

This is precisely the point where a normal person would review arguments, perhaps wonder a bit about where the right to kill comes from, or question how it is that what one wants to do lines up so well with what is *celestially allowed*. Scott will have none of that. His very next step is, "The killing of animals is found throughout the Bible," and that's it. The Bible says it's fine, so Scott's moral responsibility is done. In an earlier chapter, he sums it up even more crassly: "I hunt because it is a privilege. It is a right (see Gen. 9:3). It is a blessing."

And that's not even the most blatant summation of his position. It's actually down-right responsible when put next to this gleaming declaration of moral self-absolution: "God has instilled in the heart of many people ... the desire to match wits with some of his finest creatures. If we do not pursue what God has wired us to do, we do him a dishonor."

This is what Christianity in America has come to – the idea that, if you really want to do something, then you have the right to do it. Otherwise, you'd be dishonoring God, obviously! You want to murder those beavers that have never done you a lick of harm? Great! Have at it – never doubt for a moment that every twisted whim you can conjure from the depths of your sadistic God complex fantasies shouldn't be acted upon, and constantly. Because constant self-gratification is what Jesus is All About.

We should be thankful that these books exist, really. More self-aware authors might realize that advocating against "unfair advantages" on one page and then going on to describe one's collection of electronic fish finders, hunting cameras, precision engineered weapons, genetically engineered hunting companions, industrial-grade camouflage, fine honed optics, and extensive array of decoys and scent traps is grossly and grotesquely hypocritical, and avoid putting it in their books, thus depriving the rest of us of that insight into how deeply Christians will allow themselves all manner of luxurious self-indulgence so long as they can gloss it with a baldly disingenuous statement of principle later.

More psychologically informed authors might not want to draw quite so close a connection between their fantasies of being pursued by God and their actions on the hunting fields, but that rich sexual imagery is perhaps the closest the rest of us are ever going to get to the truth of day-to-day religious fervor.

A man with an eye towards public relations might not be quite so blatant about drawing parallels between the need to get kids to hunt early and the need to get them hearing about Jesus early, thereby revealing the latter as every bit as much a process of violent desensitization as the former. But Scott, rather than avoiding the unfavorable comparison between numbing a child to death and eroding their soul by the notion of sin, proudly proclaims his role in establishing a combination hunting/preaching youth camp with the express aim of hitting kids from both directions before they can build up any defenses against his righteous onslaught.

Some have interpreted this Renaissance of Death Christianity as the herald of a new wave of recreational critter murder in the country, but the more you look at it, the more it seems little more than the Jersey Shore of 2013 – a new breed of loathsome individuals who captivate the country by their unwavering commitment to personal horridness for a little while, puffing themselves up with the great contribution they are making to their cause, not realizing all the while that their spirited grotesqueries are cracking the very foundations they're trying to save. We have given them as much exposure as they need to destroy themselves with, and so long as their utterances continue to replicate the determined cluelessness of Scott, that day shouldn't be long in coming.

SHAME TO SAVE:
THE PINK CROSS AND CHRISTIANITY'S CURIOUS OBSESSION WITH PROSTITUTES

(Originally Published In *The Freethinker*, April 2013)

In 2008, the Pink Cross Foundation was founded by an ex porn-star who had the goal of redeeming others in the porn industry through the word of Christ. Perhaps it makes for a titillating story, but it's hardly a new development. Ever since Jesus accepted a rather sensual foot oiling from a prostitute, Christianity has had trouble being of one mind about the workers of the pleasure profession. Witches and blasphemers, Jews and heretics - these it historically has had an unflinching instinct to eradicate, but when it came to the prostitute, there has always been a double conscience wavering between ill-informed attempts at reform and politically-minded persecution, both of which are woven into the mission statement of today's Pink Cross.

The Old Testament didn't suffer from this dual mindedness. The Hebrew forefathers were locked in a struggle to supplant the heavily matriarchal religions inherited from the Babylonians. Their greatest competition came from the persistent worship of female divinities, and the temples devoted to them where the lower echelons of the female priesthood also operated as temple prostitutes. For the patriarchs, prostitution meant competition. Asherah was being worshipped by more and more Hebrew families as the wife of Yahweh, and the conservative elements of the male priesthood would have none of it, increasing their invective against female priests, divinities, and the prostitutes associated therewith. So, organized religion, which once worked hand in glove with prostitution, came to be its greatest critic, but less on grounds of morality than out of a ruthless desire for political dominance. It was okay to rape women (as long as you married them after and paid the father fair coin), but it was decidedly not okay to let them speak or act as representatives of divinity.

And then came Jesus.

Or, more properly, then came Mary Magdalene. No single figure has sent Christian theology into more fits of self-censoring panic than this prostitute turned disciple. The early history of the Church can be more or less neatly gerrymandered between those who wanted to admit her as a significant figure in the story of Jesus and those who wanted to bury her as far as the records would allow. In several Gnostic texts, Mary Magdalene is portrayed as fully qualified to interpret the teachings of Jesus while at the same time being a fully sensual figure, refusing to denigrate her body or physical pleasure in general. These texts threatened the power base of St. Paul's followers, men who scorned the body as weak and polluted and women as nothing but vessels of sin. Influenced by Orphic traditions, and counting among their number many able wheelers and dealers, this group managed to work the vote at the Council of Nicea in 325 to exclude any texts which hinted at Gnostic influence, giving us the Bible we largely have today - a testament not so much to the ideas of Jesus as to the political fears and philosophical prejudices of St. Paul's descendants. Again, the body and its champions, the prostitutes, were sacrificed that a group of over cunning men might maintain its theological control.

But it's one thing to say that prostitutes are out, and another thing to make it so. Over the centuries, the Catholic Church realized that there was money to be made in them there prostitutes, and took upon itself the business of organizing the trade. The city of Rome in particular was zealous in fostering the industry, keeping up a registry of thousands of sex workers and funding its more grandiose religious projects on the back of their labor. After the philosophical battle with the Gnostics was decided, prominent theologians of the rank of Thomas Aquinas recognized in prostitution a necessary component of civilization, while the priesthood benefited not only from their money, but from their skills. Sex workers had places in religious festivals and in the halls of power. While not as respected as in Babylonian or Greek times, the highest echelons of the profession were nonetheless powerful forces in their communities.

Leave it to Protestantism, then, to ruin everything. With its unerringly dreary instinct for building power on a morbid obsession with the crushing of anything that promotes life, the Protestants rabidly attacked the Catholic Church for its support and organization of a sex industry, setting off waves of small town violence against anyone suspected of loose sexual morals. In city after city, prostitutes were beaten, shaved, and had their ears chopped off before being stripped and kicked out of town. Because the Pope was far away, and the prostitute at hand, she had to bear the brunt of the religious mania that swept northern Europe in the sixteenth century. The Catholic Church joined in since, after all, how much easier was it to set the masses loose on the harlots than to actually rethink the core of the Church's architecture? Both Catholic and Protestant vied with each other to see which could be crueler to the pleasure classes, torturing thousands of poor and uneducated women by way of gaining political clout. It was a bloodbath in bad faith that Christianity was not to recover from.

In these paroxysms of hysteria, centuries of societal progress by women were effaced. The slow and steady gains of the late Middle Ages, when a new code of conduct which allowed women to speak as equals at the dinner table and everybody to regard their bodies as not strictly evil, were wiped out in the grand game of proving which theological system was most pure in thought and deed. The body was once more reviled, with prostitutes being the living instantiations of the devil's arts.

It was a novel situation for the trade. Whereas Hebrew scholars and the early Church fathers heaped their venom on prostitution because of its association with powerful competing strands of thought, now the profession was attacked by all and sundry precisely because it was so powerless. It was an easy target, a convenient battlefield before the seventeenth century carried the conflict between the religious systems to a whole new level of destructive extremism.

If modern Christianity has a gift for anything, it is for finding contradictory terrible viewpoints from its storied history and improbably stitching them together into a new system that is more horrendous still. Enter the Pink Cross. The project of former porn star and current self-proclaimed prophet Shelley Lubben, the organization and its "prayer warriors" harness the message of Jesus in their attempt to rescue people from the porn industry, and to combat the consumption of pornography in the world generally. As is usual with these sorts of foundations, there are a few useful things that it does. It is currently working towards the passage of a bill that will require governmental inspection of porn studios to ensure safety and health standards are maintained (though, of course, we all have learned to be ever so slightly nervous when the words government, health, and sex pop up in the same sentence).

But for the rest, the Pink Cross is a fundamentally sixteenth century institution. There are two pillars to its mission in the world - one is to spread the message that "Porn is not glamorous." It is a vile profession that demeans everybody it touches, and makes you, by virtue of being in it, miserable. And then, in case that message doesn't stick, they follow it up with the notion that, even if it is something that you enjoy doing, pornography as an institution is destroying the world family by family, and so you still have to leave it. So, presented with say a twenty year old porn star, Pink Cross's first tactic is Shame, and if that's not successful, their second tactic is More, Different Shame.

I don't think I've ever said this before, but these people really need to take a page from medieval scholasticism. For all of their faults, most of these scholars realized that people really enjoy sex, and that, no matter how lamentable you find that trait, it is something which takes very dark turns if you try and turn it off. In the age after the war against Gnosticism but before Luther's body-hatred and Victorianism's perpetual case of the vapors, people just had sex from time to time, sometimes with prostitutes, sometimes not. It's sort of central to our continuance as a species, and just like we'll always enjoy watching tv shows about precocious offspring spouting one liners to their witless parents whether or not it's the best use of our time, so will we spend some treasured moments out of our busy week watching other people have sex. And if we aren't horrid people for doing that from time to time, as the medievals realized but we have come to forget, then they certainly aren't horrid for producing the films.

Do some people take it to extremes and neglect their families? Certainly. But that's hardly cause to put the burden of society's familial ills on the shoulders of a class of professionals trying to carve out a living wage while they can. So, as to the second prong of Pink Cross's attack, it amounts to little more than trying to whip up outrage that people are really quite interested in sex in its various manifestations. But it's not that outrageous. Aquinas knew it. Augustine knew it. And we'd all be better off not backpedaling from stuff that *fourth century Christian theologians* had already admitted about sexuality, I rather think.

Which leaves the first pillar - Porn Is Not Glamorous. 'Aren't you tired of feeling ashamed of yourself?' the site all but purrs with empathy. 'Well, luckily for you, Jesus has a plan to make you feel good about yourself again.' This is clever stuff. Because who is really making people in the pleasure industry feel ashamed of themselves? Perhaps the people who just gave over half of their website to detailing how porn is destroying the modern world. It is a classic Christian strategy - making you feel ashamed of something you weren't particularly ashamed of, and then offering a way out of that shame by joining the organization that set up the structures that allowed the shame to happen in the first place.

It's the religious equivalent of the boyfriend who tells you that you won't ever find anybody else because you're fat, and then, in the midst of your tears, graciously accepts you as you are, provided you keep cleaning the house and going to work to support his online casino addiction. A cheap psychological trick, but an effective one, particularly on people suffering from esteem issues to begin with.

If one cared about the workers of the porn industry, really cared about them rather than one's fame as Jesus's right hand man, wouldn't it be better to work towards removing the stigma that are attached to that industry, to do your part to dial down the knee-jerk reactions that have been causing civilization to react with such uncalled for vehemence to prostitution and pornography since the Reformation? To make these people's lives better without making them first submit to the deity system you happen to think makes you important? Perhaps the day for that is coming, but in its way stand organizations like Pink Cross, combining Pauline views of sexuality with Lutheran shame tactics, all wrapped in a false layer of empathy which says less, "Let me make your life better" than, "Let me validate my own choices by compelling you to be more like me." And on that day we shall finally have achieved the impossible goal of achieving a balanced view of human sexuality which starts to approximate that of the *Ancient Babylonians.* One can hope.

FEUERBACH ... TO THE FUTURE!
OR, HOW TO REVOLUTIONIZE PHILOSOPHY
AND GET ABSOLUTELY NO CREDIT.

(Originally published in *Philosophy Now*, July 2014)

For most people, Ludwig Feuerbach (1804-1872) is the grey but necessary spackle shoved between the foundational blocks of Hegel and Marx in the edifice of modern philosophy. The phrase "transitional figure" haunts Feuerbach literature, as if he were little more than a just-functional emcee holding the stage until the Real Act came along. This is hardly a just fate for the man whose critique of religion revolutionized philosophical theology, and who then pushed that critique into an all-out war against philosophy itself every bit as dramatic as those of Marx and Nietzsche later in the century.

Ludwig was born on July 28, 1804, in Landshut, Bavaria, into one of those large, broad-minded, and liberal German families that not only existed in the era before Bismarck, but positively throve. His brothers included a philologist, a mathematician, an archaeologist, and a jurist, so it is perhaps not too surprising that Ludwig would later make his name in philosophy as the man whose watchword was the infinite potential and diversity of the human species.

Like many intellectuals of his time, Feuerbach arrived at philosophy via the gateway drug of theology. In 1823, he attended Heidelberg University as a student of religion but was soon lured to Berlin and the big-stakes philosophy being wrought there by Schleiermacher and Hegel. He was intoxicated by Hegel's ability to take massive intellectual systems and explain them in terms of man's collective effort to understand itself. Even though he would spend most of his life passionately demonstrating the harm that Hegelianism does to humanity, he would never entirely escape the spell of the great man's dialectic thinking.

It got him into trouble almost immediately. After five years of searching unsuccessfully for a permanent university post, Feuerbach fired off *Thoughts on Death and Immortality* in 1830, a merciless, ironic, and just downright fun broadside leveled at the Christian notion of personal immortality. You can hear him chortling still while laying down lines like, "The entire pietistic or modern mystical theology rests only on a game of ball. The individual throws himself away only in order to have God throw him back again; he humbles himself before God only in order to be reflected in him. His self-loss is self-enjoyment, his humility is self-exaltation. He submerges himself in God only to surface again intact, and, refreshed and renewed, to sun himself in his own excellence." This is classic Feuerbach rhetoric – an incisive inversion of the accepted order of cause and effect aimed at bringing our loftiest notions back to their all-too-terrestrial origins.

It was, of course, an incredibly dangerous thing to write in the increasingly reactionary atmosphere of the time, and so Feuerbach published it anonymously, which delayed but did not prevent the cold hammer of retribution from falling. After his authorship was found out, the doors of professional academia were closed firmly against him, and he would live his life with the wolves of penury always nipping at his heels.

For the next seven years, writing from the depths of poverty, he produced three works on the history of philosophy that included a reconsideration of the epochal thought of Spinoza and Leibniz. For Feuerbach, these two figures represented a decisive turn in the history of thought, their notions of God as a pervasive mind inhabiting all creation opening the way for a staggeringly rich and tantalizingly contradictory pantheistic conception of the universe. As he would later summarize in *Principles of the Philosophy of the Future*, "Pantheism is the naked truth of theism. All the conceptions of theism, when grasped, seriously considered, carried out, and realized, lead necessarily to pantheism." And yet, so fraught with destructive significance is the unification of thought and matter in the deity that, ultimately, "Pantheism is theological atheism." By making God extensive with the universe, pantheism allowed humanity to see clearly that God is an alienation of our own nature, and thus brought to a close the first stage in man's self-rediscovery.

Some respite from his financial worries came in 1837 with his marriage to Berta Löw, whose wealth from a porcelain factory would keep Feuerbach snug and cozy until its bankruptcy in 1860. From that position of relative ease Feuerbach launched a flurry of hard-hitting blows straight to the gut of traditional philosophy. In 1839, he renounced his Hegelianism once and for all in the *Critique of Hegelian Philosophy*, seeing the future of philosophy not in abstract idealist speculation about the nature of mind, but in a strictly materialist evaluation of anthropology.

Then, in 1841, he published his master work, *The Essence of Christianity*, the book that ensured his survival in the philosophical pantheon regardless of what you think of his position about Hegel. In it, Feuerbach painstakingly sets out the attributes of God and shows how they are all nothing less than representations of the species-being of humanity. God is humanity's way of portraying itself, as a whole, to itself, an act of alienation that had to happen in order for us to overcome mere individuality, but whose time is done. "Man first of all sees his nature as if *out of* himself, before he finds it in himself. His own nature is in the first instance contemplated by him as that of another being. Religion is the childlike condition of humanity."

All easy enough to say, but where Feuerbach excels is in the rigor with which he chases down each divine attribute and traces it back to its species-generated source. Even the morbidly religious Karl Barth, who recommends that the best way to criticize Feuerbach is to "laugh in his face," has to concede that "In his writings – at least in those on the Bible, the Church Fathers, and especially on Luther – his theological skill places him above most modern philosophers" and, "No philosopher of his time penetrated the contemporary theological situation as effectually as he."

And this is what you intimately feel when reading *Essence*, the words of a man who has made the contemplation of religion his life's work, offering us his dearly bought insight into its twisting psychology. The infinities present in the deity are the result of our own feeling of infinite potential, as a collective, and the dictates of our ever-evolving conception of reason. As humans, we survived because of our capacity for goodness, and were so pleased with that capacity we made an ideal of it, paradoxically denying its existence in ourselves even as we hoisted it into the sky as a necessary attribute of our deity. We denied ourselves personal goodness in order to venerate it the more, and with the passing of time actually became convinced of our own worthlessness as against the purity of God. Along the way, we forgot that the very existence of goodness as a God-attribute signifies our basic goodness as a species.

Feuerbach wants to remind us of what we were before we deified our favorite qualities: "You believe in love as a divine attribute because you yourself love; you believe that God is a wise, benevolent being because you know nothing better in yourself than benevolence and wisdom, and you believe that God exists, that therefore he is a subject – because you yourself exist, and are a subject."

It's a book of titanic import, filled with delectably quotable lines like, "You are terrified before the religious atheism of thy heart!" But it is only the first step in Feuerbach's revolution. For, Feuerbach explains, philosophy freed us from the abstractions of religion only to encase our attributes in another, even more sinister, layer of abstraction. We shall not truly be free of alienation, he concludes, until we slip the bonds of philosophy.

He makes his case in two books that followed hot on the heels of *Essence*, 1842's *Preliminary Theses for the Reform of Philosophy*, and 1843's *Principles of the Philosophy of the Future*. In them, Feuerbach starts his turn to a more aphoristic style of writing that crackles with a proto-Nietzschean intensity. He portrays our self-knowledge as a being locked away from our view for centuries until it was finally rescued by philosophy. At that moment, however, instead of handing it back to us, its rightful owners, the philosophers took a long look at what they had in their hands and said, "You know, this won't *quite* do. We'll fix it up really nice for you, don't worry," and then proceeded to leech it of anything resembling an actual, human trait in the name of idealistic consistency. And so, in the end, we were worse off than before, because at least with God we had some tangible elements for us to recognize ourselves in, whereas idealist philosophy took anything smacking of a mere sensation-bound self and refined it beyond all recognition.

Feuerbach wants to strike out on a new path, and in doing so he defines the project for the next half century of philosophy: "The new philosophy has, therefore, as its principle of cognition and as its subject, not the ego, the absolute, abstract mind, in short, not reason for itself alone, but the real and whole being of man. Reality, the subject of reason, is only man. *Man* thinks, not the ego, not reason. Thus, the new philosophy does not rest on the divinity, that is, the truth, of reason for itself alone; it rests on... the truth of the whole man."

Feuerbach put out the call, and the response was immediate and fevered. Marx and Engels were among the first to answer, and, even though they went on to criticize Feuerbach for not going far enough in his materialism, there is no doubt that their revolutionary work is an extension of his own foundational concerns about the project of modern, post-idealist philosophy.

With the failure of revolutionary reform in Germany in 1848, Feuerbach's life took a marked downturn not remotely helped by his hankering after the much younger Johanna Kapp or the ransacking of his home by police on the hunt for incendiary material. He had one more significant book in him, the hefty *Theogonie* of 1857 which expanded his religious ideas beyond the source material of Christianity to include classical and world religions. But with the bankruptcy of his wife's factory in 1860, Feuerbach was left to spend the last twelve years of his life largely a broken man, living off of donations, detached from the current philosophical trends, and constantly ill of health.

In 1830, Feuerbach had thrown his professional career away with a book that intertwined a radical critique of religious psychology with long sections of philosophical poetry, all delivered with the rhetorical instinct of a prophet. Forty two years later, in one of the great hand-offs of history, he died the same year that a new poetry-spouting psychological philosopher, Friedrich Nietzsche, published his first work, *The Birth of Tragedy*. What had begun as a revolution tentatively explored from within the teeth of Hegelianism had exploded during his lifetime, largely because of his efforts, into a thorough-going attack against the business of philosophy itself. If we are, today, a generation of self-obsessed, online-status-checking maniacs, therefore, both the good and ill of it can be laid at the feet of the Bavarian theologian whose life work was to give us back, at long last, ourselves.

FURTHER READING:

English interest in Feuerbach is primarily as a linking figure between Hegel and Marx, so finding books in our language dealing solely with his life and thought is a somewhat frustrating task. Marx Wartofsky's 1977 *Feuerbach* is the best you're going to find, though

110

it is much more weighted towards an evaluation of his use of dialectic and other such specialized philosophical concerns that aren't of particular interest to a non-academic. So, the best place to start is really Feuerbach's own works. *Philosophy of the Future* is a slim volume full of wit and punch that makes for an ideal starting point. From there, *The Essence of Christianity* is a natural jumping point, though I'll caution you against the George Eliot translation, which is lovely on the whole, but full of *way*-distracting Thee and Thou constructions that have to be actively ignored if you're going to make any headway with it.

THE SCIENTIFIC SOUL:
WHAT NEAR DEATH EXPERIENCES SAY (AND DON'T SAY)
ABOUT IDENTITY

(Originally Published at *The New Humanist*, February 2013)

It has been a hard century for the soul. From its former role as the unquestionable master of our actions, emotions, memories, and behavior, it appears now as a wispy monarch without a kingdom, sustaining itself on the scraps left it by neuroscience, evolutionary biology, and genetics. And yet, if you've been watching the right places, you might have noticed that it has been making something of a determined comeback in the last decade, its fate tethered to the curiously rising star of Near Death Experience research. A small group of psychologists have used NDEs to drive a wedge in the materialist conception of identity large enough for the disembodied self to assay an entry into the scientific debate.

The bible for this school of thought, which continues to be more or less uncritically quoted as having scientifically established the incorporeal soul, is 2007's *Irreducible Mind* by Edward and Emily Kelly, with contributions from a handful of others. It is a good book to have in a fight, weighing in at 643 pages with another hundred in bibliography. There is no doubt at all that these are people who have painstakingly done their work in accumulating hundreds and thousands of atypical case studies over the past thirty years. And we owe them thanks for that- nothing spurs science to figure things out to the next level of complexity quite like a puzzlement.

As the Tycho Brahes of unusual biological phenomena, there is nothing to fault them for here and much to admire. But Tycho had the splendid good sense to turn his astronomical data over to Kepler for interpretation, while the Kellys try to fill that role themselves, and this is where the problems start creeping in.

Put generally, the viewpoint of the authors is that psychology did itself a massive disservice when, early in the twentieth century, it forsook the idea of a non-corporeal explanation of consciousness in favor of first behavioral psychology and then rigidly materialistic neural network theory. While they (at times begrudgingly) pay respect to the insights gained from these approaches, they nonetheless feel that the dominant position of materialism in the scientific establishment has pushed back by a century the progress that could have been had by studying psi-phenomena scientifically.

And there is much quoting of William James.

In the case of NDEs, they have personally collected files on nearly a thousand instances, and have come to the conclusion that this body of data represents unequivocal proof that an immaterial self exists. Their first argument is that the rich experiential cocktail of an NDE, with its bright lights and tunnels, out of body experiences, peaceful sense of serenity, vivid life memories, and conversations with the deceased, is something far too complex to have been mixed by the mere brute matter of the brain. Keep that argument in mind - NDEs are too complex to be explained materially - we're going to need that later.

The authors then turn to review mainstream explanations for NDEs, curiously restricting themselves to thirty year old psychological explanations and a handful of more modern physiological ones, without paying much more than a nod to theories based in evolutionary biology. So we learn that oxygen deficiency can produce a pleasurable sense of leaving the body, and that increased carbon dioxide levels can produce tunnel vision with bright lights, spikes of access to past memories, and peaceful feelings of connection with God. Further, we find neurochemicals that produce a feeling of travel through a tunnel and communing with the divine, and that electrical stimulation of certain parts of the brain has produced out of body sensations. It's an impressive body of findings, made all the more so when you see that they don't quote any non-sympathetic study made after 1997.

What's more troubling than the omission of a decade of data, however, is the conclusions they draw from all of this. Instead of seeing that, hey, a lot of the very strange psychological occurrences characteristic of NDEs can be brought about by purely physical means, the lesson they take away is that no single chemical factor causes *all* of the characteristics by itself, and therefore physical explanations cannot and will not be able to explain NDE phenomena. They reject out of hand any attempt to explain NDEs as a combination of several of these chemical and biological factors working together, mocking them as "ad lib" and unscientific attempts to piece together a working theory after the fact.

Here's where their first argument comes in - one moment NDEs are described as too complex to be caused by the brain, and the next, when one tries to explain NDEs by piecing together discoveries from physiology and neurochemistry, the attempt is rejected as *too complex*! This is putting inquiry in something of a straight-jacket, since if we aren't allowed to have complex or multi-faceted answers for complex phenomena, we aren't going to get very far. The only thing that will satisfy the authors is, apparently, if we find a batch of neurons somewhere that, all by itself, causes every NDE characteristic.

And that, as the authors well know, will never happen. Just look at the number of brain regions and chemicals involved in the motor response to a possible threat - a stimulus is sent to the lateral and then central nuclei of the amygdala, which then sends signals to neurons of the ventral tegmental area, which in turn release dopamine into the nucleus accumbens, which allows the activation of the pallidum, which allows for the initiation of movement by the cortex and brain stem. All of that to Just Start Moving- the demand that the entirety of the NDE response be localized to one region of the brain or one chemical in order to not be considered an ad lib fabrication is utterly unreasonable in light of all we have learned about the networking of synaptic systems. Mental events are incredibly complex, and to ask for a simple neural solution to them is to willfully ask the impossible in order to slip the immaterial soul in the silence that follows.

I hardly have words for what comes next. After rejecting a multiple neural region model for the NDE, they *employ* a multiple neural region model of consciousness in their very next argument. Near Death Experiences, they rightly point out, involve accessing memories, processing language, and crafting elaborate out of body scenes that incorporate pieces of the action around the patient. To do that requires a lot of mental coordination and activity - so how, they ask, is this possible for a brain which is basically dead, which shows minimal to no gamma activity of the type associated with conscious, memory-creating processes? And that's a good question, except for the fact that we have no data which shows that NDEs actually do occur during the time when the brain is flatlining. We know for sure that there are many cases of NDE spectrum characteristics occurring when the brain is in full health - as when mountain climbers describe seeing their life flash before their eyes in the midst of falling. But since we don't know for sure when, say, a cardiac patient actually experiences their NDE mentally, the hypothesis that it is during the time when their brains show the least activity is little more than a convenient guess. Further, the idea that the brain is entirely without electrical activity during the closing moments of life is one which has come under increasing scrutiny as of late, particularly with Lakhmir Chawla's 2009 finding that the dying brain experiences a sometimes minutes-long spike in electrical activity just prior to death. Is it the right type of electrical activity to fit the effects we see in NDEs? More studies need to be done, but the fact that it is there at all shows that the brain still has a few tricks up its sleeve.

It's a trickiness which evolution has honed to a fine degree over the past few hundred million or so years. With the exception of the effectively immortal (but very humble about it) *Turritopsis nutricula*, the success of life on our planet is based upon the ability to die. For my genes to be passed on by my offspring, I have to relinquish my hold upon the resources that my descendants will need to survive. I have to die. Even as evolution has provided us with a thousand behavioral and neural adaptations to keep ourselves alive on a day to day basis, they are all shackled to a body which bounds gleefully deathwards. Recall the massive neural machinery set into motion when I just PERCEIVE a threat - is it so inconceivable that a brain which could develop that sort of response would also have a way of dealing with the imminent arrival of death itself which would draw on every trick in the mental playbook, from a comprehensive replaying of past memories to the creation of a soothing mental space populated by all the people we thought we'd never see again? Could there not be an evolutionary advantage to throwing the dying body into a Xanadu of pleasantness when one is clearly past the ability to help one's self? Except for a brief sentence that precedes two pages of battle with 1980s Expectation Theory, the Kellys fail to acknowledge any physical model which considers NDE symptoms as intentional. That these could be partly accidental (the pairing of oxygen deprivation and carbon dioxide saturation leading to euphoria, tunnel vision, out of body experiences, and lights) and partly an intentional adaptation (activation of memory centers and wish fulfillment) is simply not considered.

Instead, we have a model of the self as fundamentally incorporeal as the explanatory mechanism of the NDE. And yet,

NDE symptoms occur in only twelve percent of severe cardiac or resuscitation events. If we all have an incorporeal soul that is being filtered through our body, shouldn't these experiences be far more common? The Kellys borrow from 19th century psychic researcher F.W.H. Meyers in answering that only those with a sufficiently permeable barrier between their physical and immaterial mental selves are able to experience the phenomenon. Now, a physical model would explain the relative scarcity of NDEs on the basis of chemical conditions, semi-rare genetic dispositions, and perhaps the mechanism of neuron potentiation. The Kellys explain it by a nineteenth century notion of a gate between soul and body that for some reason opens all the way only for some people sometimes.

Do we have a full physical model of Near Death Experiences? We do not. However, the combination of physiology, neural network theory, and evolutionary biology is solving the little puzzles one by one. The pace isn't perhaps what the Kellys would prefer (patience is not one of Edward Kelly's strong points - his tale of abandoning neural computer modeling in the 1970s because punchcard-based computers weren't able to instantly mimic human linguistic behavior to his standards being a somewhat amusing incident of jumping ship a TAD early.) But just because we don't have an answer right now doesn't mean we get to shove the incorporeal soul edgewise into the gap. Or, as Antonio Damasio said in a slightly different context, "The possibility of explaining mind and consciousness parsimoniously, within the confines of neurobiology as currently conceived, remains open; it should not be abandoned unless the technical and theoretical resources of neurobiology are exhausted, an unlikely prospect at the moment."

So it seems the soul, our long-suffering hero, will have to put its visions of restoration aside for a while yet, NDE research having proven rather more Atterbury than Monck. And though, when the answer is found, it will undoubtedly be an astonishingly complex but sensible material one, it must be said that that answer will owe much to the research accumulated and symptom criteria compiled by the Kellys, van Pommel, Greyson, and Grosso.   Science is complicated like that.

BULLIES FOR JESUS:
THE SPREAD OF THE GOOD NEWS CLUBS

(Originally Published in *American Atheist Magazine*, 2013)

It is the quietest of invasions. The sort that covers a core of pure malevolence with an innocuous facade of hand-made posters, home-cooked brownies, and affable "How could you ever think we'd do something like THAT?" smiles. Since 2001, when the Supreme Court validated their right to do so, the Child Evangelism Fellowship has been planting after-school programs called Good News Clubs into the very heart of our public school system. Their Empire now stands at 3500 schools, and is growing every day through the Fellowship's efficiently organized and End Times Passionate national campaign.

To the public, the CEF portrays the Good News Clubs as merely handmaidens of morality enhancement with some light Biblical instruction on the side. The sobering reality is that the clubs are, quite explicitly, vehicles by which the CEF is attempting to proselytize non-Christian children at our public schools, using their own classmates as the "harvesters" (their term) of these lost souls. When a new club is established in a school, it is helped on its way by volunteers trained at the CEF's Children's Ministries Institute, an academy which trains shock troops in the most effective methods of seducing children into surrendering themselves to Christ.

One of the first things I did in preparing to build our case to present to the school district was to read through the training material that these volunteers are given. A fair amount of it is available online so as to facilitate the fastest possible training and diffusion of the clubs, and it makes for chilling reading. What is immediately clear is that these are people motivated by a sense that Jesus himself is commanding them to impress upon children their sinful nature, and to compel them to see the world, including their fellow non-saved classmates, as fundamentally evil and broken. In the pamphlet *Why Evangelize Children?* this is made especially clear. The pamphlet makes the case that, "It is clear from the Bible that a child who has not trusted Jesus Christ as his Saviour—no matter how young he is—is therefore spiritually dead, a sinner by nature and action, and that he is outside God's kingdom." (p.35) Luckily, the author continues, it should be easy to convert children because they are so susceptible to shame and guilt: "We all know from experience and from our own memories of childhood that children's hearts are tender, and that they can be very sensitive and feel guilty concerning sin. They are more sensitive than adults and feel guilt more easily than adults."

The answer, then, to evangelizing children is to purposefully and strategically riddle them with guilt and fear until they succumb. And, lest you feel worried that making children feel fear so that they believe in the same things you do is deeply messed up, the author reassures us that this is entirely in line with the Biblical plan: "It is clear ... that Moses believed it was possible for **all** four groups, including the children (the little ones), **to fear the Lord**." (p. 26, emphasis is theirs.)

Manipulation of fear and guilt, dehumanizing non-believers – these are the tools with which the volunteer is armed as he or she goes into a classroom after school hours and is given free reign over the minds of kindergartners and elementary school children. One of our parents sat in on a meeting and counted fifty nine uses of the word sin and two instances of the children being made to label themselves as sinners. But it doesn't end there.

As Katherine Stewart revealed in her 2012 book *The Good News Club: The Christian Right's Stealth Assault on America's Children*, these trained first wave organizers do not limit themselves to the after-school activities of the GNCs, but volunteer in classrooms so that the children associate them with the school's authority structure. The result is that, when the volunteers go on to tell the kids after school about the horrors awaiting non-believers in Hell (which they do, and encourage the children to repeat to their non-Christian friends), their words have that extra touch of "It must be true, an adult from my classroom said it" that children are so ill-prepared to defend against.

These children, however, aren't the real targets of the groups. That honor belongs to the children of non-Church families who are ordinarily out of the reach of the long arms of the CEF. They see the public schools as their way of approaching these children but, darn it all, they can't, as adults, harangue the children directly on school property. But what they CAN do is train other children to do the work of proselytizing FOR them.

And that is precisely their strategy. By dangling points, prizes, and candy in front of their members for each non-Church student they drag to the GNC, they effectively create an on-campus army in their own image to do the work that they are prevented by law from doing themselves. Joseph Rockne, a parent at Loyal Heights Elementary, described what he overheard of a GNC meeting at his daughter's school in an interview with Stewart: "They had their club meetings next door to my daughter's classroom. There are accordion walls and you can hear that it's all about, 'If you recruit your friends you'll get candy and prizes.' They coach the kids to exert pressure on other kids."

It is a loophole so deviously grotesque that nobody thinks to protect children against it until it is too late. The CEF establishes its clubs so quickly and efficiently, and its shock volunteers are so expertly trained, that by the time parents in a district realize what is really going on at their school, the organization is so firmly implanted as to be all but immovable.

Many have tried to dislodge them only to come up against the full legal artillery that the CEF's deep pockets are able to field. Administrators who have other things to be worrying about are harried by CEF lawyers while local pastors are pressed into service to make the parents of the GNC children feel like martyrs under attack by the vicious secular world. PTAs that used to work together for the greater good burn themselves out in paroxysms of mutual distrust and ideological posturing, all but crippling their ability to actually help the students succeed. Jeanne, another parent at Loyal Heights, describes the poisoned atmosphere that formed at her school: "When parents were picking up their kids, you could see that groups divided along faith lines had formed. Parents weren't intermingling anymore. Parents who supported the GNC were sticking together, and parents who opposed it stuck together."

And in the meantime, the students twist in the venomous wind, victims of the CEF's almost reptilian sense of opportunism and tactical advantage. I want you to put yourself in the shoes of an elementary school student for a moment. You're on the playground, trading Yu-Gi-Oh cards or jumping rope (kids still do that, right?), when three of your friends come up to you.

"Why don't you go to the Good News Club after school?" they ask, eager for the prizes they've been promised for every new recruit they bring into the fold.

"I don't want to," you might answer if you're unusually brave. "I don't know," if you're a normal kid terrified of peer rejection.

"Well, you should, because we all have sinned, and the club teaches you how not to go to Hell," they press, quoting from the literature they've been given which teaches them in vivid detail about the destruction of the non-believers during the End Times.

You could respond, "That's not true!" but then they will point to the signs for the Club that the school has been pressured to allow on the campus, or the flyers that your teacher has put into your hand advertising the club's meetings (in my own school district, the Superintendent allowed the distribution of CEF propaganda in student packets, citing district guidelines), or the fact that the meetings are held At School. "See," all of these bits of data imply to a young mind unused to the fine distinctions of Official Recognition, "It's in our school, and if it's in school, it's TRUE."

Is there a six or seven year old kid in the world who wouldn't crumble under that kind of pressure? Playgrounds, where kids aren't supposed to deal with anything more nefarious than a breach of four square etiquette, are being shamelessly recast by adults who should know better as acceptable zones of religious conflict. As if being a kid weren't difficult enough, now our children have to deal with the one place where they're supposed to be safe from ideological pressure becoming a war zone in an orchestrated holy battle.

This is clearly not a matter of Morality Enhancement, as the CEF claimed when bringing its case before the Supreme Court. This is a narrow band of zealots seizing an opportunity to rake as many children into their clutches as they can before the clear illegality of their actions catches up with them. As the Columbia Midlands GNC states on its website, "We don't know how long we will be able to openly share the Gospel within the Public Schools, so that is why it is our goal to establish a Good News Club in every public elementary school in our district."

It is hard not to feel a simmering outrage at these tactics. The CEF saw that children had a refuge from indoctrination, the public school, and set about systematically destroying that safe harbor, weaponizing the school's own students as part of the process. And no matter the result, the CEF wins. If the GNC at a school flourishes and grows, then its base of believers swells. If it encounters resistance, then the public school ceases to function under the weight of the conflict, and the CEF can check another institution off its enemy list. To an organization that subscribes to such a deep-seated hatred of humanity as lies at the core of End Times zealotry, anybody and anything destroyed in the process of elevating the elect become merely tokens of glory, the foundation of refuse upon which God's chosen must stand to enter Heaven. Whether they thrive in a school or break it is therefore all the same to their cynical estimation of humanity's worth.

So, yes, outrage is easy, but it is also what the CEF is largely counting on to fulfill its larger goals. They want and need atheists, Jews, and Muslims to react sharply to their needling advances. They need people who worked together before suddenly separated by an unbridgeable gulf. They need the GNC parents to feel like

121

their way of life is under imminent and real threat from their neighbors and friends. That is why we must be proactive in our response to the problem, to cut off the CEF's lines of ingress before their strategy has a chance to unfold to its calculated conclusion.

That's where you come in. If your school hasn't been invaded by a GNC yet, take a look at its facilities use policies. Making sure that the wording unambiguously prevents the establishment of institutions like the Good News Club that encourage discrimination or emotional bullying is a good place to head them off at the pass. Unfortunately, what lawyers can make, other lawyers can unmake. The best place to start, I think, is simply letting people know that this organization exists and publicizing its own statements of intent. Most parents who sign up for the club simply don't know what it wants to do, and would never approve if they had been informed ahead of time of its goals and intentions. The CEF lives and grows on stealth and misinformation, on presenting a fluffy-bunnies-in-the-garden-of-paradise face at PTA meetings and an iron doctrine of damnation in its meetings with children. It is resolutely and purposely a creature of the shadows, capable of surviving only if it sets down its roots before light is shone upon it.

So, share what you know. Read Katherine Stewart's book, and loan it around. Send out a few links on Facebook to your parents' group by way of getting their warning antennae up early. This is one of those cases where a little bit of shared knowledge before the deluge can go a long way. Who knows – the school you save may be your own!

Base Considerations:
A Number Lover's Critique
Of Numerology

(Originally Published in *The Freethinker*, September 2013)

Mathematics is the purest and most beautiful form of poetry available to the human mind. I not only say that to my students at the beginning of each new semester, but I actually happen to rather believe it too. A great proof can combine elegance and chaos, the eternal and the infinitesimal, within a few lines of text that make haikus look positively verbose. Savoring those lines is, for me, every bit as heady and breath-arresting as wandering through Wagner's harmonies or dancing with Diderot's impish devices. So, I understand where Numerology, with its deep and abiding love of number and pattern, comes from.

Mathematically, however, it is utter rubbish. Most critiques of this belief system focus on the weaknesses it shares with astrology – its lack of precision in defining its terms, for example, which allows everybody to come away from a numerology session feeling that their unique soul has been enumerated for the first time, when in fact selective memory is simply playing its usual role as hand-maiden to chart-filling hucksters. That is entirely true, but what really upsets me about Numerology is the thoughtless mathematical apathy that it exhibits when using the numbers it purportedly understands so well and reveres so much.

The fundamental principle of Numerological theory is an interesting one – it would make for a good bit of universe building in a comic book or episode of the X-Files. Basically, after we die, we survey our lives, see the things we didn't accomplish spiritually or professionally, and then encode those unrealized goals within the name and birth-date of our future self. Upon being reborn, we forget everything that we knew as spirits, but so long as we know how to decode our name and date of birth, we can recover the information that was lost to us. It's our previous life's coded message in a bottle to our current selves. As a fictional premise, it's actually rather cool.

The problems start filing in quickly, though, once we go into the mechanism of Numerological decoding. Everything is based on all facets of humanity and the universe being reducible to the single digits 1 through 9, with 0 thrown in from time to time when the formulas force its presence. Each numeral has an associated character attribute which tells you not only your inner nature, but the goals you have to set for your future. With the 0, this is a base 10 system, which is the one we happen to use in our day to day lives, but it certainly isn't a universal or necessary way of thinking about numbers. The Babylonians used base 60, the Celts base 20, and, if we are to believe Voltaire, Charles XII flirted with the idea of making Sweden a base 8 system since ammunition cartridges contained 8 shots. And computers, of course, represent all numbers with a base 2 system in which only the digits 0 and 1 exist.

Base 10 is only special because it's common, and it's only common because we happen to have ten fingers at this stage in our evolution. Picking the numerals of this system as the foundational blocks of the universe makes perfect sense if you are a Westerner caught in your culture's base prejudice, but it is entirely arbitrary to anybody who actually cares about how numerals and numbers relate to each other. More disturbingly, it means that the Fundamental Character Attributes of humanity will be different for different cultures, Brits having 9 possible inner natures and life paths, while Babylonians somehow get 59. I love the Epic of Gilgamesh as much as the next fellow, but I don't think that those characters are *six times* more emotionally refined than those of, say, Shakespeare.

So, Numerology is a system of belief whose first step is based on an arbitrary but convenient whim. Where does it go from there? There are two widgets that do most of the heavy lifting, and these are the Alphabet Table and the concept of Numerical Reduction. The table tells you what numerical value to assign the letters in your name, and carries with it the echoes of base 10 prejudice we've come to know and love:

```
1 2 3 4 5 6 7 8 9
A B C D E F G H I
J K L M N O P Q R
S T U V W X Y Z
```

Pretty it isn't. 9 only gets two letters in the English system, while 8 is stuck with Q and Z. The only thing to say in its defense is it isn't as awkward as this system comes off in Cyrillic which, because of its 33 letters, ends up having 3 spaces left over at the end instead of 1, or the Greek, whose 24 characters also leave 3 to spare. And then, of course, this approach makes no sense whatsoever in a pictogram-based writing system...

The end result of this arbitrary shackling of the modern Roman letter system into groups of 9 is that certain attributes which are generally well distributed amongst humanity are forced into artificial rarity for certain ethnic or cultural groups. Americans and Brits don't have the number 8 come up a lot, the odd Quentin notwithstanding, and yet 8 importantly represents Law, and so we are to believe that our nations uniquely tend towards collective lawlessness. What this alphabet table ends up doing is prejudicing the character traits that happen to line up with your culture's favorite letters, and so sacrifices the actual diversity of humanity in favor of a desperate clinging to numeral consistency.

If it were just the base 10 thing, or just the sloppiness of the alphabet table's assumptions, though, I'd have let it all go peacefully. It is in the operation known as Numerical Reduction, however, that Numerology's true indifference to mathematics makes itself ghastly obvious and quasi insulting. For example, in making one calculation, I have to find the sum total of the letter values for my first name. This assumes that there IS a standard spelling of my name, something that has only been true for industrialized societies within the last few centuries or so, meaning that this supposedly universally applicable numerological method is entirely useless for the vast majority of historical mankind.

I'm lucky enough to be born in the modern era, and have a written record of my name's original spelling. It's DALE, so numerically I get $4 + 1 + 3 + 5 = 13$. But wait, that number is greater than 9! I'm not allowed to use numbers greater than 9, so Numerology has to find some way to break 13 down. The device that does this is called Numerical Reduction. All you do is take the digits of your name sum, and add them together. So, in my case, I'd go $1 + 3 = 4$, and THAT would be the number I use in the relevant calculations.

But of course that doesn't always reduce to a single digit either. RAHA, for example, has an initial sum of 19. When we "reduce" that, we get 10, which is still not acceptable. Numerology's answer? Reduce again! So that, finally, we arrive at 1. What does that 1 really represent, though? What does it mean, mathematically, to add the digits of a number? In Raha's case, the initial reduction to 10 meant that there were 10 powers of 10 in his original name sum (9 ten to the zero powers and 1 ten to the first power). That's it. Then the next reduction down to 1 tells us the number of powers of ten in the number that represents the number of powers of ten in his original name sum.

deep breath

So, the number which is supposed to stand for the deepest content of your soul is basically just a running tally of powers of 10, a number which, I'll remind you, isn't considered significant enough to deserve a character attribute being associated with it. This disconnect between the insistence on the exclusive power of the numbers 0 through 9 and the constant hidden reliance on the rejected number 10 runs throughout the structure of Numerological analysis. Faced with the problem of Name Sums producing answers that don't fit into their 1-9 scheme, the founders of Numerology just grabbed the easiest mathematical operation at hand, addition, and started running wild with it without stopping to consider just what adding digits together willy-nilly actually *meant*. When I add two normal numbers, say 6+8, that tells me the number of total objects I have. When I add two digits of a number, it only tells me about the number of base powers that exist in the number, and so all of the information encoded in the *order* of the digits is lost. 312 comes out exactly the same as 123. Numerical Reduction as an operation blanches the diversity of the number spectrum, draining numerals of the meaning that comes with being placed in a given order, which is a victory for the dogmatic "1 to 9" hegemony of Numerology but tastes bland on the tongue of anybody who actually loves the spice of the numerical world.

Faced with a base 10 system in their culture, the early numerologists saw a chance to make something philosophical of it. Nine character attributes seemed doable, so they pushed ahead. The number of letters didn't quite cycle in groups of 9, but, eh, close enough, and they kept going. The name and birthday sums they computed often resulted in numbers that were greater than 9, but, heck, if you add the digits to each other enough times, eventually you will come out with something 9 or smaller, so they continued to shamble forward, their gait catching on each half-considered compromise they left trailing behind them. The entire project of Numerology strikes me as the work of a person aiming for perfection and stopping at Good Enough. If you want to do due reverence to the power of numbers in nature, get yourself a copy of Roger Penrose's epic *The Road to Reality*. Numerology, however, is a game best consigned to the schoolyard of history.

BECOMING HEINOUS:
HOW THE BAPTISTS WENT FROM HEROES TO ARCH-VILLAINS IN THREE SCANT CENTURIES

(Originally Published in *The Freethinker*, March 2014)

In the roll call of modern religious grotesqueries, few groups figure so prominently as the Baptists. Homosexuality correction centers. Hunting camps. Abortion clinic violence. Godhatesfags.com Creationist textbooks. All of these, and so many more humanity crushing ideas, have sprung from the collective evil genius of the modern Baptist movement, and in particular the Southern Baptist Convention. How did a movement which, at its founding, stood for the most progressive and liberal ideas of its age, descend to a state of such shambling self-parody?

The answer lies in the twisting brambles of United States history. The first Baptist church in America was founded in 1639 by one of the truly and legitimately great men of this nation's past, Roger Williams. He was unique in our increasingly blemished pantheon of colonial figures in that he did not believe the government had the right to enforce infractions of religious practice, and in his desire to deal honestly with Native Americans. Of course, such a man had no place in the religiously authoritarian structure of seventeenth century Salem, and he was driven into the woods, quite literally, to survive as best he could.

Survive he did, however, and he founded our first colony which held religious freedom as a central organizing principle, where the content of your mind would not interfere with the safety of you or your family. This was a Baptism of profound conscience, founded with a concern for equality and intellectual freedom, and its subsequent history bore out these concerns. When slavery ran rampant in the South, it was the Baptists and Methodists who stood in the front ranks against it.

And yet, the Baptist church was, even then, at its moment of greatest heroism, slowly nurturing the seeds of its own decline. The true explosion in its membership occurred with the waves of Revivals that swept America in the eighteenth and nineteenth centuries. The emphasis on emotion, on the subjective *experience* of religion, attracted droves of followers, and not only from the educated classes, where these movements usually thrash themselves out. Thousands were told that

128

what they experienced as true *was* true, and once that sapling of a notion was planted, it inevitably outgrew and overshadowed the more fragile undergrowth of compassion and tolerance that Williams had risked everything to establish a century before.

Southern planters and their families *wanted* slavery to be okay, *felt* that it must be so, and with the official sanction of Awakening-wrought theology, were able to convince themselves that it was even godly, and the preachers followed suit. In these torments of self-justification, the Southern Baptist Convention was born. The religion that began upon the most advanced principles of human dignity became the deft accomplice of gross degradation.

Now, to be fair, the SBC did apologize for its overwhelmingly racist origin story (though not until 1995). However, they don't appear to have actually learned anything from it, structurally. The same underpinnings of blustering confidence in the righteousness of one's own life prejudices remained, even when the subject of that prejudice shifted. The genius of Baptism as a religious denomination is its dressing of personal revulsion as a matter of mere scriptural adherence.

In essence, they provide a brilliant proxy for your own hatred, allowing you the full scope of that hatred practically while still claiming a benevolent soul personally. "We don't hate the sinner, we hate the sin," is the classic line of a movement filled with people who want to keep their low-hanging beliefs but not lose their friends. It's immensely self-deluded, of course, but also a very powerful combination for those who want the security of traditionalism but can't stand to be judged themselves. It's a flexible position ideally suited to keep awful practices alive.

This is why Southern Baptism has served for so long as the last refuge for social and religious ideas that more contemplative branches of Christianity have long since abandoned as untenable upon the briefest of reflections. Their current position statements are a veritable time capsule of the accumulated dross of American prejudice:

"We affirm God's plan for marriage and sexual intimacy – one man, and one woman, for life. Homosexuality is not a 'valid alternative lifestyle.'"

"A wife is to submit herself graciously to the servant leadership of her husband even as the church willingly submits to the headship of Christ. She, being in the image of God as is her husband and thus equal to him, has the God-given responsibility to respect her husband and to serve as his helper in managing the household and nurturing the next generation"

"We ask the people of the world to conform to Christ and His Word, and not to our merely human traditions."

"Procreation is a gift from God, a precious trust reserved for marriage. At the moment of conception, a new being enters the universe, a human being, a being created in God's image. This human being deserves our protection, whatever the circumstances of conception."

Notice the artful framing of that last phrase, which somehow makes of a rape a miracle without even having the principle to name it as such. This blend of random prejudice parading as scriptural adherence and personal moral cowardice has been with the church for a century and a half now, and has found its fullest flowering in that nadir of humanity, the Westboro Baptist Church. They maintain the site godhatesfags.com, picket funerals, and in every way are so thoroughly loathsome that even other Baptist churches can't publically be seen to tolerate them.

And yet, their difference is just one of tact and method, not of belief. Westboro's approach towards social truth and how it is revealed and upheld is not substantially different than that of mainstream Baptism. Unlike with other religions, which have developed supplementary principles of morality against which personal opinion must be checked, the only requirement in the Baptist stated platform is the ability to find a line of scripture that approximately matches your opinion. There is no secondary check, no way to know if you've gone too far or considered too little. Search through the Basic Beliefs section of the SBC's website, and you'll find a good deal about political hot-button topics, and nothing whatsoever on how to be a basically good person.

This lop-sidedness is, I have to admit at least some happiness in reporting, finally putting the brakes to Baptism's twentieth century juggernaut. It is still the largest Protestant denomination in the USA, but it is now experiencing a membership *decline* for the first time since the nineteenth century. Putting all of their efforts into the creation of an all-hatred-yet-all-innocence façade stitched together by sumptuous amounts of doublethink was very effective for a world where adversarial thought was the order of the day.

That's not really the case now, in a world intimately reliant upon cooperation for its basic functioning. The luxury of writing off different strips of humanity that we could afford in, say, 1952 or 1985, is too dear now, and fewer and fewer people are willing to buy themselves such a strange-fitting self-conception at the price of their own mental flexibility.

Maybe the SBC will get smart and return itself to the high level of its seventeenth century betters. More likely, it will continue its policy of taking a century and a half to realize specific errors without noting the common factor that binds them all. But when that time comes, when it's finally ready to apologize, to gays and women and teachers and doctors, will there be anybody left to listen?

MEDIEVAL 2.0 :
THE UNEXPECTED AND
TRAGIC RETURN OF COLLECTIVE GUILT

(Originally Published in *American Atheist Magazine*, 4th Quarter 2012)

And can you then impute a sinful deed
To babes who on their mothers' bosoms bleed?
Was then more vice in fallen Lisbon found,
Than Paris, where voluptuous joys abound?
Was less debauchery to London known,
Where opulence luxurious holds the throne?

- Voltaire, *Poem on the Lisbon Disaster*, 1756

When Voltaire wrote of the devastation caused by the Great Lisbon Earthquake, it was still widely believed that, as part of God's perfect plan for the universe, the innocent must occasionally suffer horrors. This was solid, main-stream theology with an august pedigree stretching back nearly a millennium and a half. Voltaire and his comrades sought to end it and, thanks to their unique genius and wit, they were successful. That is, until recently. From Katrina to Aurora, AIDS to 9-11, the notion that it is acceptable and just for God's wrath to be visited upon the innocent has resurfaced with an alarming rapidity and voracity. How has this happened, and how can our knowledge of its first appearance guide us in responding to its current reemergence?

In 410 CE, the Eternal City of Rome, which had resisted invasion for eight centuries, fell to Alaric I, and in the ensuing orgy of murder, destruction, and rape, it was the job of the theological community to explain how God had allowed all of this to happen just thirty years after the Empire adopted Christianity. The need produced the work, and Augustine's *City of God* stood as the definitive answer to why God permitted the innocent to suffer and die in such overwhelming numbers. He had counsel for everybody - for the starved and starving: "Those whom famine killed outright it rescued from the ills of this life, as a kindly disease would have done; and those who were hunger-bitten were taught to live more sparingly." For the violently slain: "Of what consequence is it what kind of death puts an end to life, since he who has died once is not forced to go through the same ordeal a second time?" And for victims of rape: "Neither those women then, who thought over-well of themselves by the circumstance that they were still virgins, nor those who might have been so puffed up had they not been exposed to the violence of the enemy, lost their chastity, but rather gained humility; the former were saved from pride already cherished, the latter from pride that would shortly have grown upon them."

Really, then, the sacking of Rome, by Augustine's account, was the best thing that could have happened to everybody involved - a free lesson in frugality and humility, courtesy of the All-mighty, and all it cost was the brutal death of one's loved ones and the repeated, savage violation of one's own body. It all sounds entirely horrid to our modern ears (mainly because it IS horrid), but there was a system of theological reasoning behind it which marched under the banner Sin Saves the Universe. It was Sin, according to this tradition, not Virtue, which turns the wheels of creation towards perfection.

The thought, as it was assembled by Isidore of Seville, Thomas Aquinas, and others over the succeeding centuries, ran something like this: If we are to obtain blessedness on our own merit, we must have Free Will. But, if we have Free Will, there must be a path away from blessedness if our choice to be good is to be meaningful. Therefore, God endowed us with a capacity for sin and permitted that we use it, and since he is Very Clever, this permission must be part of some larger and perfect plan. But if sin is allowed with all of its ill consequences, it must be an *exceedingly* important part of that plan, and so each sinner has more than purely individual significance. Therefore, by medieval reckoning, each act of sin *can't* be an isolated and independent act by a deranged mind - it *must* have an impact that ripples across the community and a purpose beyond the individual sinner.

When the sinners sins, it affects the innocent as well, with just perfection the result. By bringing chaos, the sinner allows the Good to overcome it and show their righteousness. By persecuting the true believers, he allows for the creation of glorious martyrs. By suffering torments for his wicked acts, he serves as an example. And, by bringing destruction on his city, he provides the gateway for the redemption of all. This is Augustine's point in its final evolved form - that sinners and the destruction that God brings through them are necessary in order that The Elect might grow and perfect themselves. As the authors of the *Malleus Maleficarum* put it in 1484, "If there had been no sin,... then there never would have appeared what debt of grace in good works is due to God, ... and many other things without which the universe would suffer great loss."

It took the eighteenth century's revolutionary conception of justice to chip away at this monument to the beauty of catastrophe, this love song to suffering. After *Candide* it was no longer possible for a theologian to say the phrase "the best of all possible worlds" without provoking knowing laughter from all sides. By deflating the concepts of Sin and its handmaiden Disaster as the positive guiding forces of humankind's destiny, the philosophes also rescued the sinner from the epicenter of God's divine plan. The caprice of Nature and man's as-yet-unrealized sense of responsibility towards his fellow man more than explained the travails of the human race without recourse to claims of perfection that beat against common sense and experience. The debate was, to all appearances, definitively settled.

So it remained until the ignition of the Culture Wars. First we heard of AIDS as God's punishment of homosexuality and vice. Pat Robertson saw Katrina as God's retribution for America's abortion policy, while Generals International was somehow able to twist the BP oil spill into a sign of God's disfavor with our treatment of Israel. More recently, we have witnessed an unhinged youth kill a dozen movie-goers in cold blood, and that too, according to Truth in Action spokesman Jerry Newcombe, is a result of God visiting upon innocents what the immoral in society have wrought. It's the thirteenth century all over again.

Or is it? For the better part of twenty years we've been employing Voltaire's techniques in the attempt to fight back the rising tide. You even see *Candide* quoted from time to time on the internet chat boards where these debates get thrashed out, but to no avail. We are treating this as a rematch of a fight we won before, and that is precisely why we aren't making the impact we think we ought. As we've seen, the punishment of the innocents evolved by the Church theologians of the Middle Ages had as its central thesis that disaster and sin were brought into the world to serve an ultimately higher good purpose, one that had an aim beyond the suffering of those involved. To combat such an idea, highlighting the arbitrary, malicious, and deeply unjust structure of nature and the world worked well.

This new wave of collective guilt enthusiasts, however, work from a different starting point, even if they arrive at the same conclusion. The assumption is not that innocents suffer because the world is secretly perfect, and that free will works towards that perfection even (perhaps especially) when it falters. Rather, innocents suffer because free will was a mistake, and people have doomed themselves and their civilizations beyond redemption by their use of it. The goal is not making people better, even by St. Augustine's perverse notion of "better", and punishment is not something undergone on the way to the bigger point God is making. Punishment IS the bigger point, it is the last stage of The Big Plan, a dress rehearsal for the glorious day when Everybody who isn't of the elect is going to be dragged down for eternal suffering.

How does one argue with people coming from such a dark place? The medieval Scholastics at least thought their beliefs to be reason-derived, and so could be approached through reasonable argumentation. Voltaire and Company, by using reason to demolish the machinery of the old theological system, effectively drove the successors of the Scholastics onto the shoals of Faith, where we find them still today. It is axiomatic that you can't argue against faith any more than you can box with a spider web. But perhaps you can find out Why that faith is so important, and offer something better in its stead.

If, as appears to be the case, this new generation is concerned that our use of Free Will is heading us towards disaster and away from the principles of Good Living, then maybe it is not in abstract moral argumentation, but in the potential of modern life, that we shall find our answer to them. We need to show how the Secular Turn, and the freedom of action and variety of choice it has brought with it, has allowed *everybody* to live closer to the best ideals of their notion of morality, that just as Humanists are better Humanists than they have ever been, so too now are Christians better able to live their most cherished (or at least most publicly proclaimed) principles than at any time before. They can offer the hand of Christian charity without wrapping it in the iron glove of dogma, and so approximate the principles of their founder in a way that a thirteenth century missionary could never understand. They will most likely never be bouncing and bonny atheists like ourselves, but perhaps in seeing what modern humanity is offering them, they will grasp what they in turn have to offer it, and we may all get over the notion that anything in this world or beyond it justifies the suffering of another living being.

(Peasant) Girls
Just Wanna Have Fun.

(Originally Published at *The Humanist*, July 2014)

Heresy-wise, it's hard to beat the early Thirteenth Century. In Northern Italy, Southern France, and throughout Germany, thousands of individuals rose, as much disgusted by the Church's excesses as inspired by its attempt at self-reform, and crafted local theologies that were part ancient tradition, part Christianity, and entirely revolutionary. For a century, the Cathars and Waldensians, Passagians and Arnoldists organized a threat to Catholicism so great in appearance (if not in fact) that the Church saw no way out but to let loose the Dominicans and the dread force of Inquisition.

In the midst of this battle for scriptural orthodoxy were the common people, hungry for a way out of the spiritual impasse of worldly Catholicism. Lone humans, making what sense they could of the conflicting authority around them, often guided more by their innate moral instincts than by a fundamental need to preserve some dogmatic core of belief. None speak more eloquently to this trend than Grazida Lizier, a commoner from the South of France whose entire record of existence consists of a few scant pages of testimony taken down by Cathar-hunter extraordinaire Jacques Fournier in 1320. In those lines, a humble mind sets forth what she understood of the universe and its workings, and in a few devastating lines unmakes the cocksure dominance of Catholic orthodoxy.

But to understand why she was being questioned in the first place, we have to talk about Cathars. Which is just as well, because they are lusciously fascinating. They were dualists, which is to say that, faced with the problem of the overwhelming evil present in a world constructed by a supposedly good God, they split the cosmos in two, declaring that everything material was actually constructed by Satan, who peopled his world by imprisoning the souls of God's angels in flesh, while God dwelt in an ethereal, entirely Other realm.

Now, the Old Testament is *rather* clear about Jehovah making the physical Earth, which meant that Cathars variously believed that (1) The Old Testament ought to be thrown out entirely, or (2) that it is correct, but that the Jehovah of that book was actually Satan.

Personally, I think that option two explains *a lot* about the Old Testament's unilaterally horrendous moral sense, but the Catholic Church understandably didn't see it that way, nor did it particularly like the Cathar claim that Jesus could not possibly have been a real man, but rather was an essence made to appear as a man. Their new spin on an old problem, combined with their vows of complete austerity (it was common Cathar practice to, after receiving their final baptism, starve themselves to death to avoid pollution of the things of the world) made the movement wildly popular in both Southern France and the Italian realms still under the influence of Arnold of Brescia's revolution against Church authority.

The problem was that the Church didn't really have a firm grasp on what heresy was, or how it was to be dealt with when the Cathars and Waldensians started flowering in the late twelfth century. There wasn't a standardized set of questions to ask, or a routine procedure to follow when trying to determine if a thought was heretical or merely eccentric. Catholicism was caught thoroughly flat-footed as the Cathars and other heretical sects lurched past them in the hearts and minds of a Europe growing weary of the Pope's fumbling half-measures towards basic decency.

Jacques Fournier, who would go on to become Pope Benedict XII, was a man determined to bring order to the hunt for heresy, and wandered through Southern France, interrogating the Cathars that his ring of informants ratted out to him.

In 1320 he met Grazida Lizier, a peasant from Montaillou, questioned her, incarcerated her for two months, and then questioned her again. This was all of a piece with the rest of Grazida's storm-tossed life. She was born around 1298, and at age fourteen her virginity was taken by the local rector, Pierre Clergue, with the full knowledge of her mother. He continued using her for sex until marrying her, at the age of fifteen, to a pliable man who looked the other way whenever Clergue came to sexually appropriate his wife. Grazida's husband threw her out of the house when she was nineteen, not because of her adultery, but because she wouldn't join his religious sect. So, she was forced to make a living as a bar-keep, at least until age twenty-one when she was arrested by Fournier as an adulteress and possible heretic.

Clergue was a Cathar, and in between sexual encounters, he imparted to Grazida some of the tenets of his religion. And then Grazida did something altogether remarkable for an adolescent in any age - she held up each of those Cathar beliefs, weighed them against her own internal moral compass, and crafted a new, wholly individual accounting of how the universe worked. It's worth quoting at some length from the original inquisitorial document:

Asked if she believed whether a man sins who has sex with a woman not related to him by blood, a virgin or not, in marriage or out of it, only because it is pleasing to both, she responded that, although all carnal unions of men and women are displeasing to God, however she did not believe that those performing such acts - so long as both derived pleasure from them - commit a sin.

Asked if she believed that those who act well and live sanctified lives go to Paradise after death, while sinners enter Hell, and if she believed there to be a Paradise and Hell, she responded that she didn't know, but she heard it said, that there is a Paradise, and she believes it; she also heard that there is a Hell, but this, she said, she neither believed nor disbelieved... since it is an evil place. Asked in the same manner about resurrection, she said she neither believed nor disbelieved, although she frequently heard it said that we shall rise again.

Let's stop for a moment to appreciate the inventive boldness of Grazida here. On one hand were the Catholics, insisting absolutely in the existence of Heaven, Hell, resurrection, and the sinfulness of sex outside of marriage. On the other are the Cathars, dismally opposed to all sexual unions, Hell, resurrection, and anything of the Earth. And in between those massive boulders of absolutist dogma is this peasant girl who asserts, in the very face of a Catholic inquisitioner that sex is sex, and though it might displease God, it's certainly no sin as long as everybody is enjoying themselves, that Heaven is probably real, but Hell is kinda shaky, as she can't conceive of why a good God would have made such an evil place, and that our bodily resurrection seems like a longshot as well.

And, while Grazida's testimony is among the most frank in its assessment of current theology, it is by no means unique. Fournier's records include accounts of women who believe in the general salvation of all men, those who completely deny any afterlife at all, and those who experienced moments of total disbelief in God himself. Indeed, Fournier's reports were on the tail end of a troubling wave of information, starting from the early thirteenth century, documenting a surge of heretical sects throughout France, Italy, and Eastern Europe. Something needed to be done, some organization empowered to draw up regulations for the identification and prosecution of heresy.

In 1252, the Pope granted the Dominicans the right to use torture in weeding out heresy and after that it was off to the races. With the help of obliging monarchs in France, Aragon, and Germany, and the creation of a standard inquisitorial processes, the Cathars and Waldensians were driven underground such that, by

1320, when Grazida was being held for questioning by Fournier, the movements were shattered husk of their former selves.

And yet, in spite of the organization of the Inquisition, the viciousness of its techniques, and the alliance between Rome and monarch in the prosecution of heretics, the strands of heterodox doubt were still vibrant enough to produce Grazida Lizier, and a host of others like her. As a brave rebel princess once remarked to an Imperial officer, "The more you tighten your grip, the more star systems slip through your fingers."

Though the Cathars couldn't organize effectively any longer, the circumstances that created the Cathar heresy were still very much present and indeed worsening thanks to the torture-licious exuberance of the Dominicans. The worse a place they made the world to live in, the more plausible did Dualistic theology become, and the stronger Dualism became, the more doubt there was about the validity of theological posturing generally. Grazida was created in that space between orthodoxy and its combatants, a bold testament to how the lunge towards hegemony leaves a million scrambling microscopic heterodoxies in its wake, if you take the time to look.

Further Reading: The translation of Grazida's testimony above is my own. The original Latin text (along with that of several other women collected by Fournier) is available in the appendix of Peter Dronke's wonderful *Women Writers of the Middle Ages*. For those interested in medieval heresy, a great sourcebook is Walter Wakefield and Austin Evans's *Heresies of the High Middle Ages*, which contains 640 pages of original documents in English translation relating to the Cathars, Waldenseans, and everybody in between. There is also a novel about Grazida and the persecution of the Cathars, *The Good Men*, by Charmaine Craig, which I admit to owning but never having read. Cover's nice, though.

PART III:

Good Reads,
God Reads,
And Their Rare
Intersection

STRANGER THAN YOU DREAMT IT:
A STROLL THROUGH THE CURIOUS HEART OF CHRISTIAN ROMANCE NOVELS

(Originally Published at *The Twilight of Nearly Everything*)

The best thing about romance novels as a genre is that they are, page for page, the most unashamedly honest books you can read. They express the longings and frustrations of immense swaths of the population untainted by the distancing irony that black tie literature so often sheepishly passes off as refinement. As such, there seems no more ill-conceived notion than welding together this most frank of literary forms with Christian thematic material, which is founded on the sublimation and execration of the very needs that romance novels serve.

And yet, the Christian romance novel has a pedigree stretching back half a century, encompassing everything from crass financial opportunism to sensuo-theological amalgamations of the creepiest sort. What began as a modest form reflecting back on an idealized godly past soon fell victim to the Culture Wars and reshaped itself into a shrill platform of seething bigotry thoroughly willing to drown its hapless central characters in a wash of ill-fitting ideological posturing.

Most trace the beginning of Christian Romance to Janette Okes' s 1979 novel *Love Comes Softly*. It follows a young woman suddenly widowed in the depths of the American frontier. Before she has time to grieve, a pioneer, also recently widowed, asks her to marry him so that she can be a mother to his young daughter. In return, she will have a place to stay until the next coach heading East arrives. From there, the novel falls out pretty much like a less charming version of *Little House in the Big Woods*, with plenty of descriptions of the practical routines of life in the wilderness, including one dismally imagined comedic set-piece involving chicken butchering about which the less said the better. God shows up in the pioneer's prayers from time to time, but no more often than one would expect from a person in that time and place.

The Christian elements are entirely appropriate for the setting and never over-stay their welcome in the name of authorial zeal. It is a book from the tail end of that slim era sandwiched between Elmer Gantry and Jimmy Swaggart when religion was a purely private matter of reflection, and not the cudgel against unfamiliar lifestyles it has since become. And, while I wouldn't say it is a *good* book, I would say it is at least minimally aggravating with moments of genuine enjoyment to be had. Unfortunately, this oasis of comparative literary restraint was not to last. The new romance authors who emerged from the Eighties took the form and used it as their base from which to advance the cause of Christian fundamentalism, creating books of unparalleled, and consequently rather fascinating, awkwardness in the process.

Lori Wick's *Sophie's Heart* and Francine Rivers's *Redeeming Love* top most people's list of the most important contributions to the genre to come out of the nineteen nineties, and it's easy to see why. They are both works of an entirely different stuff than *Love Comes Softly*, seething and bitter books with scores to settle jammed uncomfortably into the mould of a romance novel.

For Wick, there is no violence against her characters that she won't commit in the name of expounding her version of Christianity. But before we get to that, I have to ask your indulgence to stop for a while to reflect on the style of the book, because I've never seen its equal in terms of its unfailingly miserable grasp of conversation. Here, I've made a little quiz for you. I'll give you a piece of dialogue from the book, and you pick who is saying it:

"Whether or not you think we need someone, Craig, we do. I'm sorry it's taken so long for me to see this. Nevertheless, I will expect your cooperation in the matter."
A man talking to his business partner about a change in the company.

A woman telling her subordinate about the need to bring in a new employee.
A man talking to his children about hiring a babysitter.

"Nicole's never happy with anyone, and she's so protective of her cousin that I wouldn't wonder if they get married someday."
A middle-aged woman trading gossip with her neighbor.
A grandfather commenting wryly about the relation between two distant family members.
A sixteen year old girl from the eighties talking with her friend.

"I know, but what a way to go."
An elderly veteran talking about his friend who died in a parachute incident.
A middle aged Church volunteer describing a parishioner who passed during a sermon.
A ten year old kid talking about her father's wallet.

"What time shall we go?"
Winnie the Pooh
A nineteenth century fop who stumbled his way into the novel.
The friend of the girl from question 2, also a TEENAGER FROM THE EIGHTIES.

      If you answered c to all of these fine samples, then you are curiously in tune with Lori Wick's odd notion that everybody in her book ought to talk like her, regardless of their age. The boundary between narrative voice and casual dialogue simply doesn't exist. Catch phrases that she uses in her descriptive paragraphs regularly make their way into character's speech patterns without any particular concern about the bleed-over. But the crowning achievement is the central character's manner of speech. Her name is Sophie and she is a professional UN translator fluent in five languages who comes to the United States from her native Czechoslovakia in search of a better life, and yet after nearly a year of being in the country, Wick still writes her English dialogue entirely in the And Now Natasha We Look for Moose and Squirrel vein, dropping all definite articles and having her struggle mightily with the most basic accusative personal pronouns.

This tone deafness to the cadences and vocabulary of everyday speech, however, is the real saving grace of the book, because without it comically tumbling about the page in the nearest literary approximation of the Keystone Cops we are ever likely to have, what remains is brutally ugly. Wick's adults are all bigots of the most insidious flavor. She goes out of her way to give each of them at least one line in which they evaluate people as Christians first and humans a distant second. Sophie, praying to God as she does every other page, says after meeting the family whose house she is to serve in, "I'm ashamed that I didn't ask ahead of time if they believe in You, but I'm so glad it's true." The implication being, what, that she'd tell this family grieving from the loss of their mother to go screw themselves if they turned out not to believe in God as she does?

But it's okay, because everybody else is equally horrible. The father of the family, talking about his dead wife to their daughter: "I am sorry that I didn't handle things differently. We should have courted longer, set up standards for our whole marriage. I feel we floundered spiritually far too much, especially in the last few years before she died. We really drifted from church activities, and our hunger for God seriously waned." Yes, that's a father telling his daughter that he regrets the purely romantic one-on-one time he spent with her recently passed mother, because their eyes should have been on God instead of each other. That deceased bitch.

And even Sophie's driving instructor, after not seeing her at the early service of the Church that apparently everybody she meets in this town goes to, gets his digs in: "His [mind] was wholly taken up with Sophie. It concerned him that she would sleep in when she should have been in Church." This is before their second lesson, he has known her for all of one hour, and we are all apparently entirely fine with his unilaterally determining what she should or should not do with her time. But that's the way of this book – you don't build friendships with people, you build *fellowships* with them, with one eye always on your scorecard with God. You don't work on actual relationships with people of a different faith, lest they pollute you (the father flatly refused to even consider dating anybody but Bible Believers in his college days). And they can't be just any Christians, of course – Sophie starts off in her new town (somewhat incongruously for an immigrant from Czechoslovakia, but Wick doesn't seem to care) hunting down a fundamentalist Church "that preached salvation by grace plus nothing."

Having a Czech immigrant fervently hunt for an American fundamentalist style church is not the only instance of Wick using her characters in improbable ways to make a religious point. Mini speeches about the benefit of Christian schools, embarrassing dialogues highlighting the superiority of creationist explanations for the universe's origin, and the obligatory concern about lawless teenagers all limp into position, pushing aside the main story as they make their way to center stage, leaving an awkward sucking gap when they finally depart. There is romance, in the sense that a man and a woman are developing a relationship throughout the course of the book, but it is a relationship everywhere twisted by the overbearing need for gross servility before an omnipresent Lord.

Francine Rivers sticks closer to the romance novel form in *Redeeming Love*, taking the normal tropes and driving them into a dark corner of the human soul, one so bleak and humanity-hating that only Christianity could possibly thrive there. One of the classic storylines in romance novels is, "Girl has rotten life. The right man comes along. Girl has great life." Not particularly subtle, and it tends to fail the Bechdel Test rather superbly, but it works and people seem to enjoy it. Rivers takes this structure as her starting point and drags it to a place only a Christian author would care to go.

Her protagonist, Sarah, starts off the unwanted offspring of an affair between her prostitute mother and a married man who can't stand the sight of her. After he abandons them, the mother turns to street prostitution and dies in a shack, whereupon Sarah, at the age of 8, is brought to a mysterious man called The Duke who, it is implied, abuses her sexually for the better part of a decade before she escapes out West, nearly starves, and ends up working at a brothel where a Christian farmer finally rescues her after the brothel's hired muscle savagely beats her almost to death.

Understandably, she hates men, and despises her life, all of which make her particularly susceptible to Christianity's influence. The farmer who rescues her has regular conversations with God, who is apparently very interested in having hour-to-hour input on the handling of this farmer's new bride while being totally hands off about the other horrendous stuff happening all around. "Sure, there are Chinese immigrants being worked to death a hundred miles away, but I *really* need to sort out this guy's sex life." It's that "God is responsible for everything good and nothing bad" logical inconsistency so common to believers that the rest of us just have to accept as a charming foible lest it drive us utterly mad.

To continue, the farmer is a romance novel cut-out: handsome, patient, knows how to cook, and likes watching the sun rise. He wins her over slowly, letting Christianity play the Good Cop to the world's Bad Cop. It is swapping one form of control for another, and perhaps a worse deal at that, trading being a prostitute in body alone for one in both mind and flesh.

Between Wick's pervasive bigotry and Rivers's bleak view of a life lacking God's regular and verbal intervention, the Christian romances of the nineties show a full willingness to carry on the belligerence of the teeth-gnashing No-Longer-Silent Majority even if their heroes and heroines stumble into monotonic detestability in the process. Even these, the purportedly best meldings of romance and fundamentalist Christianity, seldom claw their way to a genuine emotional statement without immediately dissipating its impact in a mass of preposition-crippling Christian catch phrases.

In short, it didn't work very well artistically, and others took the note, one of the most notable being Dee Henderson, whose O'Malley Series of Christian Romance/Suspense novels launched in

1999 and have shown the world a new way of doing the genre. I admit to only having read *Danger in the Shadows*, the prequel to the series, a tale of a mystery writer (yes, another mystery writer writing about mystery writers) who falls for an ex football star who… you know what, it doesn't matter. Because Henderson's solution to the Wick Problem is astonishingly simple: write a secular suspense novel, then shuffle in lone and shivering references to God about, oh, every ten pages or so, and call it good. It's the novel equivalent of South Park's summary of Christian music: "Just take a popular song, and replace the word Baby with Jesus." If you were to remove every reference to God from this book, it wouldn't change the plot or tone of the book one jot. What you'd have is a by-the-numbers suspense remarkable only for certain contortions performed in the name of alcohol not being present. (One of my favorite is when the writer character has the football star over for a pasta dinner and offers him the romantic choice between Fruit Juice and Soda. Nothing complements angel hair *quite* like a cool can of Mountain Dew: Code Red).

Business-wise, it's smart. I read the book through and found it entirely palatable, and a glance through her online reviews seems to indicate that this smattering of randomly flung God references is sufficient for her Christian base. It will allow Henderson to survive and adapt in ways not open to Wick and Rivers, though I suspect that Wick, with a hundred MILLION books in print, isn't too worried.

This was supposed to be a happy article. I envisioned sitting down with a handful of Christian romance novels, and being delighted to find that, deep down, they show the same fundamental needs and desires as their secular counterparts. The heartbreaking fact is that they do. There is writ upon each page a longing and loneliness and need for companionship every bit as animal as in the most basic Harlequin Romance. But between that longing and the object of its desire there is erected a tortuous maze of Holy Adjustment where every impulse is reinterpreted and each touch of friendship weighed on the scales of theological purity so that, by the time the lovers finally fall into each other's arms, they are staring not into the living eyes of a loving human, but the remnants allowed them by a capricious god and resent-laden author. Watching these books unfold has all the grim fascination of ritual suicide, as the authors gut themselves and their best literary instincts for the meager recompense of considering themselves, to use Wick's juttingly misshapen but unintentionally apt phrase, "used of God."

Holy Writ, Accessorized:
The Rise of the Gimmick Bible,
And What it Means for Christianity

(Originally published at *The New Humanist*, June 2013)

There was a time, spoken of with hushed reverence by a generation rapidly passing beyond the veil, when the centerpiece of a home was its family Bible. It carried not only the word of God, but the record of one's ancestry as well, each generation carefully scrawling a few lines on its translucent pages that summed up the total of its accomplishments and disappointments in life. It was an object of almost mystic power – I remember shuddering when Mr. Tulliver asked his son Tom to take down the family Bible and write his curse against Lawyer Wakem therein. After that act, there was no going back or, as I eloquently expressed it to myself at the time, "Damn, Shit Just Done Got REAL."

And yet, when you visit a Christian bookstore now (and you should every so often, if only to peruse the posters section) what you find is that the few beautifully bound and printed Family Bibles are stuffed off in a corner somewhere, their only hope of purchase being the odd octogenarian who might buy one as a present for her desultory offspring (and which they will inevitably donate to the local library the very moment she is gone, citing lack of space). The trend now is towards specialty Bibles which Christians see as the salvation of their species.

When I was in high school, I was presented with one of the first of these, *The New Student Bible*, a garish and cheaply produced paperback done up in an odd amalgam of goth black and Malibu Dreamhouse purple and pink to attract "the youth." It was such a meager and uninspiring

149

thing that I wrote it off completely as a doomed fad. For a decade, that volume faithfully served as a replacement for the right rear foot of my couch, not realizing in the least that its brethren were rather more heroically conquering the holy writ landscape.

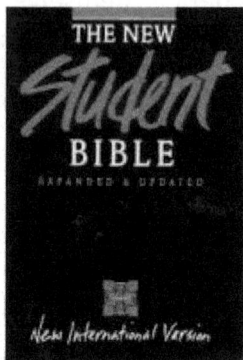

In the ensuing decades, Bible publishers seized on the best wisdom of Apple's marketing department, and rushed to produce not only a separate Bible for each member of the family, but a different Bible for each stage in that family member's life. You start out with a Children's Bible done up as a comic book so that somehow the idea of eradicating entire civilizations and eternally torturing people who disagree with you will seem heroic rather than deeply twisted.

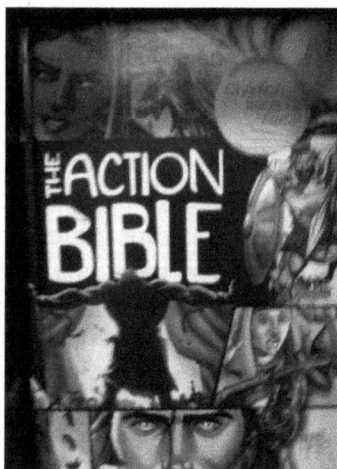

But kids are kids and they'll put up with just about anything that ends in the phrase, "and there's CANDY when you're done!" (Come to think of it, so will adults... just substitute "Heaven" for "CANDY!" and there's not much, historically, that we haven't been talked into doing.) Teens are a trickier proposition, and that is why a disproportionate amount of resources have been devoted to crafting Bibles that might appeal to what are deemed their core values. These Bibles are sad, sad things, conjured by committees of earnest Caucasians who perceive teenagers dimly if at all through the occluding mists of talk radio and indifferently conceived magazine articles on The Facebook Generation.

Let's begin with the teen-targeted covers. Here are a couple, one that seems artsily alternative aimed at teenage girls and one that looks like an aggressive protein bar label for the fellows.

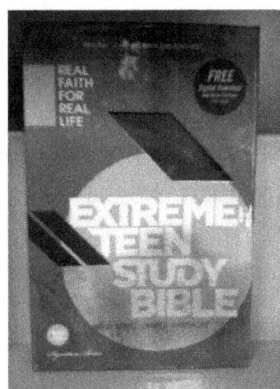

Inside, you'll find the text of the Bible interspersed with a variety of gimmicks. These include activities that you can perform, one of my favorite being a ritual that is in every way ripped from a *Buffy The Vampire Slayer* style Wiccan meditation, just with Jesus pasted over the Hecate bits. Because sitting on the floor with candles and chanting and stuff, that's what the kids like, right? More cravenly, one of them features occasional "Text Messages" – side boxes with information that amplify the text, at the bottom of which "This information has been scanned and is free of all known viruses. Please forward to your friends" has been inserted through one of those processes where a higher-up's polite laughter is misconstrued as an editorial decision.

I'm being somewhat deliberately mean about the ham-fistedness of these books, but I assure you, as mean and sarcastic as I am, it is nothing compared to the fierce eye-rolling criticism they are going to come up against when put in the hands of an actual teenager. Far better to just slam a musty copy of the King James in their hands and hope that it is retro mystical enough to catch their fancy. By portraying the Bible as essentially one long text message from a deity who hasn't quite figured out how to self-edit, these publishers are putting it in direct competition with the thousand other similarly draped media productions screaming for teenage approval. Given the choice between a secular source that honestly wants to engage with their concerns and a Bible that is cynically aping an interest in order to keep itself stumbling along another couple of centuries, there's little doubt about where a modern adolescent will turn.

Let's say, though, that you are a female Christian, and somehow weather the storm of Christianity's awkward pawing at your adolescent loyalties and come through it all a Christian still. Congratulations, you have graduated to the wide variety of Women's Bibles currently available!

And what a delight they are. In place of the gimmicky text messages, activities, and blank "Creative Space" that abounded in the teenage Bibles, you will be treated to a series of essays that purport to twist the blatantly and purposely anti-feminine message of the Old and New Testaments into something approximating statements of self-affirmation. Here are a couple of my favorite instances:

"God created man – male and female – in his own image. What an awesome reality that is. There *I* am in the first chapter of the Bible – a woman – distinguished from animals, distinguished from my male counterpart."

This is taking an awful lot of comfort from the relatively banal act of object differentiation, and ignoring the hefty mal-distribution of power that more or less immediately follows (the bunnies don't come off much better than the women in the ensuing power structure, it turns out, for all their having been "distinguished" from each other.)

The winner, though, is this frothingly worshipful essay on Male Power which is the first side-bar in the *WOMAN'S Study Bible*:

"God has gifted men with great capacities for responsible leadership. This can be channeled positively into the church and all walks of life through teaching, leading by moral example and supporting righteous causes. Masculine power when sanctified can be used in a positive way, such as in the lives of great men through whom God provides leadership... How wonderful that God balances this image of dominant masculine strength and power with the example of the Lord

152

Jesus who was moved by compassion, loved little children, cried at the death of his friend and gave his life so that others might live."

At least the first quote, from the *Women's Devotional Bible*, attempted to massage the meager material of the Old Testament into something like a positive message of identity. This commentator, however, had a chance to set the tone for what followed, and decided to turn the dial all the way to Victorianism of the "Really all of my accomplishments are thanks to my royal consort, Albert" variety. Because, presumably, the Bible isn't quite explicit enough about male hegemony, so we need extra articles to really tease those subtle sub-texts out from the page for the advantage of the devout female reader.

Luckily, though, you'll only need that Bible for a short while, as eventually you will find a partner in Christ to cleave unto, which clearly necessitates a new Bible:

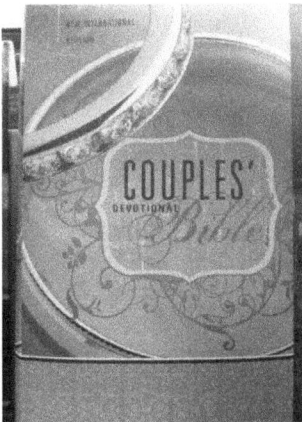

This one is actually kind of fun in so far as it is the love child offspring of a one night stand between the Holy Bible and a Harlequin novel. Turn the lights down, put on some Barry White, and read along with me:

"They fit together so beautifully, these two [Adam and Eve], that their lives intertwined. One can only imagine the special times they shared: the first time they made love, their first sunrise together, their late-night walks through the garden. How God must have delighted in these creatures he had made to expand the harmonious, loving relationship enjoyed by the Trinity itself!"

Ohhhhh yeahhhhh…. Although I'm not sure if it's comforting or way creepy that, every time I get it on, I'm expanding the harmonious relationship of the Trinity. I can't help but think of some ethereal Scotty dialing into Jehovah with a panicked cry of, "I've been watchin' the levels, Sir, and unless we get more couples madly humping, I cannae say if we'll have enough power to pull off the Second Coming!" And the bumper sticker "Snogging: God's Celestial Battery" is *pretty* catchy.

Continuing on, there might come a point in your life when you go utterly "The Jackdaws are after my teeth!" insane, which is the only time that I can possibly see this Bible being attractive:

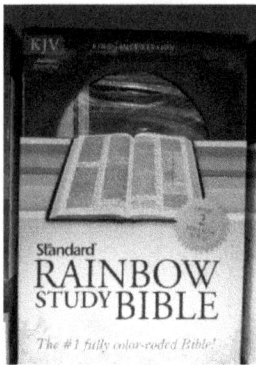

Ah yes, there's nothing as conducive to calm contemplation of Biblical truths than having nine out of every ten words slathered in one of twelve thematically dedicated colors. "Hooray, it's got somebody else's highlighting in it, that will make it ever so much more convenient to read," is what I hear pretty much any time one of my friends gets a used book in the mail and finds it swimming in neon yellow. That 2 million of these have been sold is baffling, but there it is.

And thence death-wards:

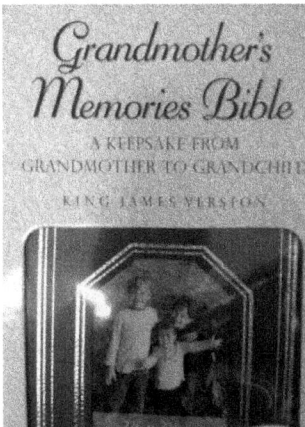

Grandmother's Memories Bible
A KEEPSAKE FROM
GRANDMOTHER TO GRANDCHILD
KING JAMES VERSION

Awww. Well, with that you can close the book on your specialty-Bible consuming career. Now, what if you're an adult Christian male? Sadly, there's not *all* that much for you. Maybe because it's been determined by some marketing division that you don't like having things explained to you that you think you already know (the spiritual counterpart of "stopping for directions"). More likely because the Male Devotional Bible is basically... The Bible. Since that already makes up 98% of the material of all the other specialty Bibles, collecting male-centered essays to pop in the margins of the male-dominated Old Testament is just so much wrapping of bacon in bacon, a grotesque example of Textual Excess that is so unnecessary that I have no doubt it is feverishly in the works.

What does this dilution of the Bible into a series of transitional accessories betoken for Christianity? For the Christian publisher, it's a short term good. Why sell a family one volume of leathery portent when you can sell them five disposable gimmick Bibles instead? For secularists, it's a long term good. The more a religion tries to make its central texts relevant and accessible to modern readers, the worse off it will fare. Obfuscation and intimidation are what a holy text need to survive as something more than just one book among many, and those are the last things that *The Extreme Teen Bible* has to offer. For Christianity, this trend is yet another canary that has, in the good words of the Pythons, curled up its tootsies. Accessories are trendy – popular items that catch humanity in a moment of confused inertia and give it something to affect interest in for a few months – they are created to be superseded. Crafting Bibles with supersession built in is to open the gates of your religion to a diffuse, meandering spirituality that ends in effective non-belief. So, let the cash registers ring while they may, for there is nothing more sure of creating a future humanist than putting any of these books into the hands of a thinking human being.

WHY CAN'T THE ENGLISH
TEACH THEIR GODS HOW TO SPEAK?
FIVE CENTURIES OF BIBLE TRANSLATION FOLLIES.

(Originally published at *The Twilight of Everything*)

Part I: The Problem.

I'm glad you could all make it. I, your god, have something crucially important to tell you about what is expected of you, and your purpose on this Earth. Before I do that, though, I couldn't help but notice you all speak the same language, and it's making you a *little* complacent.

So, I'm going to go ahead and make you all speak something radically different. Let's call it a team building exercise. Then, I'm going to wait a bit, let's say two thousand years, before telling *one* of you *half* of my very important message.

Whoever that guy is, he should really get the word out somehow. Try charades. People love charades.

I've got lots of stuff to do though, so I'll probably need another couple of thousand years before finding another one of you, preferably the one with the worst possible history of keeping reliable records, and imparting the second half of the message to him, a half which will, for the most part, contradict everything that I told the first guy.

Whoever that second guy is, if you could go ahead and lose not only whatever of my first message is still around, but write what you remember, or think you remember, or would like to have remembered, about the second half on something highly perishable, that would be great.

Questions? No. Fantastic. I think this is really the best possible way to get my message out, and am thrilled to have you all on board.

If there is anything in the Bible which demonstrates Jehovah's lack of omniscience, it's his bumbling and erratic marketing campaign. It is a strategy that begins on a misstep and concludes in farce.

To start, Jehovah, after scrambling the world's languages at Babel, has to pick one of them for the first half of his message. Now, if there is a language in world history that you Absolutely Do Not want to start a religion in, it would be Hebrew. That choice alone ensures that the majority of the vowels in your message will not be written down, but will have to form part of an oral tradition for a thousand years until somebody finally gets around to some manner of codification.

For Hebrew, that definitive codification did not happen until the *tenth century*. Christianity, of course, couldn't wait that long to appropriate the Hebrew Bible, and impatiently started translating the Tanakh into the universal language of Latin about six centuries before the standard Hebrew vocalization appeared. Lacking that standardized text, Jerome, the man who brought us the Latin version of the Bible which would stand unchallenged for the better part of twelve hundred years, had to make do with the bits and scraps of manuscript, tradition, and commentary he had at hand.

His major sources included Origen's 3rd century CE *Hexpala*, which places a Hebrew manuscript alongside several different attempts at translation into Old and Modern Greek, and the *Septuagint*, a 2nd Century BCE translation of the Tanakh into Greek that served as the primary source for Biblical translators for millennia after Origen's source material became scattered to the winds. And he did his best, translating the Hebrew, with the advice of previous Greek translations, into Latin, ensuring a sort of twisted, transposed half-existence for the Hebrew text even as its manuscript copies blinked out of existence.

For centuries, then, the word of Yahweh was wrapped up in a Latin translation understood only by a swath of the population so narrow that it makes The One Percent appear positively inclusive. If God's message was, "Go forth, and spread the word, after translating it a couple of times, ultimately into a language that only a super-privileged portion of the population can understand!" then things were going swimmingly.

Eventually, however, people smelled a rat, and a veritable orgy of translation gushed forth in the sixteenth century on the heels of Luther's German Bible. Each country had its own dramatic version of the process, but few rival the convolutions the text endured during its translation into English. Not only did English translators face all of the problems of their Continental comrades – a shriveled and incomplete manuscript base, the slow grinding away of meaning that necessarily occurs to words long in circulation, and the unavoidable misquotations and contradictions that are just part of the Bible, no matter what version you look in – but they also had to deal with fractures within the Protestant tradition that were entirely unique to England.

There's a lot of back story here, but the basic idea is that you had the power structure put in place by the king and maintained by his successors, which was Protestant but still highly hierarchical, and you had the tradition that felt that, to eject the name of Catholicism while still keeping bishops and elaborate rites was not going nearly far enough. And each of them created their own English Bibles, the Separatists leading the way with William Tyndale's foundational 1525 translation of the New Testament. For daring to put the Bible into English, and worse, for daring to use vocabulary that suggested bishopry was not in fact part of the Bible's plan, Tyndale was put to death in 1536, before he had a chance to complete his Old Testament translation.

From there, the race was on, but let's not lightly pass over the very critical point that Vocabulary Choice just cost a man his life. I'm not too interested in the pathos aspect of that so much as how radically different the Bible becomes by simply choosing one probable word over another. Use "congregation" instead of "church" and you rock the very foundations of Western religious practice. This is why translation is such a horrid thing to rely upon - the men who translate your works, by thinking in a different language, cannot and will not understand you on the points close to their hearts or yours. Distinctions which were critical to you will be lost to them, and distinctions that they are willing to shed blood for after millennia of shared experience won't have even been thinkable by you from your historical position. What Tyndale's death ultimately shows us isn't the sublime beauty of martyrdom or the resolute dickishness of

Thomas More, but the deep futility of translation as a mechanism of transmitting a message.

The history of English Biblical translation largely bears this out. By the 1560s, the Separatists had created their crown jewel while in exile, the Geneva Bible, which included not only large chunks of Tyndale's anti-establishment phraseology, but also extensive commentaries and references intended to drive their point home. To counter, the Church of England put together its own translation, the much-bemoaned Bishop's Bible of 1568. Translation had become a weapon of theological war, with vocabulary choice its ammunition.

The King James Bible we have today is the ultimate peace treaty in that conflict. It was a massive undertaking which included primarily pro-bishop translators, but also many moderate Separatists as well, working together to produce something minimally offensive to all concerned. A good idea of how synthetic their ultimate work was is given by Adam Nicolson in his quite lovely book *God's Secretaries*, in which he sets off in brackets the Biblical versions that a particular wording is borrowed from:

"You are also helping [Bishop's] together [Geneva 1557] by [Bishop's] prayer for us [Tyndale], that [Tyndale] for the [Geneva, 1560] gift [Great Bible] bestowed upon us [Geneva 1557] by the means of many [Tyndale] persons [Great], thankes may bee given [Tyndale] by [Geneva 1557] many on our behalf [Tyndale]."

The majestic rhythms of the King James Bible, then, are a patchwork sewn from the half dozen or so major English translations that came before, always with the goal in mind of producing a sense of irresistible grandeur. As a text, it has become so influential that it's hard to evaluate. Does it sound so powerful (at its best) because it is great prose, or was its style simply at the right place at the right time to impact our developing language's notion of what greatness sounds like?

I liken it to attempting to evaluate the Beatles catalogue musically. I can't do it – the music is so a part of my biographical and cultural heritage, so woven into what songs ought to sound like, that I get

160

caught in self-referential circles that end up saying little more than, "Yes, this Beatles song is musically good because it sounds like the Beatles, and they wrote good things." They came along when pop music was establishing its own evaluative criteria, and are inextricably woven into that criteria. Likewise, the King James Bible, which was for centuries the *only* book you could find in many households, had a part in determining what counted for majesty in language in a way that we won't escape for a good long while yet.

Even if the KJB does represent a triumph of wordsmithing, what it certainly does not represent is a vindication of God's plan for his message. Written in its lines are the demands of a king for compromise Of A Certain Sort, and the translators delivered that beautifully, staying on-message with what King James expected of them, and wrapping it all in the most imposing but comprehensible words available to them at the time, even when, as later translations have shown, they didn't *quite* understand what they were rendering.

Since then, our manuscript base has grown (The Dead Sea Scrolls alone jumps us from the 900 CE Aleppo Codex, our best source prior to 1946, all the way back to the 1st century CE), and our knowledge of how languages work has exploded. Unfortunately, part of that explosion is the realization that cross-cultural translation is inherently flawed and mostly doomed when it comes to really gaining insight into understanding the text *as it was then understood*. But, even with that admission, we have at least learned enough to improve on some of the passages hazily grasped by the great sixteenth century translators, and have even been able to carry out analyses to allow us to unravel the multiple authors of the Tanakh, and order historically those of the New Testament in a way that sheds light on their various motivations.

Enter the farce. Let's face it, the translations that we've made since the King James, even when armed with all this new knowledge, have been, unilaterally, crap. Those aimed at a literal translation speak to nobody, and those which attempt to render ancient Hebrew in Modern English are necessarily flat and awkward, utilizing as they do the vocabulary and associations of a largely secular and technical grammatical structure and word base to attempt to convey moments fraught with religious significance. Here, I'll flip open *The Living Bible* to a random location and write down the first thing I see:

"As Jesus was going on down the road, he saw a tax collector, Matthew, sitting at a tax collection booth. 'Come and be my disciple,' Jesus said to him, and Matthew jumped up and went along with him." (Matthew 9:9)

Quite. And think, if that's how tawdry and ill-fitting the text is now, after only a century of secular-technological thinking being the standard, what it will be like in four hundred years, when translators don't even have the scintilla of everyday religiosity to fall back on that is still part of our present cultural-linguistic heritage?

Each year, we grow further and further from being able to understand the deeply held beliefs of the wandering Hebrew tribes or Jesus's fellow political revolutionaries. By translating those texts, we were not so much reproducing their message as restating our own, and for a while that breathed a modicum of fresh life into these crumbling and increasingly foreign texts. But with each fresh attempt, the gap between our mindset and theirs became ever more painfully apparent. We can see the original intent stirring in shadows, and try to jam it into the mould of our own experience, but we'll never really know it as it was. And that's fine, if you think of it as just another book, but if you are a Christian, shouldn't you expect a bit more from your all-powerful deity than two books half-heartedly delivered, followed by a shrug of the shoulders, and silence?

When Big Evidence Isn't:
The Statistical Pitfalls of Dean Radin's
Supernormal

(Originally Published in *Skeptical Inquirer*, Jan/Feb 2014)

We all want superpowers. I don't think there is a single person my age who didn't, as a kid, close their eyes and reach out towards some random object, hoping to will it into their hands with The Force. And while most of us stopped trying to manifest supernatural powers, hardly any of us ceased *wishing* we had them. In that spirit, Dean Radin's new book, *Supernormal: Science, Yoga, and the Evidence for Extraordinary Psychic Abilities* attempts gamely to use science to revive our belief in our superpotential. That it fails to do so is a result of Radin's tendency to laud showy results over responsible ones, leaving the inquisitive reader utterly unsure about what to trust and what to leave behind.

Most people coming to this book are looking for the evidence promised in the title. Unfortunately, they're going to have to wait, as the first third of the book is primarily a drawn out lament about parapsychology's lack of recognition by the academic community, and its rejection by skeptics. We are offered a hundred pages of Radin *saying* that skeptics are wrong rather than *showing* that they are, with repeated assurances that he'll get to the proof... later. Had he retitled the book "Dozens of pages of bitching about Michael Shermer, and THEN some evidence about Yoga" he could have saved us all a great deal of time.

Eventually, however, Radin purges himself of bilious resentment and is ready to get down to the business of providing the long-awaited evidence. Or rather, non-evidence, for he begins with an analysis of the Big Siddhis – those manifestations of yogic mastery that sound highly improbable to modern ears, like levitation, invisibility, and self duplication. He sets out to answer the reasonable question, "If the yoga sutras are a faithful account of the supernormal abilities of the human body, why can't I YouTube, right now, a hundred videos of yogis making themselves disappear in controlled situations?"

Radin's answer is that the sutras instruct yoga masters not to show off their perfection of the siddhis, lest it affect their ego. So, they refuse to demonstrate their mastery in order to keep themselves from the possibility of taint. This is a curiously selfish thing to do for a being supposedly concerned about minimizing humanity's suffering. Faced with the opportunity of demonstrating the power of yoga to overcome the Thousand Natural Shocks of fleshy existence, and thereby potentially help untold millions lead better lives, the yogi chooses to do nothing in order to preserve his personal purity, which is sort of a dick move. In the final analysis, we are left with two choices, either the big siddhis are real, and yogis are selfish jerks who value their own magnificent purity over helping their fellow man, or they aren't, and these yogis are simply charlatans or charmingly delusional. Either way, it doesn't look too good.

The real, statistically analyzed evidence doesn't come until *another* 30 pages later, with Radin's chapter on precognition. Right out of the gate, he produces a study which demonstrates the existence of psi effects with odds against chance of ten million billion to one! Except it's not a study, it's a meta analysis carried out in 1989 by Charles Honorton and Diane Ferrari in which they took all of the studies of forced-choice recognition (think of Bill Murray's experiment in the first scene of *Ghostbusters* but without the shocks) between 1935 and 1987 and combined them into one super-study. I was intrigued by the profoundly high number quoted by Radin, so I looked up the initial paper, and found that Radin's representation left out a number of significant caveats in the original.

For example, the studies gathered by Honorton and Ferrari are, by their own admission, "extremely heterogeneous" with z scores ranging from -5.1 (extreme negative correlation) to 19.6 (extreme positive correlation). The studies are all over the map, with some highly uncharacteristic outliers. This made the paper authors uncomfortable, and they responsibly shaved off the top and bottom 10% of their data to get a better idea of what most of the studies were coming up with. That results in an effect size of .012, half that of their original result. This is very small, but it is still an interesting number. The fact that Radin decided not to report it, but rather to report the .02 result from the extremely heterogeneous data, is troubling. Why neglect a responsible, but still intriguing, result, in favor of a larger result that even the original authors were uneasy about? And if this is how he reports data from readily available studies, how can I, as a reader trying to figure out what the evidence actually says, entirely trust his reporting on numbers for the studies he references which are much harder to find? With his very first statistically measurable study, Radin made a choice that casts a pall on all the numbers he will go on to convey, numbers that are far less towering than ten million billion billion to one.

Ultimately, he decides that these forced choice tests aren't the thing to test what is really happening with pre-cognition, and moves on to free-response experiments, where a subject is asked to describe the randomly selected location of an agent miles upon miles away. Of the 653 tests performed at Princeton, he selected a single example to show just how successful these tests were. This is his polished gem, his shimmering exemplar of the very best possible result obtained. It's worth quoting in full, because it lets us know what passed as a "success" in these trials, and therefore informs us of how confident we should be in the reported odds. This is what the subject described as the agent's future location:

"A rather strange yet persistent image of [the agent] inside a large bowl – a hemispheric indentation in the ground of some smooth man-made materials like concrete or cement. No color. Possibly covered with a glass dome. Unusual sense of inside/outside simultaneity. That's all. It's a large bowl. If it was full of soup [the agent] would be the size of a large dumpling!"

Radin reports the actual location of the agent as "the radio telescope at Kitt Peak." The problem being that there is more than one radio telescope at Kitt Peak, and they look rather different. The most significant is the VLBA radio telescope run by the National

Radio Astronomy Observatory, and is in no regard similar to anything that the subject mentioned. If you decide to keep digging until you get the result you want, you stumble upon the much smaller KP12m radio telescope run by the Arizona Radio Observatory, which is as close as Radin is going to get. It features (1) No indentation in the ground of any sort, (2) a white fabric retractable dome, (3) the colors white and silver, (4) *a giant thirty two foot telescope sitting right in the center of it.* The subject's response, then, is a mixture of plainly wrong positive statements, an absence of the most significant feature of the observatory (namely, its telescope), and a somewhat correct statement about the rough shape of the building (it isn't technically a hemisphere, but we can let that go).

This is not an average example chosen at random from the study – this is the single best piece of data that Radin could find from a study extending over two decades, and it is a mess. If this is the sort of thing that qualifies as a sing-it-upon-the-mountaintops success, little wonder, then, that he reports the odds against chance at a whopping 33 million to 1. As American standardized testing learned years ago, the best way to improve results is to redefine success.

The rest of the section is a cataloguing of other studies with ever-declining odds-against-chance that demonstrate a front-loading of favorable data, something which journalists tend to do but that scientists oughtn't. The most telling detail is the disappearance of error bars in his graphical representations of data. Radin is all too happy to include them when they make the data look good, as in his skin conductivity experiments, but then they have a tendency to disappear where they would make the data look very bad, as in his lab's occipital lobe experiments. It's a curious omission, compounded by his weakness for presenting outlier-responsive means in these graphs when medians would have been more responsible, if less dramatic.

It is one of the deep ironies of this book that it begins with such extended flights of frustration about skeptics' response to parapsychological data, and then spends its middle section doing everything that one can possibly do to rouse a skeptical response – misrepresenting report data, lowering success criteria, and playing a somewhat loose game with how rigorously confidence information is presented. I find it all titanically aggravating. I very much want to know what the data is, and how trustworthy it is. I would gladly take a small but sure result over a larger but fishy one, but there is something of the showman in Radin that gravitates towards the latter, leaving the reader who wants to *think* about the data, rather than merely accept Radin's interpretation thereof, with nothing to take away from the experience except frustration at what might have been. Radin is ever in this book his own worst enemy.

The subsequent sections are largely a repetition of the pattern established in his precognition chapter. In the telepathy section, we have another hand-picked trial example along the lines of the dismal radio observatory one, and it is only mildly more compelling. There are more meta-analyses which accomplish little more than casting doubt on the rigor of the whole statistical method of meta-analysis. Take for example this characterization of several different studies of ganzfeld telepathy experiments: "Of the seven meta-analyses, six reported statistically significant evidence with odds against chance ranging from a modest 20 to 1 to over a trillion to 1." The seventh study, he goes on to add, found no statistically significant evidence at all.

What are we to make of this egregious spread of reported odds? It stands to reason that, if I ask a chemist what the mass of a mole of oxygen is, and he says, "Studies suggest somewhere between one gram and a trillion," I would probably have *pretty* good cause to doubt the mass-determining mechanisms of chemistry. Meta-analyses appear to be the ideal subject of scientific debate – by combining dozens or hundreds of previous studies, they allow us to have a truly massive set of trials to work our statistics on, and at the same time seem to offer balance in so far as irregularly positive studies are often balanced out by uncharacteristically negative ones. However, there is a dire power within a meta-analysis, secretly wielded by the author, and it is this highly subjective power which lends each analysis its unique end result.

Put simply, the author gets to weigh how much an experiment counts to the aggregate through his evaluation of its quality. Ray Hyman, the author of one of the seven ganzfeld meta-analyses mentioned by Radin, highlighted how this weighing process often bends data towards desired outcomes in an article for Skeptical Inquirer in 1996:

" I did a meta-analysis of the original ganzfeld experiments as part of my critique of those experiments. My analysis demonstrated that certain flaws, especially quality of randomization, did correlate with outcome. Successful outcomes correlated with inadequate methodology. In his reply to my critique, Charles Honorton did his own meta-analysis of the same data. He too scored for flaws, but he devised scoring schemes different from mine. In his analysis, his quality ratings did not correlate with outcome. This came about because, in part, Honorton found more flaws in unsuccessful experiments than I did. On the other I found more flaws in successful experiments than Honorton did. Presumably, both Honorton and I believed we were rating quality in an objective and unbiased way. Yet, both of us ended up with results that matched our preconceptions."

In other words, if you want a study to count less, you tend to find more flaws with it, and if you want it to count more, you tend to gloss over flaws that might exist. In a normal study, this power would wreak comparatively minor havoc, because the trial number is low enough that a modest result doesn't lead to massive odds-against-chance numbers. However, when you exercise this power with millions of pieces of data, the impact is colossal, and the odds-against-chance skyrocket, resulting in "trillion to one" type numbers whose immensity belies their tenuousness.

There is perhaps phenomenal data within these studies, but Radin's tendency to reach for the astronomical keeps him focused on meta-analyses wherever he can get them, and, as the wild variation in results shows, there just isn't enough standardization of method in this approach yet for us, the readers, to really trust what is going on. Radin has a tendency to veer between hyper-specific reports of individual trials that are entirely unconvincing and massive Billions Upon Billions meta-analyses that grow progressively less trustworthy in the telling, and does himself disservice thereby. Every time I found myself wondering, "Is there really a new physical principle at work here, or perhaps an extension of a known but ill-defined one?" that curiosity was soon stamped out by the author's proclivity for over-reaching.

Radin's intention with this book is to convince us average folks of the existence of supernormal abilities. In my case, it didn't succeed. After a certain point, I felt that my trust had been abused one too many times, and Radin Fatigue set surely in so that data that might have been convincing presented on its own became suspect when issuing from the pen of the fellow who had taken me on so many rides already. I come away from this book not convinced, but not unconvinced as to certain details either, and if Radin can adjust his expectations from "convincing people" to "not unconvincing them" then, well, he might have a good night's sleep yet.

ATHEIST BOOK OF THE MONTH?
ELIZABETH SCALIA'S *STRANGE GODS*
AIMS AT MODERNITY BUT KNOCKS OUT JEHOVAH

(Originally Published in *The Freethinker*, August 2013)

We are not spending enough time thinking about God. That is the central idea of Catholic blogger Elizabeth Scalia's new book, *Strange Gods: Unmasking the Idols of Everyday Life*. For that matter, it stands, quite proud of the fact, as the *only* idea in a book which just barely manages one hundred and sixty pages by dint of a generous font size and a firm belief in the character-building value of incessant repetition.

That idea and its development through ten plodding and utterly predictable chapters are not, by themselves, just recompenses for the few hours one invests in reading the book. And yet, for reasons utterly unintended by the author, it is a fascinating read. It turns out that, in attempting to expose the psychological damage wrought by the "idols" of modernity, Scalia inadvertently wove a condemnation of Christianity and Jehovah so damning that it wouldn't surprise me in the least if the book turned out to be a stunt by an atheist in disguise.

Scalia's big thing is the clearing away of any belief, ritual, or possession that interferes with one's line-of-sight on God. Each chapter of the book is devoted to a detailing of a fresh idol. Chapter four is about wealth, five about technology, six a lamentably conceived chapter on coolness and sex, and without even reading the book, you already know everything that she is going to say on these topics and their relation to a life well lived. By the fifth chapter, I was playing a game with myself of writing down what I thought her points and examples would be before reading each chapter, then checking them off as they thudded to ground with the inevitability of gravity on the page before me. Her advice is often good, though the monodimensional reasoning behind that advice rarely is (yes, we do feel diminishing returns in a life devoted to material consumption, but not so much because we are robbing ourselves of Jesus Time as because that's how neurochemical reward pathways work).

What I never expected, though, was that, with each definition she offered of a reigning idol, each laying out of its assumptions and flaws, she would precisely and unintentionally define the Judaeo-Christian God as the greatest and most false idol of them all. The first time she did it, in a chapter about how our ideas and expectations are idols, I thought it an oversight, an accident of ill-chosen vocabulary:

"We cling to resentment or feed jealousy until it grows into something we burnish daily with our justifications. We get it to glitter in our minds like something alive, like a genuine force outside of ourselves. We go so far as to proselytize our grudges to others through spin, gossip, and even lies – see my anger, my resentment, my jealousy, and my spite! Acknowledge it with me; let us have communion in our shared umbrage!"

This is a fair representation of rankling indignation, but how could any writer miss the fact that nothing benefits from these psychological motivations more than Christianity, and nothing instantiates them so much as the Judaeo-Christian God? How do you use the word 'resentment' twice in three sentences and not realize that you are conjuring the ghost of Nietzsche's analysis of Christianity's genealogy in the process? Turning resentment and jealousy into a force outside of yourself (God the Judge on the Day of Reckoning), proselytizing that resentment to others to cudgel them into holding the same fears and loves that you do (Go Forth and Spread the Word), changing shared umbrage into a source of communion (It Will Be Easier for a Camel to Walk Through the Eye of a Needle...) - these are, phrase for phrase, a retelling of the negative side of Christianity's initial appeal and growth. Really, the very idea of Hell itself is nothing but group resentment and umbrage given divine sanction.

171

I expected a follow-up, "Of course, one might say these things about Christianity too, and here's why one would be wrong" but it did not come. Scalia was apparently thoroughly unaware that, in describing the psychology of our enthrallment to our worst ideas, she had just neatly paraphrased Christianity itself. Everybody's entitled to one slip in self-awareness though, so I continued on, swallowing more sentences with phrases that make "burnish daily with our justifications" sound positively elegant (the winner, by the way, for ungainly imagery goes to this gem: "Justice and mercy are the right and left sides of the horizontal beam of the crucifix, upon which a constant tug of war ensues." I'll let you unpack that at your leisure.)

But the inadvertent body blows to the gut of Christ kept coming.

In warning us against the Internet: "She [a friend of Scalia's who uses Facebook to keep up with the world] pushes away the real world and escapes to the illusions. She rejects what is sometimes dreary, like other people, to delight herself and bathe in the regard of the better, less-troublesome, handpicked others of the Net." The internet is bad because it distracts us from reality and other people by holding out an illusory paradise filled just with those people we like. This, I shall remind you , in a book which says that we are too distracted by reality and other people and should be focusing more on the paradise awaiting the elect few who choose God. So, ignoring reality is awful except when it's The Best Thing Ever.

In bemoaning trendiness, we are told that, "its only membership requirement is that one be immediately and unquestionably in tune with the conventional wisdom of the day (or the week), and against the establishment, as it is continually redefined." Defining one's self adversarially... the only requirement for joining being that you unquestionably believe whatever person is pulling the strings at the moment... if this doesn't bring the history of Catholicism rushing to mind, it will when Scalia quotes, as she often does, from Retired Pope Benedict's injunctions to mistrust the offerings of the secular world.

Suffice to say, uncritically quoting the Catholic trend-setter par excellence while bewailing uncritical trendiness is so blatantly self-contradictory that I can't help but suspect Scalia is batting for our side here.

Continuing on in that chapter: "There was a constant call for conformity, a continual demand to disdain, and a lessening of human feeling. She was not at liberty to betray simple excitement and enthusiasm, which, though human and true, were not considered to be cool emotions." Replace "cool emotions" with "sufficiently God-directed" and you have here Scalia outlining the central problem of her *own book*, with its constant call to Catholic conformity, to disdain anything, human or otherwise, that gets in the way of God, and a resultant lessening of human feeling in the name of cultivating a feeling of oneness with the divine. I am sure that she would respond that tending exclusively to one's connection with God makes you more in touch with humanity rather than less, but, using her own terminology, it seems rather the case that she is letting the idol of God block her access to authentic humanity so that the "idol" of authentic humanity doesn't block her access to God.

In warning us against the idol of "having plans" she tells us, "To be inflexible about deviating from the plan is to erect a roadblock, an encumbrance – an idol – and put it in the way of what the Spirit might be trying to do with us and for us." This bit about the dangers of inflexibility in the face of change is, of course, located smack in the middle of a book devoted to a rigid cultivation of commandment-aligned inflexibility in the face of modernity and its temptations. There is hardly anything less open to life's variation and potential than the willful crafting of knee-jerk execration in the face of the world's offerings.

But my absolute favorite, the most stunningly anti-Christian set piece ever written in a desperately pro-Christian work, is this sparkling treasure, which aims for putting us on our guard against group identity and ends by masterfully demonstrating precisely what is so sick at the core of Christianity:

"One thing that can hinder growth is our willingness to attach labels to ourselves and adopt identifications, particularly with groups, to whose ideas we've become attached. In doing so, we cease to ponder, cease to wonder, cease to think... When we over-identify with an idea or hermetically seal ourselves within the seemingly safe cocoon of groupthink, we stop knowing much at all. Everything we think we know is surrendered to the collective from which we gladly take our identities and our self-definitions."

Is that not beautiful? If my copy weren't from the library, I would tear that page out and frame it as a testament to humanity's exquisite capacity for double think.

Taken in sum, what Scalia's critique of the idols of modernity and the harm they do to the growth of the self really contains is a condemnation of Christianity in all of its facets. As defined by her, there is no more harmful idol to humanity than the Judaeo-Christian god, and so the entire effect of the book comes off as, "You have to abandon all of these false idols that are hurting you, so that you can fully engage yourself with this astoundingly false idol who will utterly gut you."

Scalia wants us to choose the self-harming idol which she happens to like best, and that's a very human thing to do. There are points in the book where she almost seems to turn the corner, as when she realizes that over- attachment to particular religious rituals or incantations can verge on the idolatrous. But she always stops short before the core of Catholicism and the person of Jehovah. That God is an instance of humanity pouring its resentment and hope into an illusory construct in order to make its own prejudices and insecurity divine, and that Catholicism is the groupthinkalicious, reality-hating vehicle of that act of deitysmithing is quite beyond her willingness to consider. It is a truth unthinkable even as she watches her own pen lay out both the accusation and evidence. She is devoted to the notion that God's love is real and that it is worth subsuming all other aspects of humanity to. It is her addiction, one that the analytical part of her brain is clearly rebelling against even as the chemistry of religious addiction forces her to deny all such insight.

As atheists, therefore, we have much to learn from this book, about how closely the die-hard Christian's worldview is predicated on beliefs that, with the slightest flick of self-realization, drive straight to the core of religion itself. When David Silverman went on The O'Reilly Factor and declared that everybody is an atheist waiting to happen, I was skeptical about the capacity for non-belief being that generally distributed, but upon reading this book I wonder. I wonder...

"THE HORROR HELD HER": THE RELIGIOUS DISNEYFICATION OF THE HARLEM RENAISSANCE

(Originally Published in *The Humanist*, 2014)

Right now, in a hundred book clubs spread across the United States, the literary history of the Harlem Renaissance is being rewritten by a thousand Discussion Questions of good intent but devastating effect. As a result, a movement that once brimmed over with radical ideas that shuddered before no idol is turning slowly into a sanitized collection of feel-good tales that aim at little beyond the portrayal of adversity overcome. Hardest hit are those works that feature stinging portrayals of religion's role in racism, the legacy of their authors muted in the name of marketability, producing a vision of the Harlem Renaissance that it is long past time to correct.

In particular, I'd like to focus on a couple of female authors who bravely faced up against three-fold discrimination to say their peace, and who have been coldly rewarded for their bravery in our own times. To be African American in the 1920s was hard enough, to be a female author in the publishing industry somewhat more daunting, and to be one who held that religion perpetuated rather than combatted the worst excesses of racism was to be in scant company indeed. And yet, from that handful of authors we have some of the most beautiful, disturbing, and profound works to emerge from the Harlem Renaissance.

The crown jewel of this tradition is, without a doubt, Nella Larsen's slim marvel of a novel, *Quicksand*. First published in 1928, it was hailed instantly as a milestone, W.E.B. DuBois dubbing it "the best piece of fiction that Negro America has produced since the heyday of Chesnutt." And yet, two years later, on the heels of a groundless plagiarism accusation, Larsen's career was over as suddenly as it had begun. For the next three decades, she lived in total obscurity, never putting pen to paper again. Her great work, however, has never entirely slipped from common memory as it is one of those books that, once read, stays lodged within the wheels of your mind.

It is the story of Helga Crane, daughter of a racially mixed couple, whose education and restlessness drive her from misery to misery. Unable to find herself at home under the crippling omnipresent racism of the United States or in the accepting but somber bosom of her mother's native Denmark, she comes to believe that happiness and companionship are simply things that she will never know. Then one day, broken by disappointment and drenched by a sudden storm, she finds her way into a small church. In other books, this scene would play out as a moment of triumphant salvation, but in Larsen's masterful hands the grotesquery of the conversion process, the breaking down of the human spirit under false promise, has all of the brutal earmarks of a rape scene:

"The yelling figures about her pressed forward, closing her in on all sides. Maddened, she grasped at the railing, and with no previous intention began to yell like one insane, drowning every other clamor, while torrents of tears streamed down her face. She was unconscious of the words she uttered, or their meaning: 'Oh God, mercy, mercy. Have mercy on me!' but she repeated them over and over. From those about her came a thunder-clap of joy. Arms were stretched towards her with savage frenzy. The women dragged themselves upon their knees or crawled over the floor like reptiles, sobbing and pulling their hair and tearing off their clothing. Those who succeeded in getting near to her leaned forward to encourage the unfortunate sister, dropping hot tears and beads of sweat upon her bare arms and neck."

Thrown violently out of equilibrium by the "confusion of seductive repentance" (a deliciously apt phrase if ever there was one), she convinces herself into marrying a Southern preacher who breaks her will and vitality through serial pregnancy, scolding her for lack of faith whenever she complains of the weariness of her used-up and worn body. Lingering near death after a failed birth, she realizes finally the insidious role that religion has played in manipulating her race.

"The cruel, unrelieved suffering had beaten down her protective wall of artificial faith in the infinite wisdom, in the mercy, of God. For had she not called in her agony on Him? And he had not heard. Why? Because, she knew now, He wasn't there. Didn't exist…. Life wasn't a miracle, a wonder. It was, for Negroes at least, only a great disappointment… The white man's God. And His great love for all people regardless of race! What idiotic nonsense she had allowed herself to believe. How could she, how could anyone, have been so deluded? How could ten million black folk credit it when daily before their eyes was enacted its contradiction?"

Small wonder that, impelled by a desire to do justice to the female writers of the Harlem Renaissance, the Oprahs and television networks skipped easily over this small, uncompromising volume, and lighted instead upon the more easily digestible, less rancorous works of Zora Neale Hurston and Dorothy West. Justice, yes, but let's not alienate any key demographics (though, confession time, I do rather unambiguously love West's *The Living is Easy*).

Such thinking also explains the unfathomable lack of interest in reviving the works of Ann Petry. Her debut novel, *The Street*, was published in 1946, and was the first novel by an African American woman writer to sell a million copies. And deservedly so. *The Street* delves into the question of race not from the point of view of politics or personality, but from that of structure, a penetrating look into how the physical realities of living and working space, perpetuated over half a century, succeeded in diverting a whole race into an inescapable spiral of urban hopelessness. It is a challenging book that does not settle for easy resentment or racial slogan-smithing, and its portrayal of religion is completely dismissive. God is a hypothesis that Petry, Laplace-like, has no need of. His only appearance is in the form of a golden cross that one of the characters nails above her bed to act as a talisman against her lover's walking out on her. It is a fetishistic object bought from a witch doctor that only works because of the superstitious paranoia it engenders. Beyond that, there is nothing any supernatural power can do to alleviate the crushing weight of place and time.

Petry wrote her last novel, *The Narrows*, in 1953, and in it allowed herself much more explicit statements about how religion interferes with basic decency. The central story of the book revolves around a romance between an African American male and a white female, both of whom combine unreflecting selfishness with overwrought erudition to an unappealing degree that would wreck the novel were it being written by less of a master than Petry. Fortunately, as in *The Street*, Petry spends large swaths of the book focusing on the sub-stories of her secondary characters with a faultless eye for psychological detail. Chief among these is Abbie Crunch, adoptive aunt of the lead male, a woman whose default approach to life is righteous indignation rather than open compassion.

When her husband is brought unconscious into her home by the local bartender, she assumes that he has drunk himself senseless in spite of the bartender's insistence to the contrary. In a pique of high moral outrage, she spreads newspapers on the floor and dumps his convulsing, seizure-wracked, body on top of them, refusing everybody's advice to call a doctor until it is too late for anything to be done. It is not the last time that her instinct towards outrage will end in tragedy.

Faced with a tearful Jewish mother complaining about how the Christians at school were taunting her son with chants of "Matzos, Matzos, Two for five, That's what keeps the kikes alive," Abbie decides to hotly deny that such things could possibly have been learned in Sunday School rather than to actually comfort the distraught human being in front of her. Repeatedly throughout the book, her attachment to religious purity prevents her from extending a helping hand to suffering people, breeding unnecessary tragedy. From Abbie Crunch to a priest who simply walks on by while a young man is being unjustly beaten by the police to the garish self-aggrandizement of the local preacher who installs mega-speakers in his Church to inflict his views upon the neighborhood, the message of *The Narrows* is that decency and understanding are astoundingly rare creatures who cannot breath in the thick, inhuman atmosphere of theology.

Ironically, *The Narrows* also carries Petry's own epitaph. One of the characters explains about church membership, "When they're young they don't go to church. Then when they gets false teeth and they waterworks run all the time, they gets scared, they think that well, after all, everybody's got to die some time and so mebbe they could, too... Then one mornin' they gets up and looks in the mirror and they got gray hair and a bald spot and they kind of adds themselves up, and they got a full set of uppers and lowers and two sets of glasses and some kind of funny crick in the middle of they backs and they begin to figure mebbe they better start goin' to church." Petry would, in her sixties, have such a moment herself, and among her last published works is a children's book about the lives of the saints. That happens sometimes, but it in no way detracts from the portrayal of religion in her novels as a force of superstition and inhumanity lined up against the best instincts of man.

By omitting Petry and Larsen from the pantheon of female Harlem Renaissance authors (though Petry is admittedly something of a latecomer), the recent popularizers of the movement have cut away a large chunk of its vital force. Deciding ahead of time that the only authors due for revival would be those with uplifting messages about diffuse spirituality and self-belief that would play well on television, they have only perpetuated long-lived stereotypes about religiosity and race. These stereotypes are not only inaccurate, but actually doing active harm to thousands of young adults afraid of admitting their own lack of belief for fear that it will cut them off from their culture and heritage. Far better to demonstrate the vitality of the Renaissance in all of its shades by resisting the urge to cherry-pick its authors. Then those people struggling to come to grips with their humanism will have at long last some predecessors to look to, a feeling of common cause, and an understanding voice from the deep recesses of the past to assure them that they are not as alone as they feel.

GEORGE, GEORGE, AND FANNY:
HOW THREE NINETEENTH CENTURY WOMEN
INVENTED TWENTY-FIRST CENTURY HUMANISM.

(Previously Unpublished)

The twentieth century was a dark era for humanism. Atomic bombs and Cold War, concentration camps and mass media - all played their part in tearing to tatters all confidence in the basic goodness of humanity's guiding lights. The shame of it is that all shades of humanism were treated as one, and so the subtle philosophical treatment of some of the nineteenth century's greatest thinkers was thrown out as a matter of course along with more irresponsible and extreme positivist musings, buried en masse under the cackling scorn of Adorno, Heidegger, and the rest, who would have none of any system that spoke against our long-standing, even fundamental, brokenness as a species.

It has taken us a century and a half to get over their frantic (if understandable) over-generalizing to rediscover the marvelous humanism of the late nineteenth century, one which achieves a balance and elegance that we have yet to realize in spite of our vaunted neo-secularism. More amazing still is how the ideas that humanism is just now starting to develop were fully present in the writings of three female writers who defined a continent's conception of what the humanity-oriented life might be, both artistically and societally, George Sand (1804-1876), George Eliot (1819-1880), and Fanny Lewald (1811-1889).

The decline of Sand's reputation has been perhaps the most pronounced. She has gone from recognition as a prime figure in the history of the psychological novel and developer of non-factional humanism to a gross caricature, the vampiric lover of Chopin and dozens of others besides, who smoked cigars and wore pants while writing books we can't be bothered to read anymore. Yet, if ever there was an age that could gain from her wisdom, it is this one.

She never ceased believing in God, but she redefined what God might mean. With dogma she had no patience, but she was attracted to the idea of Love (with God its symbol) being a force whereby an individual human could become something more. She gave her life over to that notion of Love, and her writings to investigating its various forms and consequences with a sense of diversity unmatched until our own times. Above all else, she wanted to substitute the cult of the individual, which was the reigning doctrine of early Romanticism gone amok, with a cult of humanity: "My individuality is neither significant nor important. It only takes on some sense when it becomes a part of life in general, merging with that of my fellow men, and thereby becoming part of history."

She based her life in love and beauty, rather than disputation and rhetoric, and so found it possible to make strong friends and lovers of people from every stripe of philosophical perspective, the atheist and the abbé both equally welcome so long as their eye was on how to broaden the inclusivity of humankind rather than how to prove themselves always In The Right.

As much as Sand was consulted and revered in matters of gender and politics, however, it was to George Eliot that the world turned in order to understand how to cope with a loss of faith. There were plenty of philosophers around who, in one way or another, demonstrated the implausibility of a divine presence, but it was the lived example of George Eliot that drew the attention of a people desperately trying to thread their way between tradition and science in a world moving too fast.

Eliot started life as a convinced Christian of the most trenchant sort. She sneered at the frivolities of her peers and consumed a steady diet of high-flung religious tracts to sustain her own sense of moral superiority. Until it all came crashing down. Her wide reading put her in contact with the fringe of Biblical criticism emanating from Germany and, delving into the matter further, she had to admit grave doubts about the literal truth of the

Bible and of Christianity in general. At age nineteen, she took the unprecedented move of refusing to go to Church, thereby cutting herself off not only from society, but from her own family, who would never quite forgive her.

What is curious, then, is how somebody who had so fundamentally given up on the idea of God and the afterlife, could write books of such an ultimately conservative character. Again and again, her heroines and heroes only find their consummation in a return to tradition. What *was* George thinking?

Well, it turns out she was thinking rather more than most of us in the atheist community tend to these days. She realized that an atheism imposed before society had the psychological wherewithal to support it was a recipe for disaster. People need people, and so long as the structures were not in place for them to find enthusiasm in each other secularly, some amount of religious tradition would survive and even be necessary. Eliot herself continued to attend church from time to time even as she knew that every word being spoken was utterly false, even though most of the religious establishment spoke out in simmering fury against her unconventional lifestyle (living… with a married man!), because it was the place where people went to bask in each other's presence for a while, and she knew the value of it.

Hers was a tolerant and wise humanism, then, intellectually rigorous (she was the translator of both Strauss and Feuerbach's foundational critiques of Christianity) but psychologically astute, recognizing fully what a life without God could realize but understanding what it had yet to fully replace. It's a position we're finally able to understand as the initial bolt of long-repressed-anger is dissipating in the humanist community, and we at long last are looking towards the next, constructive, steps.

Fanny Lewald was known alternately as "The German George Sand" or "The German George Eliot" but, to those that read and love her, she is a thinker entirely her own. In her, we find the best of both writers – she has Sand's fierce and provocative sense of right married to Eliot's staid consideration for the needs and motivations of humanity. A good deal of which is explained by her

183

unique background. She grew up in the rich intellectual tradition of Prussia's early nineteenth century Jewish community. Her father encouraged her learning, and also discouraged any but a strictly pragmatic view or religion. As an educated woman of a persecuted minority, she thus had a double insight into the foibles and short-sightedness of which man was capable when guided by a too-strict adherence to tradition.

She converted to Christianity, motivated by the same attraction to a love-based (at least in theory) religion that sustained Sand, but had trouble writing her confession of faith when she realized that she didn't believe a word of the actual content of Christianity. The miracles, the immaculate birth, the rising from the dead, all of these struck her disciplined mind as rankly improbable exercises in legend-crafting. She muddled through by stitching together a deliciously vague confession, and went on to a writing career that investigated issues of marriage, faith, and society that were as uncompromising as her confession was dodgy.

Her novels argue for a feminism as practical as Sand's was artistic, while in her memoirs she lays out in full the possibilities of a life devoted to learning and creation, free from the prejudice of both traditional societal thinking and religious devotion. When a proselytizer accosted her asking, "Where do you find comfort and support or a refuge in the hours of suffering, distress, and temptation?" she calmly replied, "I bear what life gives me to bear, I reassure myself with the view of the conditions of human existence and the view of what cannot be changed. When I feel tempted to do something wrong, I would have no restraint, to be sure, other than the feeling of what is right in my heart and the conviction, gained by experience, that every wrong committed carries within it the seed of its own punishment." For all of our decades of agonizing over the theoretical possibility of goodness outside of godliness, we really haven't come out much better than this improvised response of Lewald's, a testament to how much further we have to go to match the level-headed and broad-minded concept of faithlessness from two centuries ago.

Similar times breed similar creatures. The Victorians, and their continental counterparts, faced a world where each day brought new challenges to cherished assumptions, and had to use the best of their experience to keep a sane sense of purpose amongst the progress and pseudo-progress. They had to figure out how to craft a radically new life that still carried with it the essence of their learned humanity. And so do we, after a century of working our confidence back up as to our basic potential for good. We could continue pridefully taking years upon years to work out what our ancestors knew as a matter of informed instinct, but why not take a few moments to wade back into that vast body of knowledge, and communicate with the kindred spirits there, giving them due reverence and credit even if it comes at the cost of our own self-touted Originality?

THE PURLOINED THESIS:
REZA ASLAN'S CRIMES AGAINST HERMANN REIMARUS, AND WHY WE FORGIVE HIM.

(Originally Published in *The Freethinker*, October 2013)

As a species, we've been beating our heads against the wall trying to find new things to say about Jesus Christ for the better part of two millennia. And for most of that time, we did little more than compile variations upon the theme of "How Perfect Was Jesus? VERY Perfect!" Two and a half centuries ago, however, a very brave and respected academic named Hermann Reimarus started privately setting down his thoughts about Jesus not as a religious or intellectual figure, but rather as a failed political revolutionary. When fragments of this work were finally published posthumously by Gotthold Lessing in the 1770s, they ignited a full-scale intellectual war ended only when Lessing was forced to hand over Reimarus's manuscript to the authorities to prevent any future publication of such scandalous ideas.

And now Reimarus finds himself inexplicably in the midst of another travesty of justice in the form of Reza Aslan's recent *Zealot: The Life and Times of Jesus of Nazareth*. Azlan has a simple thesis which, he informs us, is going to rock our world: "This book is an attempt to reclaim, as much as possible, the Jesus of history, the Jesus *before* Christianity: the politically conscious Jewish revolutionary who, two thousand years ago, walked across the Galilean countryside, gathering followers for a messianic movement with the goal of establishing the Kingdom of God but whose mission failed when, after a provocative entry into Jerusalem and a brazen attack on the Temple, he was arrested and executed by Rome for the crime of sedition. It is also about how, in the aftermath of Jesus's failure to establish God's reign on earth, his followers reinterpreted not only Jesus's mission and identity, but also the very nature and definition of the Jewish messiah."

Reading these words the first time, I all but flew to my bookshelf on the wings of trembling memory as this central thesis, so boldly proclaimed as an original departure in the field of Jesus scholarship, sounded EERILY familiar. And, indeed, pulling down my copy of *Reimarus: Fragments*, I quickly found this: "Thus the existing history of Jesus enlightens us more and more upon the object of his conduct and teaching, which entirely corresponds with the first idea entertained of him by his apostles, that is, that he was a *worldly* deliverer... It also shows that the master, and how much more his disciples, found themselves mistaken and deceived by the condemnation and death [of Jesus], and that the new system of a suffering spiritual savior, which no one had ever known or thought of before, was invented after the death of Jesus, and invented only because the first hopes had failed."

That's an almost sentence-by-sentence correspondence, and the more you read Reimarus and Aslan side by side, the more you note the former's ideas creeping up in the latter. "Maybe he somehow never read Reimarus and all of this is just coincidence," I thought, and flipped to the bibliography to find *Reimarus: Fragments* quite definitely present. Hmm.

Swallowing indignation, I pushed forward, waiting for Aslan to at long last give Reimarus his due as the originator of the Jesus as Reinterpreted Revolutionary theory. No such luck. Throughout the entirety of the book, the man who anticipated his own thesis, sentence for sentence, two and a half centuries ago, only merits two toss-away mentions buried in the endnotes.

Not cool.

However. If you can get past the atmospheric hum of ingratitude that hangs about the book, it's actually very enjoyable. I think all of us are willing to accept a re-hash of an old idea so long as it is well done, and in terms of which book I would recommend for learning about Jesus's failed mission, I wouldn't hesitate a moment in picking Aslan. Reimarus is a brave and admirable thinker, and undoubtedly the originator (along with the English deists Thomas Chubb and Anthony Collins) of some of the best ideas in Aslan, but his sentences have all the dynamism of a stack of pancakes. Aslan, by contrast, is an engaging writer with a free and exciting style that makes up for a lot of his less savory academic tendencies.

Ironically, the best parts of this book about Jesus are the ones that feature him the least. Part I is a routinely engrossing account of the relations between the Jews and the Roman Empire in the century before and after Jesus's death. In it, Jesus is almost lost among a string of similar messianic figures who rose, hearts full of zeal to throw off the yoke of Roman control by any means necessary, and fell having accomplished none of their goals. The true story here is not the individual failed messiahs but the recursive loop of bumbled Roman administration and blood-soaked Jewish banditry that finally culminated in the utter destruction of Jerusalem several decades after Jesus's death. It was that destruction, and the retreat away from messianic zealotry and towards Roman universalism that it ushered in, that drove the mythmaking behind the Gospels. By drawing our attention to the ruthlessness of both sides and the centrality of the razing of Jerusalem, Aslan (as did Reimarus before him) provides us with our best chance at understanding the early evolution of Christology.

The book stumbles once Jesus takes center stage in Part II, and for the good reason that, lacking the historical data that gave heft to the first section, Aslan has to resort to rooting through the Gospels for his claims about Jesus, and the material there is notoriously tricky to tame. Still, some inspired portraits emerge, particularly in his sketches of John the Baptist and Pontius Pilate, which show how much violence the Gospel writers were willing to do to history in order to make Jesus the Jewish Peasant into Jesus the Universal Christ. But chapters nine through eleven, which are exclusively about Jesus, stagger all about, unsure of what they want to do and why. The best parts are second and third (and, in one case, fourth) repetitions of things established earlier, and the new material flails about for pages trying to suck particularism from stock phrases of oral tradition and come to terms with, say, the difference between magic and miracle in the ancient world. There is a Maybeness to these sections, a great amount of energy and space devoted to sorting out things that might or might not be true, but that don't really shine light on the central argument either way. All in all, not much would have been lost by retitling the book *Zealots* and jumping from chapter eight straight to chapter twelve.

But part III finds its feet again with Jesus shuffled off the mortal coil, allowing Aslan to comfortably settle himself in the historical record again. It is about the evolution of the other-worldly Messiah myth as it elaborated itself under the total collapse of every one of Jesus's promises. Instead of establishing an imminent and revitalized independent nation of Israel, all that Jesus managed to do was die ignominiously on the eve of Jersualem's total destruction and subjugation. Reviving the reputation of a messiah who failed to such a spectacular degree took an elaborate and decades-long process of pilfering prophetic texts, cleansing them of their Jewish particularity, and recasting them in in super-natural rather than terrestrial terms, a PR whitewashing effort of such spectacular ballsiness that it has kept the world in thrall for millennia. In particular, Paul's bitter self-aggrandizing letters preaching a Jesus without Judaic Law were roundly rejected by the Jewish Diaspora prior to the destruction of Jerusalem, but became the basis of all Christian theology in the years after. His focus on gentile conversion, his abandonment of the rituals of Judaic Law, and his philosophical focus on the role of faith and the divinity of Jesus were all perfectly adapted to a Christianity seeking to rebuild itself in the face of total disaster, with consequences for Christianity's self-conception that ring down to the present.

Aslan sees his book as a work of rehabilitation – the saving of a noble earthly figure from the trappings of divine misappropriation. Disregarding the fact that this *revolutionary* conception is over two centuries old, I would also add that the Jesus who emerges isn't particularly more likeable than the one being replaced. Faced with a political situation he didn't like, Jesus decided to follow in the footsteps of a group of zealot messiahs whose solution was ever to shed blood first and think about big questions later (if you're having trouble picturing that, just think of the "What have the Romans ever done for us?" bit from Monty Python's *Life of Brian* and you won't err far). Jesus's first act upon entering Jerusalem was one grounded in violence that ended in his death. I don't find any of that particularly admirable, but rather see in it the real seeds of all the worst aspects of historical Christianity, particularly its haughty disdain for considering problems from multiple angles and willingness to default to the tropes of divine wrath when describing terrestrial opponents. Jesus carved out a hackneyed identity for himself by cobbling together the most effective bits from previous messiahs, failed spectacularly on his first confrontation with actual authority, and was saved by imaginative publicity after the fact. He is perhaps the most likeable of the failed gore-soaked messiahs, but put against the rich intellectual atmosphere of his time, he's a footnote graced posthumously by fortune, and that's about it.

MATH GIRLS

(Originally Published at *MadArtLab*, 2014)

"Open any math book and you'll find a ton of equations. Each one is an expression of someone's thoughts. There's always someone on the other side of the math. Someone trying to send us a message. Someone trying to make a connection. I work hard at math so I can make that connection." – *Math Girls*.

Quick, name three female Marvel characters who are good at math.

I spend an *inordinate* amount of time reading Marvel comic books, and I only came up with two: Valeria Richards and maybe Moira MacTaggert, hardly first tier characters. If you ask the same

190

question for *male* characters, the answers fly off the page: Tony Stark, Bruce Banner, Reed Richards, Hank Pym, Doctor Doom, Henry McCoy, Black Panther, Doctor Octopus, and on and on....

As a comic lover and math lover with two daughters, I have always found the paucity of science-smart female comic characters immensely frustrating. Which is why I was so excited when Bento Books announced their Kickstarter to translate and publish something called *Math Girls*, a Japanese manga series by Hiroshi Yuki and Mika Hisaka involving three characters, two girls and a boy, grappling with math while navigating the emotional minefield of high school.

My copy at long last arrived, and I fell in love. It's hard to say whether it's a book about interesting math that has a really fun romance story, or a cool high school romance book that has some really great math. Either way, it's everything I wanted. The character dynamic is perfectly balanced. Miruka is a mathematical genius who challenges the male narrator to solve intriguing problems in the most efficient way possible. He is the Salieri to her Mozart, always struggling just to keep up and constantly exhilarated by the sharp brilliance of her insights into a topic he dearly loves.

He is in turn the tutor to Tetra, a girl who represents most of us, demanding to know *why* the math we're taught in school is true. *Why* is 1 not a prime number? *Why* can't we just describe taking the absolute value as "removing the negative sign"? These are all those questions we might have had back in high school, terribly important and with very interesting answers, but either didn't ask out of shyness or did ask and were told "it's because that's what the equation says" by our harried and underpaid math teachers.

Mathematically, there's something for everyone, then. Tetra and the narrator work through some bits of normal algebra and take their time to stop and ask why things are the way they are, and there's something to learn there even for grizzled math veterans. Miruka and the narrator, meanwhile, romp gleefully through the more advanced math of pre-calculus, asking questions about trigonometric identities, de Moivre's Theorem, and prime factorizations that provide all manner of Hey That's Pretty Nifty moments.

Meanwhile, there's romance afoot. The narrator starts off thinking he is just friends with Miruka. They spend hours talking about math together, and her insistence on rigor and elegance challenges him to be the best thinker he can be, but surely there's nothing more to their relationship than that... or IS there? Meanwhile, Tetra's developing crush on her tutor blows in the uncertainty of whether Miruka and the narrator are meant to be. It's a classic set up, and that very warm familiarity is a wonderful thing to settle back into after a couple of pages of mathematical pondering, a place to recharge your batteries for the next plunge into intricate identities.

The pacing is great, the math examples chosen by Yuki are brisk and exciting, and Hisaka's art is wispy and appropriate. Most importantly, the books shows that anybody can be passionate about math, whether you are insanely gifted or struggling with the basics, there is room for something wonderful to be discovered, and I think that's a message any student could stand to hear.

The only bit of a complaint that I have is that in my edition, the Greek letters get dropped from the translated text balloons. They're there where it matters, in the artwork, so it's not too hard to figure out what should go in the blanks of the dialogue, but if you're getting it for a student, it's probably a good idea to fill in the sigmas and pis to keep them moving and reading. Hopefully, this problem has since been corrected, but even if it hasn't, we're talking about maybe 5 missing characters in 180 pages, so it's no biggie.

In short, it's a beautiful series about people, girls and boys, finding excitement and satisfaction in talking about numbers and their relations, and if we had more things like it out there in the marketplace, maybe there would be less math anxiety and more math curiosity. And that would be quite a thing.

PART IV:

Science is the New
Everything

Stop Heisenberg Abuse!
Three Outrageous Misappropriations
Of Quantum Physics

(Originally Published in *Skeptical Inquirer*, May/June 2014)

We have been living in a quantum world for over a century now, and in that time quantum mechanics has grown from a field hesitantly understood by a handful of men into a full-fledged intellectual industry. Unfortunately, where ubiquity treads, misrepresentation soon follows, and no branch of science this side of evolutionary theory has suffered more distortion from popularization than quantum theory. Trendy parapsychologists, academic relativists, and even the Dalai Lama have all taken their turn at robbing modern physics of a few well-sounding phrases and stretching them far beyond their original scope in order to add *scientific* weight to various pet theories.

It's time to set the record straight on the most egregious of these abuses, a task which is rendered more difficult by those well-meaning physics writers who try to make quantum mechanics sexier for the casual reader. As a physics teacher myself, I've been guilty of this more than once in the classroom. "Quantum physics is, like, anarchy, man. No rules! Down with Newton!" pretty well sums the trend up. But this puts the kaboom in the wrong place – quantum mechanics *is* revolutionary and exciting and breathtaking, but only after a lot of painstaking mathematics has been worked through, and a lot of Rules Followed. It's in the disregarding of those rules that miscarriages like the three following Big Lies come into being.

Lie One: "Quantum Physics says that mind determines reality, and therefore that Buddhism is right."

The Argument: Take an electron and put it in the center of a box. Now replicate that set-up a hundred times. If you were to perform a position measurement on the particle after one second in each box, what you would most likely get is a hundred different results. Not because the particle is randomly veering about like a little billiard ball, but because the act of measurement imposes a position upon what was previously a complex object of indeterminate location. The measurement created the position. And so, because observation changed the nature of the system, reality is fundamentally a construct of observation, and our minds, which we use to observe the world, are thus the creators of reality. As such, our true minds must not be part of physical reality themselves, but rather must be objects in a higher realm of existence, a realization which drags with it the whole corpus of Buddhist   principles.

Why It's Wrong: Oh so many reasons. The cardinal sin, however, is that of conflating well defined scientific terms with loosely understood popular ones.   So, "measurement" becomes "observation" becomes "thought" becomes "mind" in a chain of ever-decaying precision that admits a correspondingly ever-widening array of wishful thinking to be passed off as science.

   This is what we know: If you give me a particle and describe its environment carefully, I can craft a mathematical object, called a wave function, for you. By manipulating it, you can tell how likely it will be for a certain measurement to yield a certain result. If you make a position measurement, the wave function can be used to tell you the probability of finding your particle at, say, location $x=4$ at time $t=3$.

   What a measurement does is collapse the often ludicrously complicated wave pattern of a particle to a spike centered on one of the possible values allowed by the wave function. So, your measurement can't result in just *any* answer. It's like having a hundred pieces of paper, each with an even number on it, dropped into a hat. When you reach in, you're going to pick out an even number. No matter how hard you think about it, you'll never pull out an odd, and you will never be one hundred percent sure what the next number you are going to pull will be (unless they're all the same number, in which case you're sort of extraneous to the whole process, aren't you?).

A measurement just spins a weighted wheel of pre-determined allowed values, and spits out one of them. For the experimenter, the experience is more akin to reading a ticker-tape produced by a deranged monkey typist than "willfully creating reality."

But that's not the worst of it, because the argument totally ignores the rather titanic issue of scale. Put simply, quantum effects stop being observable when the particles involved rise above a certain size. It's actually a fun calculation, and one of the few in quantum mechanics you can do without a couple years' worth of calculus, differential equations, and linear algebra in your hip pocket. Quantum effects are typically observed when a particle's wavelength is bigger than the size of the system the particle lives in. Temperature also plays a role, and the colder it is, the more quantum effects tend to be relevant. This is all wrapped up in the formula

$$\lambda = \frac{h}{\sqrt{3mk_BT}}$$

where λ is the particle's wavelength, h is Planck's constant, k_B is Boltzmann's constant, m is the mass of your particle, and T is the temperature of the system. For an electron, zooming around a bar of aluminum, the size of the system is about 4.05×10^{-10} meters (the distance between aluminum atoms). At a room temperature of 298 Kelvins, we get $\lambda = 6.25 \times 10^{-9}$ meters for the electron, and so, indeed, electrons behave in a "quantum" manner under normal circumstances, and therefore our measurements will collapse their observable quantities down in a way consistent with the wave equation's probabilistic predictions.

However, for one of the aluminum nuclei in this system, with a mass millions of times greater than that of the electron, quantum effects don't manifest until the temperature drops to .001 K, i.e. a thousandth of a Kelvin above *absolute zero*. Experiments like this are being done, using lasers to drop the energy, and therefore temperature, of particles down to the level where quantum effects are observable even on the molecular level. However, when it comes to day-to-day, dude-in-his-room-meditating, existence, we're really talking only about particles around the mass of an electron exhibiting anything like the finickiness towards measurement that we come to expect from quantum mechanics.

Measurements do impact systems, and the mechanism behind that impact is still incompletely understood. And yet, the impact of a measurement is far less dramatic than what Quantum Buddhism would have us believe. Its "reality-creating" aspect is only in evidence for sub-atomic particles (or extremely cold small atoms), and even then it isn't so much creating reality as selecting one of several pre-determined possible states. And none of it has anything to do with consciousness or mind or any other human attribute that sounds kinda sorta like "measurement."

At best we can say, "Measurements randomly select values." But that is a far cry from "Mind creates reality" indeed.

Lie Two: "Quantum Entanglement Means that Precognition and Telekinesis Probably Exist."

The Argument: In the phenomenon of quantum entanglement, pairs of particles are seemingly able to transmit information to each other faster than the speed of light. The classic example is that of a decaying pi meson particle breaking up into an electron and a positron. The spin of the original meson was zero and, in order to conserve angular momentum, that must be the sum of the resulting particles' spins as well. What we have found is that, no matter how far away the two particles are, when I measure the spin of, say, the electron, the spin of the other particle is simultaneously fixed as well. So, if the electron is spin up, the positron will be spin down. Before the measurement, the electron had no definite spin

197

(remember, the act of measurement selects the value that actually manifests in reality), but the instant that it is measured and a spin sign is obtained, somehow the other particle "senses" it and changes itself accordingly to preserve angular momentum.

Based on this finding, then, certain popular writers in the parapsychological community have theorized that it is the scientific mechanism behind precognitive abilities. The reason that one person can sense things about a person thousands of miles away, they explain, is that his state and that of the target human are entangled, allowing for faster-than-light communication between the two. And, if information can travel faster than the speed of light, then there exist frames of reference where that information is actually traveling backwards in time, so our psychic is not only being influenced by that distant target, but by the *future* of that distant person. If entangled particles can act at a distance upon each other, why can't people entangle themselves with each other and so determine things about each other's states and futures?

Further, if a measurement on one particle changes the state of a far-distant particle instantaneously, then I should be able, by manipulating the parts of my mind entangled with an outside object, to exert an influence on it, and therefore affect it with only the power of thought, which leads to telekinesis, remote mind control, and various other staples of comic books that are picking up a steady following as areas of scientific pursuit.

But Don't Order Your X-Man Uniform Just Yet :

Again, this is taking an interesting phenomenon and twisting it into an unrecognizable heap of an idea. Quantum entanglement is the guardian of conserved quantities and the Uncertainty Principle. It ensures that the constraints on particles associated at one point in time are enforced when those particles become separated, no matter how vast that separation grows. But this only applies to constraints dealing with conserved quantities of the original system, like angular momentum. When two particles get entangled, they share a superpositional state between them which collapses jointly and instantaneously upon measurement into values that preserve the original quantity being measured.

This is a decidedly mathematical beast which quickly devolves into nonsense when taken from its native habitat. What precisely is the superpositional state into which two minds become locked? What is the mechanism of measurement that causes the collapse of one of the two people into a definite state? And precisely what is the thing being conserved, anyway? Pressed on these points, most parapsychologists will revert to allegory, and though the conversation grows increasingly lovely and whimsical as a result, it is also manifestly less sensible.

Entanglement is beautiful enough as it is without tarting it up in the freakish rouges of pop parapsychology. It is an effect which resoundingly preserves the strictest of quantum dictates about uncertainty by preventing us from doing two different measurements on two once-combined particles and using those measurements to learn more than we're allowed about the original system. Not only that, but it keeps some of our most basic quantities conserved in a manner that classical mechanics would not have permitted. Within the realm of these quantities and responsibilities, it can do incredible things (take a look at Walmsley's phononic diamond experiment to see a really clever application of entanglement on a macroscopic scale: link: [http://www.nature.com/news/entangled-diamonds-vibrate-together-1.9532]). Step outside of that realm, however, and the situation immediately devolves to little more than metaphorical flailing that only makes sense if you strip entanglement of its conservative role, which is to say, if you gut it utterly of its central operating principle.

Lie Three: "Heisenberg's Uncertainty Principle means that science has failed in its fundamental goal of explaining reality, and we should therefore open ourselves up to alternative reality-explaining language games, such as are offered by religion."

The Argument: Three hundred years ago, the phenomenal results of Newton's calculus-based explanation of the natural world caused people to rush too eagerly into the arms of mathematical science as the vehicle that would unveil the universe's mysteries. They overconfidently asserted that everything could be known through the tools of scientific investigation. In the 1920s, Werner Heisenberg brought that whole structure crumbling down via his Uncertainty Principle. Science, far from the flawless edifice it considered itself, is in fact filled with vast yawning gaps impenetrable by experiment, no matter how clever the experimenter, and so it has reached the limit of its explanatory powers. Therefore, it is time for other, less mathematical, perhaps more holistic or spiritual, investigatory processes to take their turn in the spotlight.

Celebration Premature :

What Heisenberg's Uncertainty Principle decidedly does not say is that chaos reigns in the physics kingdom. It is actually a relatively benign, but incredibly powerful, statement about what happens when two quantities don't play well together. It's worth writing it in its most general form to get a full sense of its meaning, rather than the usual position-momentum form that looks nicer but that only tells the dark side of the story:

$$\sigma_A^2 \sigma_B^2 \geq \left(\frac{1}{2i} \langle [\hat{A}, \hat{B}] \rangle \right)^2$$

What this says is that if I have two quantities I want to measure, A and B, each limits the certainty of the other's measurement in a way determined by $[\hat{A}, \hat{B}]$. This is the "commutator" of $\hat{A}$ and $\hat{B}$, and tells us how well these two quantities commute with each other, or in other words what the difference is between $\hat{A}\hat{B}$ and $\hat{B}\hat{A}$ (recall that, in normal mathematics, multiplication is *always* commutative – it doesn't matter what order I multiply 2 and 3 in, I'll always get 6. That's not always the case with the mathematical operations involved in quantum measurements).

What popular accounts of the Uncertainty Principle tend to leave out is that there are *plenty* of measurable quantities that work together just fine, for which $\hat{A}\hat{B}$ and $\hat{B}\hat{A}$ are exactly the same. The measurement that determines total energy, and that which determines the magnitude of angular momentum, for example, commute perfectly with each other, so $[\hat{A},\hat{B}] = 0$, and measuring one has no impact on the other.

There are, however, quantities that don't work so chummily, measurements of which get in each other's way unavoidably. Position and Momentum are the classic examples, though more irresponsible mischief has been wrought from the fact that Energy and System Change Time form another such pair. Here it's true that, if I want to take infinitely precise measurements of both members of a pair, I'll be in for nothing but frustration. Collapsing the position spike down to a fine and prominent peak will of necessity mess with my ability to measure the wavelength of the particle and therefore its momentum, and if I somehow do make a new measurement that figures out the wavelength, it will so change the particle's wave pattern that the original position measurement no longer applies.

Frustrating, yes, and to a generation of existentialists who found common ground with their own concerns in the word "uncertainty," much was made of it. Nearly a century later, we have generally overcome that initial philosophy-brokered Sky Is Falling sensationalism, and can take the inequality for what it is. It is an expression that allows us to know the upper limit on how badly two quantities will mess with each other's measurement. Sometimes the answer is "Not at all" and sometimes the answer is "A bit." Either way, quantum experimentalists needn't ready themselves to hand over the keys of the kingdom just yet. Ironically, and much to the chagrin of scientific detractors, the mathematical consequences of the Uncertainty Principle have allowed us deeper and more precise insights into the nature of reality than were ever dreamt of under the Newtonian model. It is not a sign that experimental physics has reached the limits of its efficacy – quite to the contrary it is a century-old testament to our continually refined sense of how the observable quantities of our universe work together.

I adore quantum physics, and welcome anybody who responsibly takes the task in hand of explaining its integral laden insights for students and the general public. It was one such book, John Gribbin's *In Search of Schrödinger's Cat*, which fell into my hands in seventh grade and set me on the road to a career as a math and science teacher. (Looking at my old copy now, there are a few things that make me cringe, but I imagine they've been corrected in the three decades since its first printing. Really, though, if you have the mathematical chops David Griffith's *Introduction to Quantum Mechanics* is the way to go.)

I can take some sensationalism in the name of grabbing the attention of students long enough to sedulously expose them to some beautiful ideas. What I can't stand is misappropriating a handful of sexy-sounding terms and then applying them metaphorically to add scientific heft to one's particular intellectual fetish. But authors (and Dalai Lamas) will continue to do so until they find themselves routinely exposed for their imprecision. I've provided the briefest sketch of some of the abuses and their worst faults, but for every one I listed there are ten left unmentioned. It is a seemingly endless battle against a lineup of feckless opportunists who never seem to diminish in number, but I figure, electrons have done a lot for us, why not return the favor?

Teasing Is from Ought:
The Four Great Myths of Traditional Chinese Medicine

(Previously Unpublished)

Few phrases set the medical community into such fits of callisthenic posturing as "Traditional Chinese Medicine." As acupuncture and alternative pharmacology work their way into the Western health care system, they are greeted variously as the saviors of a monolithic medical structure gone mad and as reckless wastes of resources. The debate is only intensified by the defensive bordering on adversarial mythos with which TCM's advocates have draped its practices and beliefs. This mythology has worked its way so deeply into the popular subconscious that an honest look at the four pillars of Chinese Medicine's machinery of self-rationalization is more in order than ever. These are:

1. *There is such a thing as Traditional Chinese Medicine.*

One of the remarkable things about the history of Chinese medicine is its ability to create a semi-working synthesis from wildly contradictory theories about the nature of man and illness. The use of demon-commanding amulets existed side by side with chi-manipulating acupuncture and exotic like-conquers-like pharmacology, all ruled by a grand set of cobbled together theoretical constructs none of which could QUITE agree on how all of these bits and pieces of inherited wisdom tied together.

Chinese Medicine, viewed as a historical whole, is therefore a glorious mess of fascinating, thrillingly inventive guesses that, once posited, tended to stick around. The Traditional Chinese Medicine that is touted nowadays bears no resemblance to this living historical creature. Rather, it is a cherry-picked amalgam of the most ideologically sound bits of tradition that was produced in the 1960s when China wanted to free itself of *bourgeois* Western science. The more embarrassing parts of the medicinal firmament (like curing an illness by writing a fake cease and desist note from the offending demon's celestial boss) were quietly escorted out the back door, as were some of the more curious rationales behind the most popular (and proletariat-friendly) procedures, resulting in an expurgated and often foundation-poor but somehow folksy structure that found favor with Westerners impatient with the sometimes plodding and deliberate pace of the Western scientific method.

The myth that this sanitized version of Chinese medical practice represented the essential core of the last three millennia of development spawned three more fables in its wake that are repeated more or less uncritically by the $60 billion TCM industry and a public that has grown accustomed to post-modernism's relentless and until recently largely monodimensional war on scientific thinking.

2. *Chinese Medicine treats the whole body.   Western Medicine only cares about fixing the cells and organs that seem the most   endangered.*

This is perhaps the most persistent myth about the relative merits of Chinese versus Western Medicine. On the surface, it seems entirely plausible. Take the writings of cellular pathologist Rudolph Virchow and put them next to the elaborate system of interconnected bodily influences that Chinese medicine has crafted over the millennia, and it's hard not to say that they are aiming at rather different things. But, before we throw in the towel, a brief look at what this holism consists of couldn't hurt.

It begins with a man by the name of Tsou Yen (350-270 BCE) who hypothesized that all natural phenomena belong to one of five classifications: metal, wood, water, fire, and soil. Each has an element that it dominates and that it is dominated by. Metal can chop wood, but can be melted by fire. Water puts out fire, but can be held back by soil. Now, add to that the experience of urbanization that China underwent beginning in the Chou Dynasty and you have the intellectual and structural underpinnings for the medicine of Systematic Correspondence outlined by Paul Unschuld in his still towering *Medicine in China: A History of Ideas.*

The reasoning goes like this: for a city to run, it needs resources brought in from the countryside. If the city uses up too many resources or if the country underproduces, the entire nation can be thrown out of balance. This governmental realization revolutionized Chinese Medicine. "What if the body's like that too?" became the question that ignited two thousand years of theoretical speculation about the body entirely unfettered by a curiosity to empirically discover what was actually *in* the body. If there are five elements in the world, and civilization, which is the mirror of man, is comprised of producers and receivers connected by roads, well then logically there must be five primary storage depot organs in the body and five corresponding organs into which they feed, all connected by resource-moving channels.

The *tsang*, or depots, included the kidneys (water), heart (fire), lungs (metal), liver (wood), and spleen (soil). This is where the appearance of holism makes its sheepish entrance. For, if the body is struck by a water-type illness, it will affect the kidneys first, and then, if unchecked, will spread to the heart, because water beats fire, and thence to the lungs, because fire beats metal. So, a physician faced with a client complaining of lung trouble is obligated to determine whether the illness is primary, born of a metal-affecting disease, or whether it communicated itself along the pathway of elements to eventually settle in the lungs, in which case treating the primary carrier would be the more effective treatment. No organ is an island.

Acupuncture spun itself easily off of this system, for if the illnesses of the body are the results of a maldistribution of resources between organ depots and consumers, then the fault might not be with the organs at all, but with a blockage of the roads between them. Acupuncture, tapping into a long-standing tradition of using sharpened pieces of metal to clear away demonological forces, rose to fill the allegorical need and, between its actual but limited medical usefulness and its extreme theoretical convenience, found a home for itself that it continues to enjoy.

Even pharmacology incorporated itself into this system. Each herb's color, flavor, and heat properties were taken as indicating which of the five elements it belonged to, and therefore which organ it would travel to in the body. A bitter tasting, "cool" medicine was considered to be Metal-type and would therefore go either to the lung depot or the associated metal consumer, the large intestine. And if, in actuality, such a drug influenced the heart and did nothing at all to the lungs or large intestine, well, maybe there was just a little bit of sweet in there after all, just too subtle to detect, and so inconsistencies between theory and experience could always be papered over.

The calendar also felt the brunt of correspondence theory, each year and day being divided into periods of elemental disposition that dictated when different types of operations could be most propitiously performed.

I've spent a fair amount of time going into this correspondence thinking because, viewed from our side of history, the structure seems so utterly thorough and universal that it is hard not to find it somewhat breathtaking. What medicine you take, when you take it, what systems it spreads through, what influences it's capable of combating – all of this is folded into one densely inter-related system. There is a tempting appearance of completeness that the West's focus on things like fatty membranes or targeted chemotherapy quite consciously avoids competing with.

So, yes, it's holistic, but it's a holism built on whimsical impatience. In its giddy rush to systemization, TCM sprang somewhat too quickly over its assumptions that the universe is made of five things, that the spleen is *clearly* the soiliest organ, or that white-colored medicine necessarily rushes towards the lungs. A few leading lights of Chinese history realized that something fishy was going on here. As the first century intellectual Wang Ch'ung pointed out, "*Ssu* corresponds with the serpent and fire, *shen* with the monkey and metal. If fire really conquers metal, why do serpents not eat monkeys?" Why indeed.

The statement, "We are going to treat the Total You, and not just your disease," which sounds very comforting and trendy, has as its background and support, then, a shadowy notion of science by allegory that is anything but assuring. Given the choice between a system that is dedicated to working slowly but surely from small, perhaps unexciting cellular and organ-based knowns up to system-wide unknowns, and one which leapt immediately to systemic explanations but didn't feel compelled to check its foundational statements, I know that I'm going to opt for the one where the monkey wins.

2.   *Chinese Medicine works with the body's natural defenses, Western Medicine merely attacks symptoms.*

Sounds really good, right? It appeals to that, "I'll use my WILLPOWER to cure myself of this flu, instead of going to these dang doctors" mentality that we all have tucked away somewhere deep inside. Unfortunately, to genuinely help augment the body's natural defenses, you need to do something to ascertain what those defenses are beyond the lovely but fanciful flights of fancy we saw above.

There's a classic story in the history of Chinese medicine, told by Wang Qing-ren (1768-1831). He was a doctor who found himself, in 1798, smack in the middle of an epidemic in Luanzhou prefecture. He tells the story in *Yi Lin Gai Cuo*:

"At that time, infectious scourge papules killed eight or nine out of every ten children. Poor families used substitution mats to wrap and bury the dead. Substitution mats are mats which replace coffins. It was the local custom to bury shallowly, with the intention that the dogs would eat the bodies. This would have the benefit of a live birth of the next child. Because of this, every day in each potter's field, there were over 100 children with torn abdomens exposing their viscera... Every day, I went to the potter's fields to closely examine the exposed viscera of the children.... I started to realize that the viscera and bowel pictures drawn in medical books were completely different from [those] of these people."

The taboo against dissection in China was even more stringent than that European doctors faced in medieval times, so to follow up on the observations he was able to make during the epidemic, Wang was forced to haunt whatever public executions happened to come his way. For three decades he collected these glimpses into the human body, finally releasing his results the year before he died.

Nowhere is the gap between what Chinese medicine thought it was doing to augment the body's defenses and what was actually going on greater than in his findings about the so-called Triple Burner. This was an organ hypothesized into existence to fill a blank slot in the elemental correspondence system and also to complete the allegory between nation and body by providing an organ equivalent to a nation's metalworking industry. It's one of those things that needs to exist in order for the math to come out right, only nobody could quite agree on where it was. Wang searched and searched, his ultimate conclusion being the revolutionarily unequivocal statement that, "I will not discuss the triple burner. There is no such thing."

Augmenting the body's natural defenses is a fine, fine sentiment. Western medicine does it all the time, in spite of popular claims to the contrary. The vast machinery of our global immunization program is nothing if not a massive effort to help bodies protect themselves. It is an effort rooted in a philosophy that Is trumps Ought. Sometimes the body possesses elegant systems to maintain its health, and in those cases Western medicine works with those systems. But sometimes it does not, and however confidence-building it is to offer cures based on augmenting defensive capacities that aren't there, it is ultimately irresponsible. We might sacrifice some of the poetry of man containing all of the cures of the universe within his person, but what we gain is the ability to pursue remedies beyond ideology, and that opening of the field of medical potential is certainly worth it.

4. *Chinese Medicine is qualitative, Western medicine is quantitative.*

The classic example of this is pulse-taking, where the multi-faceted and intricate Chinese technique is weighed against the binary, (quite literally for the past century or so) robotic approach of the West. Shigehisa Kuriyama tackled these differences interestingly in his 2002 *The Expressiveness of the Body and the Divergence of Greek and Chinese Medicine.* He points out how the Chinese would take the pulse at several different places along the wrist, and at several different depths, recording not so much the number of pulses per second, but the quality of those pulses – are they Rolling or Halting or Mouselike? The sheer diversity of descriptions, and some practitioners claimed the ability to delineate between dozens of different rhythmic patterns, Kuriyama takes as indicative of a desire to approach each patient's unique bodily fluctuations on their own terms rather than forcing them into a pre-determined system of mathematized categorization.

The Greeks and their European successors, however, were philosophically predisposed to reducing problems to their fundamental parts, and so took up an interest in anatomy. That interest revealed to them the mechanism of the pulse, a knowledge which eliminated several different possible modes of interpretation, including several found in Chinese practice. They saw a transmission of blood that flowed in a manner regularly synchronized to the beating heart, and concluded that what pulse-taking ultimately reveals is the state of the cardiac system (however imperfectly realized that system's details remained for some centuries to come). What they found set the boundaries of their theorizing in a way that Kuriyama finds limiting and unpoetic, a symptom of the West's refusal to feel things differently than they've analyzed them.

For Kuriyama, the Chinese descriptive approach and the West's pulse measuring are part of two fundamentally different ways of expressing the sense of touch culturally, one direct and person to person, the other mediated by numbers and mechanism.

But again we run into the same problem as before – Chinese pulse theory is based in element theory, that each measuring site corresponds to an organ and each type of pulse corresponds to an element. Pushing down by a distance of 9 beans tells you about the spleen, for example, and anything but a "relaxed" pulse there is symptomatic of something wrong. So, the Chinese practitioner isn't really qualitatively feeling the patient any more than a blood pressure cuff does – he is merely fitting a series of measurements into a grid that he thinks tells him what is wrong where, and that grid is beholden to a system of theoretical metaphors the foundational weakness of which we've already discussed.

The Five Element analysis of pulse in the Chinese system is therefore every bit as binary as the Western system – it doesn't take *better* measurements, it just takes *more* of them, and then proceeds to contaminate the results with theoretical baggage. It's a rigid and heavily circumscribed method masquerading as a subjective and free one, with roots not in different cultures of touch, but different expectations for what counts as a properly founded statement.

Of course, Western Medicine has not always lived up to its ideals. There were entire centuries when it let itself believe certain medical facts had been established scientifically when they had only been deduced theoretically, and the results were every bit as fanciful as the most egregious over-extensions of the Five Phases system of correspondence. But those lapses were overcome as we finally accepted that a sober accumulation of dearly bought details would ultimately produce results unavailable to medical systems that started from universal notions of what the body ought to be like and worked backwards towards what they are like. The four myths of Traditional Chinese Medicine are artfully formed to appeal to our natural impatience and inflated sense of self, but they obscure more than they elucidate, and until they are put aside in favor of more sober statements of self-evaluation, it will be impossible to openly examine just what the Chinese-Western medical synthesis could look like.

The Mammal Plan and the Good News About Atheism

(Originally published in *Secular World Magazine*, Jan/Mar 2013)

Sometimes, I envy priests. Every Sunday, they get to mount the pulpit and tell people things they manifestly want to hear: "The most powerful being in the universe is deeply invested in your life and can't wait to be consulted about everything you do and think. Not only that, but after you die, all the people who were mean to you are going to be tortured forever while you eat cotton candy with Jesus and ride the London Eye with Thomas Aquinas!"

As an atheist, I tend to deal in sober truths that precisely nobody wants to hear: "You are a mortal, though highly interesting, bag of chemicals lacking a soul or even the faintest glimmer of free will!"

Often, come to think of it, I envy priests.

But then I remember that deep within the grim facts of an atheistic worldview there is a piece of news so foundational and freeing that it makes everything worth it: Bags of chemicals we may be, but we are bags with A Plan.

Before religion, before language, before opposable thumbs, there was an idea, the greatest idea since a couple of single celled eukaryotes a billion years back decided to mix up their genes and see what would happen. That idea can be summed up in the motto: Learning Over Instinct. Whereas, say, a hagfish is born quite alone, knowing everything it needs to know to go about its hagfishy existence, a mammal baby requires quite a bit of care before it figures out how to make its way in the world. And this makes all the difference.

A mammal parent can't just lay an egg in a hole somewhere and head back out to adventure. Her children are pudgy, squishy balls of fluff that would traipse gleefully into the mouth of anything with shiny teeth given half the chance (if you have toddlers and a knife-bearing drawer somewhere in the house you know this for a fact). Nature fixes this problem by giving us mammals massive doses of happiness-inducing neurochemicals whenever we see our offspring, or indeed any young, helpless critter of our species. *Our* brains won't let us leave them, and that gives the fuzzball a chance to develop *its* brain in ways that respond to the environment more subtly than a hagfish could dream of.

(If hagfish dream - which for purely aesthetic reasons I almost certainly hope they don't.)

Humans took this idea and ran with it. It's hard to find any aspect of our development and behavior that isn't somehow tied to optimizing our Learning Over Instinct strategy. We take forever to be even remotely self-sufficient so that we have as much time as possible to figure out our unique approach to the world. We don't have many children to give each the full measure of our instructional abilities. We gather in groups to keep watch over each other's genetic investments. And we have developed well-nigh uncountable courting rituals to make sure that we are getting the best reproductive deal possible.

All of which is great, and all of which came before anybody stopped to say, "Hey, here's my idea for where thunder comes from." The Plan gives us the boundless reward of watching children grow, the instinct to lean upon each other, the hunger to keep finding out more about how things work, and the intricate potpourri of emotion that is romance and sex. And for none of it do we have the convulsions of theology to thank. It turns out that the stuff we really enjoy the most about life was there long before the gods lumbered on the stage of biological history, and will continue long after they are gone.

213

For the atheist who is somewhat troubled by the often dreary conclusions that rigorous atheism leads to, then, here are some genuinely good bits of news, courtesy of The Plan we've been following since the beginning of our pre-history:

1. Love Whoever You Want

The Plan doesn't need everybody to reproduce always. Yes, perpetuation of the genetic pool is important, but perpetuation is bound with protection as we mammals have worked it out. That means that, as long as you're helping bring people together and forging bonds of trust and dependence, you're doing your part just fine. It is the great misinterpretation of the biological atheist tradition that it is obsessed with everybody performing to their meiotic utmost all the time. Quite the contrary - reproduction is great, but The Plan requires a massive amount of scaffolding to support it, and everybody who contributes to that, by working or teaching or just serving as an example of How To Be Happy, is just as integral to the process as anybody else. And you can do that no matter whom you marry (or even if you don't marry anybody at all!)

2. Atheists have as much capacity for morality as anybody else.

This is the big one. People don't trust atheists. They don't think we can be moral. Even atheists have trouble trusting other atheists sometimes. But if morality consists in subsuming personal desire for the good of the whole, then this is something that, again, predates religion. It's something we inherited as part of the grand package of Learning Over Instinct. When we needed to sleep in the Paleolithic past, somebody else was there to stand guard, and when he needed to sleep, we relieved him. We did great things for each other before anybody bribed us with Heaven or threatened us with Hell, and we'll continue to do great things for each other long after those charming institutions are gone. Whether they call it Christian charity, patriotic duty, or just being a good neighbor, people have always found ways to be helpful to their fellow humans, because that's been part of The Plan since before there were humans to help. People are not good because of Christianity, but rather Christianity has achieved a sliver of tolerability because it has had good people in it, and good people will always find ways to be good, no matter what they believe about infant baptism or the proper duties of bishoprics.

3. Go ahead, masturbate furiously!

We don't have many offspring, so we need to make sure that we're bringing our best stuff to each coupling. As Robin Baker and Mark Bellis point out in their research, masturbating every couple of days helps we men-folk types get rid of old and lethargic sperm and clears the way for healthy, robust chaps to take their place, ensuring better chances at reproductive success. We are designed to do it, there's a purpose behind it, and it gives us something to do during commercials. Christianity, which had to be fought tooth and nail just to allow something as innocuous as traditional marriage to intrude on its ascetic God-and-God-Alone ideal, has expended oodles and gobs of resources just to keep hands off penises. But we, as atheists, can ignore all of that and get back to our second-favorite pastime.

4. There Aren't Bad Questions

As mammals, but especially as humans, we live and die on what we know about the world around us. Prudery, propriety, and superstition all place neat fences around what we are allowed to know about ourselves and our environment, and as such work against the very thing that has kept us so uniquely successful. How many children have clammed up for their entire academic career after a teacher informed them that "Such things aren't talked about in school!" or a priest that, "These questions are unnatural and have to be buried deep down inside of you so that they never come back." The good news about atheism is that all of those questions are back on the table - millennia worth of curiosity that could not be uttered are suddenly before us again, and there's not a thing to keep us as atheists from rummaging gleefully through it like children in an app store.

Eventually, of course, religion came along and threw itself headlong into a war with this approach to life, and for thousands of years it was successful in replacing the life of curiosity and interdependence with one of shame and hierarchy. Then, taking a page from the Chinese Emperor Qin Shi Huang, who in 213 BC set about burning every book in the Empire that so much as mentioned any government existing before his dynasty, religion rewrote its own history. It erased humanity's long era of living well and morally on its own, and claimed itself as the founder of man's moral and purposeful existence. It recast freethinkers and atheists as the newcomers, foisting onto them thereby not only the burden of proof in debate, but the burden of conscience in trying to take away something that, they claimed, made people happy and good. "It's your job to prove that God doesn't exist, not ours to prove that he does," went the standard refrain. It was a neat rhetorical trick for many a century, but like sawing a woman in half, now that we've seen how it was done, it's just not quite as impressive any more.

The era of religion as man's foundation is rapidly receding. Being an atheist allows us to practice humanity in its most fundamental form, to help others and ourselves unhindered by the twisting logic of abstract otherworldly reward or punishment. It may have taken us thousands of years, but we are finally back in synch with The Plan, and our best days are ahead of us once again.

Humans Are Great:
The Popcorn Function

(Originally Published at *The Twilight of Nearly Everything*)

Mathematics is the summit of everything I find wonderful about mankind. It requires the most rigorous thinking of which we are capable married to an unflinching creativity, astounding sense of space and movement, and a poetic regard for the pregnancy of words. Technically, I suppose that's a marriage on the polygamous side, but I'm all for that too. In any case, once you get past the decade-long tutorial, learning the names and rules for all the different tools, you get to start having fun trying to Break Math. Seeing mathematicians hot on the hunt for something that will tear down a millennia-long assumption is really quite beautiful, and another example of humans just being great.

One of my favorite examples of Math Gone Mad is called (among other less whimsical names) the Popcorn Function. It goes like this:

$$F(x) = \{ \; 1/q \text{ if } x \text{ is a rational number of the form } p/q.$$
$$0 \text{ if } x \text{ is irrational. } \}$$

And here is a snapshot of a part of it.

It's popularly called the popcorn function because all of the rational x's pop up to one over their denominator, while all of the irrationals stay stuck on the x-axis. Now, think back to your high school Pre-Calculus or Calculus class. You might remember a working definition of continuity that says, "A graph is continuous if you don't have to lift your pencil while drawing it." Just looking at this picture, it is hard to picture something LESS continuous-seeming.

AND YET, it turns out that this function is continuous at all irrational numbers but discontinuous at all rational numbers.

That seems a rather wildly improbable statement, and yet the proof of it is delightfully uncomplicated, and in fact is something you might want to whip out at your next cocktail party while the Catan board is getting set up. It all relies on a more rigorous definition of continuity, known as the ε-δ definition. Just written out, it looks horrid:

"A function $f(x)$ is continuous at $x=a$ if, for any $\varepsilon > 0$, there exists a $\delta > 0$ such that if $|x-a| < \delta$, then $|f(x) - f(a)| < \varepsilon$."

When I introduce this to my calculus students, there is usually a fair amount of rending of clothing and gnashing of teeth, but the idea is actually very simple: "If two x values, let's say a and b, are close to each other, then f(a) and f(b) should be close to each other too." It's the pencil requirement written mathematically – to move right a little bit while drawing my curve I shouldn't have to move up or down very far.

So, to prove that something is continuous, I have to show that, for any value of epsilon (ε), no matter how small, I can find a neighborhood of x values around $x=a$ that all end up within ε of f(a). Alternately, to prove that a function is NOT continuous at $x=a$ I just need to produce a value of ε for which it is impossible to find such a neighborhood around $x=a$.

Now, I said that the Popcorn Function is continuous at every irrational number and discontinuous at every rational number. Let's start with the easy part, proving that the rationals are discontinuous. To do it, I'm going to use a smashing attribute of the number line – that the irrationals and rationals are "dense." That means that, no matter how small a step I take from a rational number, I'm going to cross infinitely many irrationals, and no matter how small a step I take from an irrational number, I'm going to cross an infinite number of rational numbers along the way. Any neighborhood, no matter how small, of any number will contain infinitely many other irrational and rational numbers. There is just as much richness to contemplate from 0 to 1 as from negative infinity to positive infinity.

So, let's say that my "a" value is rational, so $f(a) = 1/a$. I'm going to choose $1/2a$ as my ε value. Now, no matter what value of delta I choose, there are going to be infinitely many irrational x-values within that neighborhood of a, all with a function value of 0. So, $|f(x)-f(a)|$ for those irrational x's will equal $1/a$, which is more than our ε value. So, not all points within any delta of a will end up within ε of f(a), so the function is not continuous at x=a if a is rational. Neat!

But we have barely begun to climb Mt. Nifty. Now, suppose a is irrational (so $f(a) = 0$), and that I choose some random, rational value for ε (if the fact that I'm limiting ε to rational numbers disturbs you, good, but if you really want to use an irrational ε, I can always find a rational one both smaller than it but still positive, and use *that* ε for the proof). Epsilon, being rational, has an integer denominator, let's call it q. So, all I need to do is find a delta neighborhood around "a" that definitely does not contain any x values with a denominator smaller than q.

And, it turns out, I can do that. Think about it. Let's say my "a" is equal to 2 point something something something. Now, between 2 and 3 there is only one reduced fraction with denominator equal to 2 (namely, 5/2), only 2 with denominator equal to 3 (7/3 and 8/3), only 2 with denominator equal to 4 (9/4, and 11/4), and so on. The point being, that no matter how big q

219

(the denominator of my original ε) is, there are only a finite number of rational values around a with a smaller denominator. Since there are only finitely many, one of them will be CLOSEST to "a". If I choose my delta just smaller than that distance, I am absolutely guaranteed that no x value within that delta neighborhood will have a denominator smaller than q, and as such, f(x) will always be less than ε, and so, at x=a, the function is continuous!!

And one more ! for good measure.

So, in spite of the fact that there are infinitely many places where this function is hopping up off the number line, it is actually, technically, continuous at every single irrational number. What's even weirder is that, and here I'm going to turn to the calculus-remembering folk for a bit, this function is actually integrable too, since its set of discontinuities, the rational numbers, is countable! *Electric Air Guitar Riff!*

Wrapped up in this one function is a large part of all my favorite stuff about math and about the humans who make it. There are some spectacularly clean definitions that have been seized upon by some wonderfully playful minds to create an object that breaks every bond of common sense. It's the same process or rules-brokered explosive creativity you see in Beethoven's Third Symphony, or the perspective tinkering of a Braque canvas, only rendered, at least for me, several orders of magnitude more exciting by virtue of being so ethereal, so elusively abstract.
It's like I always say: If you love poetry, you'll love math more. Eventually.

FURTHER READING: If you liked that function, there are tons of other such functions to be had out there. A great place to start is Bernard Gelbaum and John Olmsted's *Counterexamples in Analysis*, which is a book of nothing but dastardly clever things that seem to defy common sense. To get most of it, though, requires something of a background in Real Analysis, for which Charles Pugh's *Real Mathematical Analysis* is a great starting point that just about anybody can dive into right away!

IT CAME FROM TEICHMUELLER SPACE!
THE MATHEMATICAL ADVENTURES OF
MARYAM MIRZAKHANI

(Originally Published at *MadArtLab*, September 2014)

A square, who works as a lawyer in the two-dimensional world of Flatland, sits down with his hexagonal grandson:

Taking nine squares, each an inch every way, I had put them together so as to make one large square, with a side of three inches, and I had hence proved to my grandson that – though it was impossible to see the inside of the square – yet we might ascertain the number of square inches in a square by simply squaring the number of inches in the side: "and thus," said I, "we know that 3^2, or 9, represents the number of square inches in a square whose side is 3 inches long."

The little hexagon meditated on this a while and then said to me: "But you have been teaching me to raise numbers to the third power: I suppose 3^3 must mean something in geometry. What does it mean?" "Nothing at all," replied I, "Not at least in Geometry; for Geometry has only Two Dimensions."... My grandson, again returning to his former suggestion, exclaimed, "Well, if a Point by moving three inches, makes a Line of three inches represented by 3, and if a straight Line of three inches, moving parallel to itself, makes a Square of three inches every way, represented by 3^2; it must be that a Square of three inches every way, moving somehow parallel to itself (but I don't see how) must make Something else (but I don't see what) of three inches every way – and this must be represented by 3^3."

"Go to bed," said I.

This excerpt, from Edwin Abbott's lusciously nerdy 1884 satire *Flatland*, was written on the eve of Einstein's space-time revolution, and captures nicely the common sense anxiety of casting one's imagination beyond the space you happen to live in. Over a century later, four dimensions are the least of our mathematical worries, and the way forward is lit by our own irrepressible human hexagons – people with the knack for peering into abstract spaces and wrestling from them consistent laws. And of all our daring hexagons, few rank higher than the first woman to win the Fields Medal, Maryam Mirzakhani.

Mirzakhani is a scribbler of the first order – a kinetico-visual thinker who fills vast sheets of paper with sketches probing at the edges of math's biggest problems. Only 37, she has already solved enough of pure math's Insoluble Enigmas to fill two careers, and her pace shows no sign of slouching over past greatness.

Born in Tehran in 1977, Mirzakhani was from the first a courter of the unlikely. A daydreamer and bookworm, writing seemed a natural choice (and, considering the literary-artistic bents of Kovalevskaya, Carson, Mead, Friedman, and Gianotti, perhaps we can finally put to rest the old arts-sciences binarism?). Her lively talent was recognized early, and she was diverted into a school run by the National Organization for the Development of Exceptional Talent where, after a slow start, she soon became the star mathematical pupil, winning the Olympiad gold medal two consecutive years.

That led to an undergraduate degree at Sharif University, and thence graduate work at Harvard, where she produced her first mathematical masterpieces. These papers dealt with hyperbolic surfaces and moduli spaces. And that's where we get into some *MATH*.

The story of hyperbolic surfaces is, really, one of the oldest tales that math has to tell. It all begins with the Axiom That Wasn't, Euclid's 5th. From its birth, mathematicians found it an odd duck, a statement that didn't quite seem to fit with Euclid's other foundational assertions. Stated in modern terms, it simply says that, if you give me a line and a point not on the line, then there exists exactly one unique line through that point which is parallel to the original line.

And so there is, as long as the space where those objects live happens to be flat. So evident does it seem that mathematicians spent entire careers trying to bend geometry to make it fit naturally in the position that Euclid gave it. To no avail. Finally, after centuries of futzing, it was realized that one could, in fact, construct geometries where The Fifth was not true, one of which was the hyperbolic plane, most easily visualized, I think, through the version known as the Poincare half-plane, sketched rather loosely below.

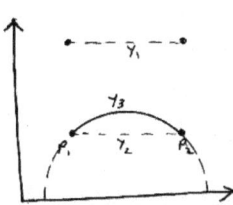

Hyperbolic Distance = $\dfrac{\text{Euclidean Distance}}{Y}$

So, the closer we get to the bottom, the greater the distance. Y_1 & Y_2 have same Euclidean distance, but Y_2 has a much greater hyperbolic distance.

Now, to get from P_1 to P_2, we don't want to take path Y_2. Since that way goes through some pretty "thick" space. The shortest distance is actually Y_3, the circular segment connecting P_1 and P_2.

In this world, all space is not created equal. It gets, in essence, thicker as you move closer to the bottom of the half-plane. My hyperbolic geometry teacher used to tell us to think of it as having the consistency of honey near the bottom axis- hard to move through- and getting progressively easier to navigate as you moved upwards. As such, the quickest way to get from one point to another directly to the right of it is NOT the straight segment that connects them (y2 in the figure) – that way you'd be running through the thickest space the whole trip. Far better to head upward, where the path is a bit easier, and then to loop your way back downward. And in fact, the path of shortest distance between these two points, called a geodesic (remember that word), lies on the semicircle through them which has its endpoints on the bottom line (y3 in the figure).

223

So, since lines in this world are semicircles, it is possible, if you give me a semicircle and a point not on it, to construct more than one semicircle through that point that does not intersect the original semicircle, and therefore is considered parallel to it. This space obeys Euclid's first four postulates, but breaks the Fifth, and introduces a slew of new geometric possibilities.

A hyperbolic *surface*, then, is a metric space (a space with a way to measure distance) where, if you take a neighborhood around any point, it is related to a neighborhood of points in the hyperbolic plane we just talked about. Such a surface contains all the craziness of the original hyperbolic plane, kicked up to the next level. These surfaces, understandably, inherit some rather interesting geometry, and it was Mirzakhani's task to tame the chaos. In particular, she wanted to break the mystery of how many simple closed geodesics of a given length a hyperbolic surface possesses.

Put more plainly, how many shortest paths of a given length are there which form a closed loop without intersecting? Let's stop and appreciate how intense that question is. It is asking for a method to determine, for an object that can't exist in real space, with geometry inherited from a brilliant non-Euclidean dodge, with geodesics ranging from the infinite to the well-behaved, how many of a given length there are going to be, which don't cross themselves, which end where they begin.

Insane. But Mirzakhani did it, and that was just part of what she accomplished as a *grad student*. From there, she has studied the world of moduli spaces, which are harder still to grasp. Oversimplifying egregiously, a moduli space is a space where each point represents some mathematical object or class of objects. Mirzakhani's research has focused on Teichmueller spaces, which are closely related to the Riemann moduli space. Basically, to get a Teichmueller space, just take a surface, let's call it X, and make *complex structures* out of sets of equivalent maps between that surface and the Euclidean plane. Doing just that lets you construct the Riemann moduli space of X, but if you add one more requirement about what it takes to call two structures equivalent, you get Teichmueller space.

In other words, a Teichmueller space is a space where each point represents a class of equivalent complex structures. That's a pretty darn abstract mental world to live in, but then to think about what happens when you put a strain on that system is something else entirely. Mirzakhani's work considered what happens as geodesics are made to flow along a Teichmueller space, discovering that the phenomenon has ergodic properties. That realization brought a whole new realm of tools to bear on the problem, and broke it elegantly from Impossible Conundrum to Solved Case.

And it doesn't end there. Work on billiard reflection with Alex Eskin resulted in a paper that opened up brand new sprawling fields of mathematical research. As ever in mathematics, work in the physical world lead to new abstract results, which themselves lead to entirely unexpected physical ramifications. Based now out of Stanford University, and with a decade and a half of tackling and solving the big problems of math behind her, there is no telling what new bizarre worlds she will unveil as her mind crisses and crosses the mathematical landscape, searching for connections where there was before only befuddlement, and in all senses being the hexagon that leads the rest of us squares to comprehend, if just tentatively, the hidden structure of the abstract world.

FURTHER READING: If you want to start getting into this area of mathematics, and have had the usual upbringing in math, a good place to start is *Topology* by Munkres. It gives you the framework for thinking about open sets, mappings, and all the good stuff you need to think about what happens as we cut and paste the edges of reality in new ways. For the hyperbolic plane, I like Saul Stahl's *The Poincare Half-Plane: A Gateway for Modern Geometry*. It develops the Euclidean stuff at a good pace before having you jump into the hyperbolic material and requires really just basic calculus and trigonometry.

Maria Sibylla Merian:
The Princess Bubblegum of 17th Century Biology

(Originally Published at *MadArtLab*, January 2014)

Biology took a while to figure itself out. For centuries, it was a mish-mash of Aristotelian sentiments and cabinets of Unnatural Curiosities whose only organizing principle was a Ripleyish sense of the weird. One of the great turning points came in 1735, with the publication of Carl Linneaus's *Systema Naturae*, a work which systematized the chaos and provided a baseline for all further biological research. Unfortunately, the rise of Linnaean taxonomy came at a cost, namely in that it all but obliterated the struggling ecosystem approach to biological study originated by one of the most fantastic figures in scientific history, Maria Sibylla Merian (1647-1717).

Merian was raised in Frankfurt which, in the middle of the 17th century, was an international center of publishing and hotbed of progressive religious and scientific ideas. Her father was a famous publisher known for immaculate illustrated volumes, and as she grew up, he taught her the secrets of his trade: how to etch copper for engravings, what natural resources made for the most vibrant pigments, and how to frame an image in its proper perspective. In short, all of the things she would need later to produce her own lush and genre-defining works of natural field history.

She was interested in insects from an early age, and felt instinctually that something was not being done justice in their representation so far. Flipping through old volumes of natural history, one can see why. What you'll find there are many gorgeous representation of animals on either blank pages or thrown randomly together into an exotic-seeming setting. Caterpillars are on one page, butterflies on another, and their natural habitat is nowhere to be found. This was the approach Linnaeus would solidify and continue – instead of thinking about the interrelationships of animals in a given ecosystem, he was interested in cataloguing structural similarities. What an insect ate didn't matter a whit next to the shape of its proboscis.

Merian's first books were a daring reversal of this trend. After painstaking field and home research, she had managed to chart the pathways of many species, and link those species with their preferred environment. The pages of her caterpillar books, then, show the typical food source and all known life stages of a given insect on the same page, providing a full sense of the species and its surroundings. It was an ecological approach two and a half centuries before Ecology was a word.

And then pietism happened. The "scientist experiences religious moment and renounces his ego-driven exploration of the universe" story happened a number of times in the religiously charged seventeenth century. The most famous example, of course, is Blaise Pascal, who was a mathematical genius whose eventual embracing of Jansenism caused him to entirely abandon scientific pursuits, his body trembling with shame every time he gave into the urge to work on an interesting problem instead of spending every last moment in prayer. But there were others, including Jan Swammerdam, perhaps the most famous entomologist in the era just before Merian, who also renounced his science as sinful in later life.

Merian's episode was less extreme. Lured by the example of the brilliant but tragic Anna-Maria van Schurman, and wanting to escape from her joyless marriage, she moved with her two daughters to live at a pietist compound run by Labadists. There, her work slowed to a trickle as she attempted to fit in with the rigorous asceticism of the community. Fortunately for us, she thought better of her decision and, after a couple of years, left the Labadists to move to the great center of European free-thought, Amsterdam.

There, some of the most influential artists were women, and scientific curiosity ran rampant. Merian's skills as a collector and illustrator of nature were respected, and she soon entered into a free and open discussion of metamorphosis and insect life with the intellectual elite of the city. It was a dizzying, mentally exciting place to be, but the local wildlife was severely limited, and most of the insects Maria saw were in the curiosity cabinets of the wealthy, far from their native environment. So, after finalizing her divorce with her husband, who had not been permitted to drag her from the Labadist collective, she sold her paintings in order to raise enough money for a grand expedition, to the jungles of South America.

This was a thing unheard of for a male scientist to do – they generally *hired* people who were heading into exotic country to collect wildlife samples and ship them back. But for a female scientist to up and decide that she was going to, on her own, at the age of 52, travel halfway across the world to slice through native jungles in search of the answers to the great mystery of how metamorphosis works was positive madness. And yet, she did it, arriving in Surinam in 1599 and staying there for two years, speaking with the native population to learn what she could of the life cycles of the specimens she found, and standing in mute awe before the explosion of life all around her.

It was (and is) the sort of place you could spend a lifetime cataloguing and still only scratch the barest surface of the teeming insect world – thousands of species of caterpillar where Europe offered perhaps a hundred, many of them only to be found in the tops of towering trees that she would order chopped down in order to investigate that hidden world above. She hoped to stay and record insect life cycles for five years, but illness brought her back to Europe after only two, but when she returned she had a treasure trove of observations unparalleled in the history of field biology.

Her field sketches and memories became the basis for one of the most ambitious volumes in the history of entomology, a massive book featuring sixty illustrated, color plates. Keep in mind this is a time when you had to hire a squad of engravers to hew each line drawing from copper, and then hand paint each individual copy of the book to render the colors. The expense was immense, but the resulting volumes set a standard for artistic merit and ecological sensibility unmatched for centuries.

Alas, it was both crescendo and coda. After she passed, later editors snuck in extra plates by other artists to boost sales, mixed up the images, and used colors not faithful to the original, so that later entomologists reading these jumbled editions took their errors as Merian's, and her reputation as a careful observer suffered a decline just as Linnaeus was achieving wonders with his system of organization that had a vastly different, and much easier to accomplish, agenda. To organize on the basis of structure required no knowledge of life cycles or environment, just a steady stream of bodies in cabinets, and Europe had far more of those than it had dedicated field biologists.

But it's hard to feel too bad for Maria Merian. In spite of an uninspiring marriage, a few years thrown away on a religious experiment, and a lot of lost time trying to wrangle funds for her publishing ventures, she lived a life more full and exciting than anybody, male or female, could have reasonably expected in seventeenth century Europe. She was born in the freest city of Germany and died in the freest of all Europe, her artistic accomplishments lauded and her intellectual rigor respected, memories of distant adventure jostling in her head with excitement about the pupae in her studio about to burst forth into perhaps never before recorded species. She was that rarest of things – a person of all talents with the opportunity to exercise them.

Like Princess Bubblegum.

We should all be so lucky.

APES IN THE GARDEN OF BOSCH:
A REVIEW OF FRANS DE WAAL'S *THE BONOBO AND THE ATHEIST*

(Originally Published in *Secular World Magazine*, April/June 2013)

As recently as fifty years ago, apes were assumed to be mechanical objects incapable of individuality, compassion, tool use, or reason. One Jane Goodall later all that changed. Her studies of chimpanzees rewrote what it meant to be human, and the brilliance of that success blotted out for some time the research of a different group of primatologists who studied our other near relative, the bonobo. Chief among these is Frans de Waal, who has made something of a life cause out of championing these primates whose advanced social behavior is so very much like our own. In *The Bonobo and the Atheist*, he tells us with wit and charm of his own experiences dealing with these animals over the decades, and brings us up to date on the most recent developments in what light the bonobos can shed on the origins of human morality.

In doing so, de Waal is carrying out a campaign against what he calls "top-down" models of morality and ethics. Rather than being handed down by God or resulting from a deliberate use of abstract reason, de Waal argues, the basics of our sense of morality are already present in primates and their emotional attachments to their community. The eventual codifying of this sense and expanding of it beyond its original borders is important, he maintains, and is a project that must be continued if humanism is to have something to offer a world turning away from religion. However, to deny the fundamental emotionality of morality, as some philosophers would have us do, is to handcuff our species to neat but biologically unfulfilling abstractions.

In story after story, de Waal strips away the illusions we have about the uniqueness of our moral sense. We see bonobos caring for the sick and elderly, adopting orphaned babies, expressing awe in the face of death, developing rules for communal use of tools, choosing to benefit others even when it harms themselves, policing infractions of the social order, teaming up to defend wronged parties, and resolving conflicts with hot bisexual ape sex rather than violence. De Waal has spent years with these animals, and when he tells these tales, he is describing friends. That sense of intimacy, of staring across the gulf of evolution and finding deep and endearing commonality with another species, makes this book one of the more beautiful reading experiences I have had in many a year.

Unfortunately, the book isn't just about bonobos and the origins of morality. As the title implies, it is also about atheism, and de Waal's treatment of the topic is lamentably as monodimensional as his treatment of primates is multi-faceted. To be fair, he admits to having grown up in a country where religious conflict was at a minimum, which allowed him to develop relatively neutral feelings about the place of religion in society, but which also prevent him from fully understanding the urgency of atheists living in, say, the southern United States. Being from California myself, where a few years ago the Mormon and Catholic churches flexed their financial muscles in an ultimately successful joint effort to prevent homosexuals from having the right to marry, I admit to not having the luxury of adopting a "Just wait and it will work itself out" approach.

What de Waal objects to really isn't atheism, but a caricature of atheism cobbled together from some of the more extreme aspects of its recent public proponents. He finds the issue of God's existence or non-existence to be "profoundly uninteresting" and conceives of atheism itself as a purely negative project undeserving of passionate adherence, equating militant atheism with "furiously sleeping." That atheism and humanism not only can work together, but must, isn't something that he considers, seeing the two as mutually exclusive approaches to life and the project of humanity. To be a public atheist is, by his portrayal, to be constantly sneering at and mocking one's religious neighbors while offering nothing substantial in return, while being a humanist is to work towards a better future by slowly integrating new sources of morality, ethics, and togetherness into society to replace religion as it falters.

Atheism is, in fact, a positive project, aimed at relieving people of the weight of monolithic authority and those who would command in its name. There are people suffering in the world because it is accepted that there are certain individuals in society who are allowed to say, "I have it on unquestionable authority that X is so." Atheism does its part for those individuals by grappling with issues of language and knowledge in an attempt to determine what precisely humans can meaningfully posit about the world around them. By broadcasting their results, atheists allow others to rise up with some confidence against the crippling Thou Shalts that they have been placed under. Once that is done, those newly freed souls may continue to march along with the broader humanist goals that de Waal so keenly desires. But they can't take that step without the groundwork in resistance that atheism has spent the last half century laying down.

In short, de Waal's project is a fine thing for a world that minimally feels the weight of religion, but it needs preparing in those large swaths of our planet where religion isn't quite the affable old fellow keen on retirement that de Waal grew up with. And that preparation work will have to be done by atheists who are willing to parse "uninteresting" issues like precisely what is meant by "god" or "salvation" and share their results. One can disagree with the tenor of the sharing, but to condemn the whole project as an uninteresting and shrill strikes me as ungenerous.

For all of that, *The Bonobo and the Atheist* is still eminently a book worth the reading. It sparkles with de Waal's love of science, primates, and humanity. If it falls short in giving atheists credit for some measure of subtlety and compassion, it is a mistake honestly made, compounded by his upbringing and a preponderance of negative media portrayals of what it is atheists do and care about. We share a common aim, "to build a better society based on natural human abilities," and there is no doubt that de Waal's work in unveiling the moral nature of primates has done its part and more in making that society possible.

THE END OF ATONEMENT:
LAW WITHOUT FREE WILL

(Originally Published in *Free Inquiry*, January 2014)

There are three things that we humans seem to really want to believe in: the existence of God, the soul, and free will. These first two constructs are being steadily eroded and it is conceivable that we shall soon see the day when soul-mongering theists are a minority. But the notion that we are meaningfully masters of our own actions is far more tenacious, and it is the rare atheist now who is willing to proclaim without reservation that Free Will Is Dead. There is an entirely practical reason for this. Whereas belief in God or the soul doesn't materially impact the structure of governance (The Electoral College is an awful idea whether or not God exists), the entire basis of human justice and law is at stake once the notion of free will starts to totter. For those of us, therefore, who do not believe in free will it is of paramount importance to put forth an image of justice that is compatible with lack of agency in order to smooth the way towards the removal of this last pillar of man's willful self-deception.

Before building a post free will notion of justice, it is reasonable to ask if we're really so sure that free will is doomed to fall. Let's start with the facts that everybody can agree on. Our genetic code is not a matter of our choice. Though there is a considerable amount of variety in which sections of the code activate and for how long during our initial development, none of that is a matter of our conscious volition. This set of genetic and epigenetic factors forms the basis of the instincts and survival reactions that we come into the world with, and there's nothing we can do about any of it.

Once born, we have a set of experiences foisted upon us in the form of native language, local community and cultural practices, and parental strategies. I was raised an English speaker in a Reagan Era small town to parents concerned with education above all else, and in none of this did I have a vote. That isn't to say that I absorbed the set of ideas around me precisely as they were given. Rather, my unchosen external experiences interacted with my unchosen neurochemical and genetic makeup to form a set of synaptic associations that are the basis of my personality.

Thus far just about anybody is willing to go. It's in the *use* of that basic personality that controversy arises. We have a choice of which actions we take and which we don't, says the free will camp. But do we really? Let's take an example. Suppose that you are walking down a street at night when you look to your left and see a stranger leaning against a wall. Whether or not you feel fear in that moment is not up to you- it is a decision made without your consent when incoming sense data is processed by your sensory thalamus and cortex and shipped to your amygdala. If the incoming signals stimulate enough AMPA receptors in the neurons of the amygdala, the fear response fires and you feel all the physical and mental symptoms of Being Afraid. If not, it doesn't.

"Well, maybe. But whatever chemical state my body puts me in, I have a range of options for how to act, and can choose one of those freely."

Let's think about that- are you free in which options are consciously available to you? For instance, presented with a stranger I might be aware of "Walk Tall And Look Tough", "Run", and "Jump Him Before He Jumps You" as action possibilities, but "Challenge Him To A Wizard Duel" doesn't come up (though perhaps it will from now on). I am not free to choose from the infinitude of possible reactions that my brain is capable of imagining - only a few crystallize in my conscious mind, ready to be chosen from. My option palette is chosen for me, as if my brain were being run by Henry Ford - "You can act however you want, as long as it's one of these."

Up to this point, the environment has pushed a situation upon me, and my brain, a product of genetics, chemistry, and past experience, has given me an emotional response (fear or the lack thereof) and a set of action options, none of which I had a real conscious hand in.

"I still have a real choice between the few action options I've been handed, though. I can freely choose to run, walk taller, or jump him."

Here I must admit there is still a good deal to be figured out, and philosophers such as Catherine Malabou have used the gaps in our knowledge to revive a post-modern notion of identity and agency based on the concept of neural plasticity. But every year those gaps get smaller. Studies by Wolfram Schultz have shown how expected reward value is coded by dopamine neurons which then have a hand in our behavioral learning, while Read Montague's work continues to demonstrate how unconscious neural efficiency pushes and determines even the most seemingly trivial of decisions. A constantly whirring chemical abacus lies within us, weighing and predicting and measuring, and in that deep calculus lies the mechanism of choice.

There is still work to be done, but just as with evolution a century ago, the data is piling up steadily on one side, reducing the possible domain of free will's activity. In previous centuries, we spoke of a self acting within a set of external and internal confines. Now, we are coming to realize that the self IS those confines. I am a grand chemical reaction tossed about on the back of the statistics of molecular combination to the day of my neuronal destruction, and that's fine.

"But, if we accept that we cannot act other than we do, how can any system of justice be possible? How can we throw a man in jail for something he had no control over, for being the unfortunate 'bag of chemical reactions' that was compelled to do something that we as a society don't like?"

It's a big question, and one so unsettling that it has driven at least one famous atheist into the arms of theism, buying back Justice at the cost of accepting God. I would argue, though, that the disavowal of agency will remove from the discussion some of the most problematic and contradictory concepts in our legal system while still allowing everyday justice to effectively proceed as before.

You have committed a crime. You fell on hard times, tried to rob a convenience store, and got caught. Bad luck. You did not choose to be born in an area where crime is perhaps more prevalent than elsewhere, did not choose the schools you attended and the influences there, and did not choose the neurochemical makeup that found the theft option compelling enough to be turned into action. And yet, here you are, on trial.

Our current conception of justice says, "You could have chosen otherwise, and you didn't. So, we shall isolate you from society so that you might be rehabilitated and serve as an example to others." A post-free-will conception of justice, while differing on the wording in many parts, would be entirely the same in effect. Our post-agency judge would say, "As you are now constituted, the extremity you found yourself in caused you to act in a way that is undesirable for the cohesion of society. You lacked an experiential basis strong enough to compel a desirable reaction, and so for the next year you will placed in a new environment which will add new experiences to your neuronal arsenal of sufficient weight to push you towards better choices in future scenarios."

What this judge recognizes is that the criminal's Internal Abacus isn't weighted in a way advantageous to society, that either from a chemical or experiential perspective, there simply wasn't enough there to push a constructive solution forward into action. Choice, retribution, atonement, revenge, accountability - these terms, within this context, are without meaning and shouldn't inform our approach towards you, the criminal. That you acted in a certain way in a certain situation tells us everything we need to know, and also what we need to do to prevent a recurrence.

Let me emphasize that this is not the "Please forgive him judge, he's just a poor child of circumstance" line of legal thinking that says that certain actions are forgivable when you take into consideration the background of the perpetrator. That conception is both too narrow and too broad. Too narrow because it assumes that only certain classes of actions from certain strata of society are forced, when in fact ALL action is forced. It presumes that everybody else has free choice in what they do, and we have seen

237

that they manifestly don't. Too broad because it brings immense and ungainly concepts like Forgiveness to bear on a problem that is much simpler than that. Strictly speaking, no action is forgivable. I can't forgive you for mugging me any more than I can forgive a rain shower for getting me wet or flowers for engaging in photosynthesis.

When we talk about forgiveness or redemption, what we are really talking about is a willingness to attempt to reprogram ourselves favorably towards a given object. "You hurt me, but I can promise to try and trust your ability to become someone who won't hurt me in the future" is about all we can offer, and then only if we have the experiential background to select that statement in the face of our own grief. But forgiveness on the order of, "It's okay, that action doesn't really count" makes no sense on the model of humanity I've been proposing. Everything counts.

"Okay, but if we leave choice out of it, how are we to tell an intentional act from an accident? What does Intent even mean since you're saying that nobody can ever really choose to do anything?"

True, we usually apportion judgment based on whether a subject *intended* harm or not. Did that salt shaker get filled with arsenic because we honestly filled it from the wrong bottle (because, apparently, we all keep bottles of arsenic around that look just like our bottles of salt...) or did we maliciously place it there? How can a judge parse the gap between accident and intention if agency is removed from humans?

Much as she does now. Given an action, she must reflect on what the deep calculus involved most likely was. With the aid of evidence and testimony, the experiential background of the defendant can be built up. From that, a judge or jury member can use her own understanding of societal practice to assess whether the accused's background and the given action are of a piece. "Can the set of chemicals, predispositions, and past experience which forms the basis of this human's action palette be sensibly shown to lead to a malicious interpretation of the given action?" isn't too far from the question that jury members ask themselves now. So again, I don't see a radical departure from current legal practice in stripping humans of their claim to free will. It's a difference of descriptive vocabulary, but that vocabulary set, in as far as it is prescriptive, is largely isomorphic to the one in current use, and so the deep structure of the system isn't in any particular danger.

It's time and past time to rise up and throw off the chimera of free will. We lose nothing by it except for words that we only ever used to inflict pain as a means of societal revenge, and gain the ability to look on with honest wonder at the operating of ourselves in the world, to be able to observe our actions of the day and say along with that fine old Fiona Apple song, "Be kind to me, or treat me mean. I'll make the most of it - I'm an Extraordinary Machine."

EMMY NOETHER SOLVES THE UNIVERSE

(Originally Published at *MadArtLab*, January 2014)

"Momentum is always conserved, except when it isn't."
In high school physics, we learn all manner of conservation laws, one at a time, when they accidentally happen to pop up, without so much as a word of explanation for WHY nature seems to care so much about these quantities. We've asked, of course, only to have our knuckles rapped for impertinence or, in our less corporal age, been referred to Google to figure it out as best we can for ourselves.

Ninety-nine years ago, a woman who was only begrudgingly allowed a university education gave us that very WHY and with it one of the most powerful tools in all of mathematical physics. Her name was Emmy Noether and she was born in Erlangen, Germany in 1882. Her father was a mathematician and she too had a marked preference for math that only grew stronger as she delved further into its open mysteries.

In nineteenth century Germany, a woman could only attend classes at a university with the express permission of each teacher. Every course that she wanted to take, she had to set aside time with the instructor and plead her case for being allowed to sit in the same classroom with the men, promising not to be a distraction and silently swallowing their regular advice to turn to more womanly subjects (Max Planck famously rejected all women applicants to his lectures out of hand ... until he met Lise Meitner).

Noether ran the gauntlet, however, with a steadfastness in the face of rank unfairness that would mark her entire career. She received her bachelor's degree equivalent in 1903 and wrote her doctoral dissertation (on bilinear invariant theory) in 1907 at the University of Göttingen.

It was *the* place to be for mathematics. David Hilbert was there. Hermann Minkowski was there. Felix Klein was there. Titanic minds who remain popularly unknown because they did their work in mathematics rather than the sexier fields of physics or chemistry, they would also be Noether's friends and champions in her battle for recognition from the University.

Noether was not only in the right place, but also studying the right field for her moment in history. She was an expert in invariant theory and group transformations, which govern how quantities change when you transform the coordinate system where they live. Newton had some assumptions about how such coordinate shifts altered measured values, assumptions which were blown apart in 1905 with Einstein's Theory of Special Relativity. In the fallout of that titanic event, mathematicians and physicists were looking for something that would link classical Newtonian conceptions of conservation with the new and strange world of relativity, and eventually with the even stranger world of quantum physics. Without such a unifying theory of conservation, physics threatened to fly apart into a chaos of special cases.

In 1915, Emmy Noether produced just such a theory, and published it in 1918 (a REAL math nerd, when asked about 1918, will get super excited and start talking about Noether's theorem and then, perhaps, as an afterthought, recall something about World War I ending that year too). And now, with your tender indulgence, I want to put on my math teacher hat for a bit and talk about that very theory, because it is truly lovely and powerful, and once you wrap your head around it, the universe just shines with snazziness.

Noether's Theorem invokes a bit of specialized vocabulary. In particular, it tells us what quantities are preserved (momentum, Energy, charge, etc) for a particular physical situation whose coordinate system undergoes a particular transformation. So, for example, if you have a falling rock, and you spin the x and y axes 90 degrees around the z axis, what measured quantities come out just the same as when you measured them in the original, unspun system? Emmy Noether's answer encompasses every conservation law that went before, and anticipated all of the ones discovered since, even those in areas of physics she couldn't have begun to imagine from the vantage point of 1915.

Consider two points in space, or two events in space-time. There are lots of ways for an object to move from one to the other, but only one that minimizes the difference between the Kinetic and Potential Energies (called the Lagrangian) for a particle making the trip. If you take that path, your KE and PE will be as balanced as possible, and we call that path "extremal". ('Cause it's EXTREEEEEEEEME... at minimizing the Lagrangian.... MAD 80s GUITAR RIFF!!)

Now, if you're on that path, and we shift the coordinate system around you (say, by rotating the x and y axes under you a bit), and the overall difference between KE and PE doesn't change, or changes only *verrrrrrrrry* slightly, then we say the motion is "invariant" under that coordinate transformation. So, if you tell me about an object undergoing a given motion, and how you want to change the coordinate system, Noether's Theorem will tell us exactly what conservation law *must* hold in that situation (given, if you're curious, by $p_\mu \varsigma^\mu - H\tau - F = $ constant).

What is phenomenal is that using this method, you can not only derive all of the conservation laws we're used to from high school physics, but a bunch of other things that you could not know from the older Euler-Lagrange equations and Hamilton Principle techniques that Noether fused in her own theorem. They explain d'Alembert's insights from a century and a half before just as easily as Feynman's ideas from three decades after her death. It was one of those grand moments in intellectual history when a shifting mass of unfathomable complexity solidified in three slick lines of text into a single over-arching theory about invariance and conservation and their role in shaping the development of the universe.

After publishing her ground-breaking work, the only material improvement Noether saw was that the university, under pressure from Einstein, Hilbert, and Klein, allowed her finally to lecture to students under her own name (until then, her classes had to be done in Hilbert's name, as women weren't allowed to lead classes). Of course, she still wasn't paid or officially recognized as a professor. In 1922, the best she got was "unofficial associate professor" and a small stipend for teaching abstract algebra, a field that she was making regular and foundational contributions to since publishing her theory.

Her life continued in this fashion, recognized by the greatest minds in physics and mathematics for her piercing insights into the theory of Lie groups and noncommutative algebras (the significance of which we are only just starting to unwrap now), but without an official position proportionate to her skills or renown. And so she marched on for eleven years, writing the laws that every abstract algebra student knows by heart, until 1933 when the Nazis came to power and she, of Jewish origin, was forced from her position. Unlike Lise Meitner, who fought to retain her place in spite of unceasing harassment at the hand of Nazi officials, Noether saw the direction of the wind and fled the country for a position at Bryn Mawr College, one that she occupied for less than two years before a failed surgery to remove an ovarian cyst ended her life at the age of 57 in 1935.

FURTHER READING:

The beauty of Noether's Theorem is almost impossible to fully appreciate until you see it at work, churning through problems in wildly separate fields of physics with the same elegant ease. My own appreciation of the Theorem's far-reaching applicability was fostered by Dwight Neuenschwander's delightful book, *Emmy Noether's Wonderful Theorem*. His buildup to the theorem itself requires really only a first year college calculus level of math fluency – if you're cool with the chain rule for partial derivatives, you're probably ready. After that, things get turned up a notch as he applies the Theorem to different fields, but he is very good at walking you through the thinking, and his insights into the historical development of invariance theory and the calculus of variations are clear and invaluable.

ATLAS Soared: Fabiola Gianotti and The Discovery of a Higgs Particle

(Originally Published at *MadArtLab*, August 2014)

In a corner of a room, tucked unostentatiously away from the notice of the raving hordes of just barely contained school children using their field trip to Berkeley's Lawrence Hall of Science to wreak havoc, there lies behind glass a hundred year old circular object no bigger than a water canteen. It's the world's first cyclotron, held together by wire and wax, and built by Ernest O Lawrence in 1930 for about $25. It is a charming relic of a time when physics experimentalists could still work profitably alone, and the ancestor of today's multi-billion dollar Large Hadron Collider, maintained and operated by a staff of thousands of scientists and engineers.

We are going to talk about *one* of the scientists who worked on *one* of the experiments performed at the LHC. She is Fabiola Gianotti, famous as the spokesperson and coordinator for the ATLAS project which, working in tandem with its competitive sibling, the Compact Muon Solenoid, announced the discovery of a Higgs particle in 2012. ATLAS alone employed three thousand physicists, with about as many on the CMS, each one of whom deserves as much attention and thanks as we can muster as a civilization, but we begin with Gianotti.

If you've been reading this series for a while, parts of her early life will sound familiar. Like Ellen Swallow and Rachel Carson, she had an early love of rambling through nature and stopping to wonder about the unique creatures her father would point out to her along the way, but, like Sofia Kovalevskaya and Margaret Mead, this curiosity was balanced by a strong attraction to artistic expression. For Gianotti, that manifested itself in the study of ancient languages, philosophy and, most importantly, music. Trained in piano performance at the Milan Conservatory, she will often end a day of physics and administrative detail by settling down to her piano at home and getting lost for a while in the elegant puzzles of the early nineteenth composers whose music integrated structure and emotion in a way that physicists and mathematicians seem to find particularly intoxicating.

It was not to piano and philosophy that Gianotti would ultimately turn for a career, however, but to physics, a field that seemed to answer the same basic questions brought up by the humanities, but in ways enticingly nuanced and fundamental. Gianotti puts the conversion down to a lecture about Einstein's explanation of the photoelectric effect. It doesn't take much imagination to guess why. In late nineteenth century experiments, it had been shown that, by shining light at a metal, you could cause the ejection of electrons but, mysteriously, and against everything people thought they knew, the intensity of the light didn't seem to matter, but the color did. Super-intense but low frequency light couldn't budge a single electron, but the faintest glimmer from a high frequency source would lead to ejection. It's a puzzle that spoke to a fundamental problem with how light was understood, and Einstein's solution, that light came in packets with energies tied to their frequency, was bold, creative, and genre-defining. How could that *not* be interesting to an intelligent person with big questions about the universe?

Gianotti earned her PhD in particle physics from the University of Milan, and at the age of 25 began her association with CERN, which at the time was coming off of its massive success in discovering the W and Z bosons. Those particles had been theorized as having a role in the weak interactions whereby protons and neutrons transform into each other, and in the transfer of momentum during particle collisions, and their discovery filled in a massive section of the Standard Model. Gianotti worked at the Large Electron Positron collider during its last years of service before it was removed from its home in 2000 to make way for the Large Hadron Collider. During those years, she conducted research into the possible existence of Supersymmetry.

That's important to talk about, because the LHC isn't just a Higgs-finding device. It also has the potential of discovering some of the high-mass supersymmetric particles that various theorists believe explain several of the remaining dilemmas in our picture of the universe. By this model, every fermion (particles that can't occupy the same place at the same time, like electrons) has an associated supersymmetric boson (particles that can occupy the same place at the same time, like photons), and vice versa. Advocates of the theory point out how some of the proposed superparticles have behavior that fits what we have been measuring about dark matter, and that, if we can probe high enough energies, we could gain insights into the realm of dark matter and therefore spark an exciting new expansion of the Standard Model.

Couple the theoretical existence of high-mass superpartners with the role of the Higgs boson as a possible mediator between standard and dark matter, and it was clear that all of Gianotti's questions about Life, the Universe, and Everything, pointed to experiments that could at last be done by the proposed Large Hadron Collider. It would be able to crash hadron streams together with enough energy to produce, if only for a moment, rare high mass particles. By the time it was shut down in 2013 for a scheduled upgrade, the LHC was colliding two 4 TeV beams, for a total output of 8 TeV, enough energy concentrated at one point to form massive particles like the Higgs (remember, mass and energy are equivalent, so if you want a big particle, you need to concentrate a lot of energy at a single location – crashing together hadron beams traveling at nearly the speed of light does just that!)

Gianotti worked initially as the physics coordinator at the ATLAS project of the LHC, a five-story tall wonder of engineering that boggles the imagination in just about every respect. One of its purposes was the discovery of Higgs particles which, even if you make them, decay in 1.56×10^{-22} seconds. So, there is no way you are possibly going to see one directly. All you can see are its products, but catching those possible products amidst the billions upon billions of other particles being shot out by all the other collisions happening requires sensory equipment of untold precision, and data mining algorithms of ruthless speed and efficiency (if you kept ALL the data produced by ATLAS, it would take mere seconds to fill up the most massive data storage centers on Earth).

It was up to the team of three thousand physicists, data experts, and engineers to solve these problems, while at the same time dealing with demands from funding governments, the public at large, and particular alarmists who wanted to shut the entire project down. And it was up to Gianotti upon becoming spokesperson and overall coordinator to balance all of those tensions while keeping the world informed about what was happening. She fielded the endless questions about whether the LHC would create black holes that would destroy the Earth, traveled to explain the work of the device to the press and government, all while still wearing the hat of an experimental physicist.

And that's precisely why I wanted her to be first in our look at the scientists of CERN, because that balance of administrative, collaborative, public relations, and scientific work is something that everybody engaged in modern physics has to confront as they move from lab drudge to full scientist. Her visible career as ATLAS spokesperson is the career of all scientists, writ large. We have a romantic notion of science as consisting of exciting moments lingering over experimental apparatuses, but the truth is actually more heroic than that. The self-sacrifice of a great mind chained to a mound of paperwork and an endless gamut of departmental meetings, when all it wants to do is find a quiet place and THINK, is palpable, and a little tragic, and should be kept in mind when we talk about the "cushiness" of research positions as against the "hard and tumble" real world.

Those three thousand people, with Gianotti their shield and voice, worked and innovated and struggled and on occasion slept, and within four years had collected enough data to announce the discovery of a Higgs-like particle, and therefore of the associated Higgs field which not only gives mass to the particles that interact with it, but also disturbs the symmetries between particles of the Standard Model, making those particles different, and allowing for the chemistry of our universe to exist as it does.

The Higgs is the last particle required of the Standard Model, but thankfully we are nowhere near done. Two giant problems with the energy of empty space remain to be solved, as does the tremendous issue of dark matter, and when the LHC comes back online in 2015, it will be armed with 13 TeV of energy to probe those corners of reality. Gianotti stepped down from her post as spokesperson in 2013, but one thing is certain. As long as there are new layers of the universe to unveil, and as long as there is Schubert to be played at night to unwind the strands of the day, Gianotti will be there, probing the secrets of nature's fields with the best products of humanity's ingenuity, and listening for the electric chirp of discovery.

FURTHER READING:

Fabiola Gianotti was a finalist for Time's Person of the Year, and their article on her can be found here (http://poy.time.com/2012/12/19/runner-up-fabiola-gianotti-the-discoverer/). You can find a 2010 interview she gave on the questions ATLAS was investigating here (http://www.atlas.ch/multimedia/interview-gianotti.html), and a really cool piece write-up of her lifestyle and work here (http://www.ft.com/cms/s/2/d3ea9832-eee4-11e2-b8ec-00144feabdc0.html#axzz3AvOL7pBq). For the issues of particle physics that she is investigating, a great introduction is *The Particle at the End of the Universe* by Sean Carroll. It presents the importance of the Higgs field, as well as of field theory in general, with some great intuitive examples that bypass the messy math involved. If you LIKE messy math, however, Halzen and Martin's *Quarks and Leptons: An Introductory Course in Modern Particle Physics* will give you just about whatever you're looking for.

IN DEFENSE OF USELESS MATH: WHY THE NEW COMMON CORE ISN'T AS LIBERATING AS IT SEEMS.

(Originally Published in *Skeptical Inquirer*, Jan/Feb 2015)

"A re-evaluation of standards is in order."

It was the war cry of an educational system which, having long given up on improvement, decided to settle instead for a dolled-up stagnation. *Let's just try and keep things from getting*

worse, and rewrite the standards so that inertia appear as success.
Internally, that worked quite well – you tinker with the SAT to drop
the arcane bits, chop six or so time-consuming topics out of AP
Chemistry, and get the results that allow the whole shlumping mass
to shlump on another year or two.

But then organizations sprung up with the wherewithal to
test basic standards internationally, and the results have been a
consistently profound embarrassment for American teaching. The
2012 PISA results have us at a solid 30th place internationally for
mathematics, in a tight race with the Slovak Republic and Lithuania.
And, yes, there are massive problems with cross-comparing age
groups from radically different cultures, but there is a thrumming
alarm deep in those numbers that can't be disregarded lightly.

Politicians sensed gold in them thar hills, and made a
political issue out of a relatively banal pedagogical one, whipping
the country into a fervor that American education is doomed and
that the answer lies in accountability systems and a standardization
of expectations. No Child Left Behind, Race to the Top, and other
governmental programs sought to cajole and punish educators into
boosting student performance and instituted an era of standardized
test fatigue that is breeding a whole generation of students who
loathe learning math on a burning, primal level.

For the last decade, I've been a math teacher in high school
and a private tutor serving experimental, religious, boarding, and
plain ole public schools throughout the San Francisco Bay area, and
in that time I've been in the trenches with the students as they've
watched the educational system radically shift under their feet
every two years or so. And they are exhausted – they have long
since given up caring about standardized tests and many of them
make it a point of honor to put as little effort into studying for them
as possible, the only form of defiance allowed them. They know
that they are being taught in order to take tests, and the result has
been an almost complete extinguishing of any desire to pursue
math or science on a recreational level out of pure curiosity.

Every teacher on the ground knows this is the hungry viper
at the heart of mathematics education – the overbearing

handicapping of inspiration and curiosity. But that's a complicated issue to solve, involving how teachers are trained, how classroom environments are created, and how to convince the public out of their fascination with standard-based testing. It's sloppy, and politicians cannot abide sloppiness. So, when the National Governors Association flexed its considerable muscle to enact educational change, those weren't the issues focused on. Instead, the solution to standards exhaustion was to, get ready for it…. Change The Standards A Bit!

Enter Common Core, the system of educational guidelines that is being, or will soon be, used to evaluate student K-12 learning in 44 states.

Now, there are some legitimately great ideas whose time has long since come in this sprawling set of benchmarks. There's a very noble attempt to get kids thinking about the structure of "informal arguments" in order to cultivate a seat-of-the-pants sense of what is likely to be a correct answer or law. Also, the new focus on explaining *how* answers are arrived at beyond "The algorithm says to do it this way" is a wonderfully important thing that I hope the K-8 curriculum succeeds with.

Topic-wise, arcane algebra tricks are downplayed in order to bring students more in line with how professionals solve problems of, say, equation intersection. And I really like how they make students play with compound expressions. Given say, $f(x) = 20x + 5$ e^x , it's good to have a visceral sense of which components dominate for which values of x. That's something I wish more of my calculus students had coming into class, and which Common Core is seeking to inculcate from an early age.

And yet. There's a cold and calculating spirit drifting through the heart of the Common Core standards that sends a chill through anybody who really and earnestly Loves Math. What becomes abundantly clear while surfing through the new standards is the titanic shift from "A Sampling of All Types of Math" to "The Math That Will Make You Money." Common Core, and the textbook company that provided substantial funding for its development, dresses this up as "providing depth instead of breadth," but the upshot is that Merely Interesting math has been discretely thrown off the pier to make room for profitable mathematics.

What you get is a huge focus on stats and modeling now, with everything else made to service those two reigning monarchs. Faced with the eternal student question, "Why bother - When are we going to *use* this?" Common Core has decided to surrender every topic that doesn't lead to, "Because it'll make you rich."

It makes sense – there is a huge demand out there for mathematicians skilled in information analysis to work in the biotechnology industry, and precious little for mathematicians who are super-interested in, say, Galois Theory. For most people, then, the change in focus will be for the good, but I can't help but feel quite sad for the few who might have cherished a love of pure math for math's sake, who were well served under a system that let them sample everything equally, and who under the new will experience 3 years of Modeling before they get the chance to strike out on their own, if any will to do so remains.

Is that elitist? Maybe, but it's in investigating those absolutely useless nooks and crannies of math that we math teachers tend to get the most excited, and I think an Excited Teacher trumps just about anything else in terms of getting students engaged with the material. More pragmatically, if the goal is to lure inspiring teachers into the public school system, the way to do that is most definitely not by shackling them to an Economics Word Problem heavy curriculum and turning class time into a series of lectures on calculator use.

This practical subservience shows up everywhere, sometimes with baffling results. In the classic Matrix – Vector tug of war, the share of matrices is expanded because those are good at dealing with large systems of equations used in modeling, while vectors are pared down to the basics in spite of their importance for students taking physics or eventually multi-variable calculus. Worse still, geometry is now a closet of horrors constructed from shards of underscrutinized good intentions.

The first standards in the new geometry curriculum are overwhelmingly devoted to transformational geometry, or how rotations, reflections, and translations move objects around the plane. That makes perfect sense if your idea of geometry is its money-making potential, since so much graphical manipulation is run off transformational mathematics and its supporting matrix operations. It's also a wonderful and productive approach in undergraduate courses for understanding the unities of geometry on a deeper level. But for a high school class, to define two figures as congruent if "a series of rigid motions exists which carries one object onto the other" smacks of pedagogic hubris.

Does American mathematical teaching need a rethink? Absolutely, but once again, the educational-political complex has placed all of its faith in curriculum tweaking to fundamentally change the academic landscape, while persistently ignoring larger issues that make for less stirring talking points. Common Core has taken the most intellectually exciting branch of human knowledge, mathematics, and turned it into a series of trade skills. If the great challenge is getting kids excited enough about a subject to learn about it independently of their classroom assignments, then Common Core doesn't contribute much. There are some very clever and positive additions to the standard curriculum, but I don't see any of it leading to a larger curiosity about the beautiful uselessness of mathematics at its best and most subtle. We shall have analysts aplenty and dreamers few, a rather dismal future in which teachers are there to show you how your calculator works and knowledge is something that gets you through the next benchmark test. All hail Common Core.

Part V:

The Stuff of Life

LET'S SOLVE A PROBLEM!
THE GREATNESS OF COOPERATIVE BOARD GAMES

"Hey guys, I've got a new problem."

Back in college, those were the words that energized a hall. People would stop what they were doing, grab a whiteboard, and all join together for a moment to try and break whatever thorny problem one of us managed to stumble across. Sometimes it fell quickly, sometimes it took hours, but in those moments of working through a mathematical or scientific puzzle with a bunch of other nerds while shoveling candy and over-caffeinated soda into our maws, life was perfect.

There is nothing better than getting together with a small group of like-minded folk and tackling a problem that has nothing whatsoever to do with anything actually useful. Unfortunately, life after college doesn't present too many opportunities to engage in such activities. Friends specialize out into their own branches, move off to different places, and so that singularity of purpose and expansiveness of time dissipate.

But humans are clever primates, and some of the substitutes we've come up with can, at their best, entirely approximate the cooperative intellectual rush of bygone days. For a long while, that's the place that tabletop roleplaying games occupied – Dungeons and Dragons, Changeling, Call of Cthulhu, Pathfinder, Vampire: The Masquerade, and dozens upon dozens more all gave adults the chance to meet a few hours every week and put their resources together in a creative, spontaneous setting to solve the problems concocted by their much put-upon Dungeon Masters.

And those were (and are) fantastic, and if you are refraining from looking into them out of pride, you're missing out on some truly memorable times. However, the start-up on these games is pretty hefty. You have to create your character, familiarize yourself with the often weighty core manuals, and get comfortable with carrying out character dialogue at a candle-lit kitchen table. For those who love problem-solving but didn't quite have the time to go in for the whole RPG experience, then, there rose the cooperative board game.

It used to be a somewhat rare breed in the board game genre, but has steadily grown in recent years so that a well-stocked game closet can now have a good half dozen quality co-op titles. The rules are usually pretty simple to pick up, but the coordination and cleverness required can often deliciously strain a room full of the brightest brains. Here are my top four picks, and if you have a favorite, do drop me a line!

4. Shadows Over Camelot: You and your friends take up the role of the Arthurian knights to take on the manifold challenges threatening Camelot. It can be a BRUTAL experience, as no sooner do you tie up one quest than three others go absolutely critical requiring all of your combined mental dexterity to resolve. Definitely the hardest coop game I've played, but every time you end up winning you feel like you definitely EARNED your bowl of pretzels.

3. Ultimate Werewolf: Sort of co-op, sort of not. It's basically the old campfire Mafia game (sit in a circle around the fire, two people are secretly appointed as mafia goons, and one as a police officer, and the game is to communally find out who is who) but with a supernatural twist and a lot more specialty roles, so that the game can actually support up to 68 players. When I had game night with my students, we tried it out and had a marvelous time piecing together the bits and pieces of psychological clues we found, or thought we found, in each other's behavior, leading to wild accusations and much fun.

2. Arkham Horror: A classic in the Cthulhu universe, in which you and your fellow investigators have to navigate the twisting hellscape of a city slowly giving way to the invasion of the Old Ones, trying to stop the incursions of monsters and corruption before a supreme embodiment of evil awakes and wipes you off the board. Like Shadows, there's a lot here to punish you if you're careless with your abilities and movement, which means that every turn is open for intense discussion about how to achieve mutual optimization. So, there's that same intense manipulation of lots of variables, but in a really cool, creepy setting.

1. Pandemic: You and a team of disease specialists are running around the world, trying to cure outbreaks of four different diseases as they arise and spread across the globe. The rules and actions are much simpler than Shadows and Camelot, so it's a good game for people who aren't used to board games, the challenge being how to pool your limited array of abilities to halt the steady spread of plague. It takes all of 5 minutes to explain, and a typical game only lasts about an hour, but there is a lot of subtlety there so you always feel that you are being challenged as a group to find the most elegant use of moves possible, making it the ideal starter co-op game.

So, there you have it. If a bit of group intellectual challenge is something you feel missing from your life, grab any one of those, two or three friends, and have a go if only to taste again for a moment those days when all you had was time and all you needed was a delectably devilish problem to while it away with.

WHEN THE WORLD LISTENS:
THREE THINGS ATHEISTS SAY IN PUBLIC
BUT DON'T REALLY MEAN

(Originally Published in *The Freethinker*, January 2014)

Any movement that's around a sufficiently long time picks up a set of obligatory phrases for public consumption that sound all right, don't cause trouble, and that aren't *actually* believed by anybody in the movement. Commonplaces that paper over contentious beliefs and make for good sound bites. We atheists have been out of the closet long enough to have collected a mass of them rather against our best instincts, turning our public utterances increasingly into strings of scripted pleasantries rather than the free intellectual engagement we say we love.

The only way to fix the problem is to admit frankly that we often don't *quite* mean those things that we say when the cameras are rolling. We're not lying, mind you, it's just that a lot of the issues we've been grappling with are so personally painful that safe and smooth phrases which are 60% true have slowly supplanted their thornier cousins. Now there's virtue in simplicity, but we should also have it on record that, when we say these things, what we mean is far less round and obliging.

Thing One: "I'm not afraid of death, because death gives life meaning."

This comes up A LOT, is very striking and heroic, makes for good debate material, and whenever we say it, we're being lusciously insincere. Try as we might to resist the utterance, it's just so simple and effective that it sort of falls out of our mouths against our will, the atheist equivalent of "He's in a better place now." The idea that life has *meaning* beyond itself is part of the metaphysical baggage we have inherited from religion. Strictly speaking, life is meaningless. We all know it, but we don't like saying it in public for fear of seeming nihilistic and cruel, so we say stuff like this instead.

Death isn't okay. Humans know that on a fundamental level, hate it, and are willing to give immense amounts of power to anybody who will speak the contrary with seeming authority. It takes a very brave movement to opt out of that power, to say, "Sorry, death is just death. It doesn't make anything mystically better in any way, and it's going to happen to you," and leave it at that. I think we had that bravery once, and maybe we can work up to it again someday.

Perhaps, though, it's not actually an issue of bravery, but a pedestrian, workaday case of unfortunate word choice. The basic idea here is seemingly fine, namely that the realization of death lends an at times desperate, at times radiant, intensity to our appreciation of life that doesn't necessarily exist for people who think themselves immortal. In the light of that, we could amend our stock phrase to become, "I profoundly dislike death, and am genuinely afraid of it, but that fear has at least one often good result."

Less pithy? Absolutely, but a tad more honest, and in the long run, honesty always wins.

Thing Two: "Well, really, when you get down to it, I'd describe myself as more of an agnostic."

Speaking truthfully, no, we wouldn't, though the temptation to do so is always there, and the best of us succumb to it from time to time just to get by. The problem is that religions, with their monomania for questions of existence, have monopolized the defining of atheism, and THAT is the definition we have to deal with in public. Small wonder, then, that we scoot away from this foisted label and towards something more benign and less starkly defined. Religion has decided that The Big Issue is one of the possible existence or non-existence of gods, and has defined atheism as the position that takes the latter view.

That is inaccurate.

The Big Issue for atheism is not an ontological one, but a much more comprehensive linguistic one. It is not about the existence of mere gods, but the existence of religions. In so far as religions are attempts to describe spiritual beings using terrestrial language, they necessarily fail. They no sooner speak than they err. There is no way for the situation to be otherwise, language being what it is. It's like trying to use a chainsaw to solve a differential equation.

If you agree with the idea, "Whenever somebody attempts to describe the nature of a supernatural entity, including statements positing existence, he is wrong, and if that person continues to *insist* on having this knowledge, he is either a charlatan, or insane, or some provocative yet zesty comingling of the two," then, congratulations, you're an atheist. And in accepting that, you haven't just pushed gods out of the picture, but anything that attempts to use language to do things that language simply cannot do.

So, the next time you feel that cold hard press of being forced into assuming a false mantle of agnosticism to escape judgment, just take a breath and say, "Yes, I actually AM an atheist, and here's exactly what that means..."

Thing Three: "If my kid came home and wanted to join a church, I'd be fine with that."

Atheist Parenting is its own subculture entirely, charged with the particularly tricky task of walking the line between protecting children from religious bullying and preserving open-mindedness. It's incredibly difficult to do, and I have nothing but respect for those who honestly try. After all, "Now, honey, you're not going to Hell like that other kid in class said you are, but you have to remember to respect his religious beliefs," is a sentence that the mind can barely wrap itself around, let alone the tongue.

In my most idealistic heart of hearts, I'd like to think that I have complete trust in the evaluative tools my kids possess to throw off whatever a church might throw at them. At the same time, though, even though I gave my daughter karate lessons, it doesn't mean I'm going to let her join the nearest brawl out of trust that she has the skills to survive. Just like a brawl is a social event aimed at systematically hurting people, so is a church an organization aimed at systematically breaking children into a certain mode of belief. Even if you survive either process, you're still going to bear scars from the attempt.

So, no, if my kid comes up and says, "I want to start going to Church" I am decidedly NOT going to just hand her over with a, "Here, she's curious, do whatever the heck you want to her and we'll hope she shakes it off." You don't bring addicts to opium dens and you don't bring children to churches.

Am I limiting my children's scope of curiosity? Absolutely, but as a parent I do that ALL THE TIME. I'd be a really crappy parent if I didn't: "Well, I see you're curious about these knives, one year old daughter, and far be it from me to restrict your curiosity, so here ya go!" Once they've developed fully their critical thinking skills, then by all means let them taste those dark alleys of the human mind a bit more, but so long as they are in the That Nice Priest Gave Me Candy So She Must Be Good phase, to church we shall not go.

The thing is, we can communicate all of these ideas without sounding like terrible people. As a matter of fact, *by* communicating them at all, we'll sound like regular people, dealing with all of the messiness of regular life, rather than the too-sure intellectuals we often come off as. "Death sucks, and sometimes you have to be a meanie to be a good parent" will gather more people out of curiosity and sympathy than the insincere formulations that are working their way into our speech patterns at present.

The good news is that it's not too late, these stock phrases haven't become banners we *must* march under. We just have to be each other's watchdogs for a while, with a "Did you say that because you meant it, or because it sounded good?" offered every so often to keep ourselves tending towards Honest rather than Quotable, embracing complexity even when it is a rather lonely thing to do.

SOUL MAN: LA METTRIE'S GREAT STEP FORWARD AND HOW WE BETRAYED IT

(Originally Published in *The Freethinker*, September 2012)

For the non-believer, these are heady times: public debates, best selling books, and a dizzying growth in both numbers and public presence all seem to suggest that history is swinging in a generally anti-clerical direction. It is astounding, but remember we've been in this position before. In the middle of the eighteenth century religion was On The Run. A thin, perpetually ailing notary's son named Voltaire was, pamphlet by pamphlet, making bishops tremble, and his words found their way into the ears of the era's greatest monarchs and statesmen.

One hundred years later, it was all gone, replaced by a religious reordering of society and public life so pervasive that we are still battling with its ideals today. What happened and, more importantly, is there a way to prevent it happening again? I can think of no better way to investigate the mystery than to start with the career and ideas of Julien Offray de la Mettrie (1709-1751), a French doctor and author whose arguments against the existence of the soul have been all but forgotten, wiped out in the great nineteenth century religious revival and the adjustment of tactics by the philosophical community that followed.

La Mettrie, to those who know him at all, is remembered largely as a clownish figure at Frederick the Great's court whom neither Frederick nor Voltaire took seriously and who ended up dying early at the hands of bad paté. This is decidedly unjust. His early contributions to the so-called Doctor's Pamphlet War, in which he argued passionately for anatomical experience and accurate case studies over Galenic metaphysical speculation, were important in the advancement of French medicine in the eighteenth century. More than that, his 1748 work *Man, A Machine*, in the unflinching boldness with which it approached the most sacred of topics, man's possession of an immaterial soul, is possibly even more breath-taking today than it was in his own time.

La Mettrie's line of reasoning stemmed from his strict training in Hippocratean medical observation under the eighteenth century's most renowned physician, Herman Boerhaave. Against the reigning Cartesian soul-body dualism, which relied on thought experiments and logical extrapolations, La Mettrie compiled case studies and personal observations of his time as a physician to note the wide range of effects that purely physical ailments had on behavior and memory, two aspects of humans under the supposed purview of The Soul. Injury, disease, an alteration of diet, fatigue, intoxication - introduce any one of these severely enough, and the flavor of one's character starts inevitably to change. But if memory, behavior, and character are all so tied to the physical, what does that leave for a soul to actually do? La Mettrie concluded, "The soul is therefore but an empty word, of which no one has any idea, and which an enlightened man should only use to signify the part in us that thinks."

It took some time for La Mettrie's initial charge forward to be joined by the philosophe community, but within two decades after his death a united front had been formed. In 1764 Voltaire declared in his *Philosophical Dictionary* that the nature of the soul was not now, nor could it ever be, known. Baron d'Holbach followed suit in *The System of Nature* (1770) that, "Man is a being purely physical: the moral man is nothing more than this physical being considered under a certain point of view." That same year Denis Diderot pulled himself away from the publishing of the Encyclopedia for long enough to write the essay *On Matter and Movement*, which furthered the materialist program by examining how matter could have force in and of itself, without being guided by outside spirits.

Interesting ideas all, but what the devil happened to them? The story of the snuffing of the French Revolution, and with it the fervored return to that odd amalgam of Mysticism and Normalcy that would have its half-century under the sun as Victorianism and its regional offshoots, is a common enough one. The Revolution had touted its Enlightenment bona fides so vigorously that the fall of Robespierre could not but bring the fall of the philosophical school held to be responsible for his rise. Skepticism of the La Mettriean mould was dropped because it was guilty by association, not because of a fundamental incompatibility with the coming Romanticism. You don't need to look farther than the late works of Beethoven to see what Might Have Been had the fusion of Enlightenment and Romanticism not been weighed down by the specter of the guillotine.

There is hope in this for us, because it means that as long as we can resist the urge to go about beheading monarchs and invading Austria, I think we'll be okay when it comes to forming meaningful connections with whatever neo-irrationalism might rise in the coming years.

What has me more worried, honestly, is us. The real reason that La Mettrie and the other courageous innovators of his time were buried was not because he was incompatible with what succeeded him, but rather because of how the skeptical community adjusted to its waning popularity. We panicked, and to some extent, we still are. In the face of a rising tide of opposition, we saw that, to survive, an alteration of tactics was necessary.

Three roads lead out from the Enlightenment, two of which terminated in dead-ends, and one of which we continue to follow today. To oversimplify a bit, these were the paths of Nostalgia, Engagement, and Caution.

Those that took the Path of Nostalgia recognized the advances of the Enlightenment, but felt the need to dilute them through a return to previous eras of thought. In 1844, in the Supplement to the Fourth Book of his *World as Will and Representation*, Arthur Schopenhauer made the very La Mettriean claim that humans are animals, and that all of our individuality is wrapped up in our particular material body, but feels compelled to add that, underneath all of that Mere Individuality there is a basic force that operates on the species level that survives us and perpetuates everything important about us. Schopenhauer's point is actually interesting, because he is always JUST on the cusp of anticipating Darwin and even Dawkins with their focus on species and genetic level survival pressures, but inevitably pulls back again into the snuggly embrace of Kantian metaphysics. Though interesting from an intellectual history point of view, the metaphysical strands were not convincing to the skeptics, and the skeptical strands scared those with memories of the Revolution, and the effort crumbled under the weight of its own improbability.

Those opting for Engagement, meanwhile, such as Max Stirner or Mikhail Bakhunin, were largely isolated individuals of the mid-nineteenth century who were genuine materialists, but whose adoption of radical political creeds brought their pure philosophical speculations into disrepute. By harnessing their thoughts about the soul to credos of anarchism or extreme individualism, they made sure that those thoughts did not survive the heyday of those credos, so all of their very real boldness went for naught, and few today point to them as their philosophical ancestors.

This leaves us with The Cautious, whose descendants we all are. Rather than attempting to continue the fight on multiple fronts, as the skeptics of the Enlightenment had done, these men decided to pare the war down to the battles we could win, and for which there existed some degree of public sympathy. The battle against the political abuses and moral turpitude of the established Church could stay, but that against the soul had to go.

It is as if somehow we all tacitly agreed that, since people seem to really like the idea of having a soul, we would leave that alone in order to carry on the struggle to liberate people from the greater evils that stem from belief in a monotheistic god or organized church. After all, it's a victimless belief, we convinced ourselves, like Santa Claus or the Chicago Cubs. Except that, when you believe that you have something immaterial that directs you, it is only natural to believe that that essence can continue without your body, and from there it is but a short step to talking yourself into a divine curator of your immaterial essence, and once you believe that, the game is largely up.

It is not a popular line of argument - it's far more practical to just keep doing what we've been doing, from Nietzsche to Ingersoll to Hitchens, and talk about Popes and Scopes, slave morality and birth control, but that is to attack the branches and not the root. The philosophes were braver men than we in many respects, but their united efforts were weakened by the politicization of their beliefs and the pragmatism of their philosophical descendants. We learned from their experience strategies that will allow Enlightenment 2.0 a greater longevity than our first go at it those centuries ago, but we have to make sure that, in our caution and our keen sense of history, we do not leave behind more than we carry forward.

Queen Christina, Anna Maria van Schurman, and the Not-Quite-Yetness of Seventeenth Century Feminism

(Originally published at *Skepchick*, December 2013)

A former monarch seeking adventure.

A brilliant polymath repenting of her worldly knowledge.

Few moments are more emblematic of the tenuousness of seventeenth century feminism than the 1654 meeting of two of the most remarkable and learned people of their age, Queen Christina of Sweden and Anna Maria van Schurman. They were in every way two ships passing in the night. Christina had recently abdicated her throne, seeking freedom to do and think as she pleased without the constant pressure to find a mate and produce an heir. Anna Maria van Schurman, meanwhile, after a life of scholarship lauded across the whole of Europe, was beginning the long process of retreating from her former claims in the name of sectarian religious fervor. Christina could have learned much from the encounter, about the demoralizing cost of compromise and the fragility of intellect confronting tradition, but she had a continent to conquer, or so she believed.

The two would not meet again.

Christina was the daughter of Gustavus Adolphus, the mercurial monarch who reversed the tide of the Thirty Years' War and gave Sweden a place at the power brokering table of Europe. Lacking siblings, she was raised to be a queen, and her tutors encouraged her various intellectual enthusiasms, from ancient languages to the balance of European power, philosophy to Italian art. At the same time, it was clear that there was something quite different about this princess. She took to wearing male's clothing, loved rough soldier talk, and was keenly proud of her abilities as a horseman and hunter. She adored the complexities of intrigue even when she came out clearly the loser, and would spend a good deal of her life spinning wildly improbable plans for remaking the face of Europe. Nobody had ever seen anything like her, and anxiety ran high about just what she might do should the crown fall to her.

Which it did, and sooner than anybody had anticipated. At age 6, her father died. At 18, she assumed formal control of Sweden's government. At 28, she renounced all responsibilities of rulership, but declared paradoxically that she still retained the title of Queen in spite of the abdication, and demanded of the Swedish parliament a lavish annual salary. Ruler of a Protestant nation, she had formed a plan to convert to Catholicism, be welcomed into Rome in triumph, and turn the prestige of that moment into a position of established importance from which she could continue to affect European politics and patronize the arts without all of the bother of parliamentary restraint, under which she bristled, or the need to give birth to a successor, which she found instinctually appalling.

Upon abdication, she flew from Sweden as fast as her horse could carry her, bounding about the different nations of Europe, preparing for her meeting with the Pope. And in the course of those first heady travels, she stopped in Utrecht to visit the most famous female scholar of her day, Anna Maria van Schurman.

Schurman was nineteen years older than Christina, and had long ago earned a reputation as a fierce mind. Fluent in Dutch, Hebrew, French, Greek, Latin, Chaldean, Arabic, Syriac, and a handful of other languages besides, she was also known as a fine artist and precise philosopher, with intellectuals as diverse as the arch-conservative Gisbertus Voetius and ultra-modern Rene Descartes falling over themselves to extol the power of her intellect. Her 1638 essay, *Whether a Christian Woman Should be Educated*, while not the fiery call to arms of, say, Lucrezia Marinella's 1600 *The Nobility and Excellence of Women and the Defects and Vices of Men*, was an influential piece that argued persuasively and logically that all women so inclined should have the benefit of the education that she herself enjoyed. The call for female scholarship was, of course, sugar-coated in a layer of "If you let them study, they'll be better Christians and wives" reasoning, and the caveats were many, but as an exercise in pure, syllogistic reason on the side of feminine equality, it had no rival.

And yet, when Christina came visiting in 1654, Schurman's star was decidedly on the decline. Her increasing fascination with Biblical linguistics and pietistic practice caused her to doubt her own earlier boldness and to eschew the modern philosophy of some of her proponents. Descartes, on his way to become Christina's tutor in 1649 (an appointment that would end in his death at the hands of Sweden's climate, Christina's rigorous daily schedule, and his own insistence that brewed tobacco made for great medicine) stopped at Utrecht and couldn't help but comment on the futility of Schurman's belief that Biblical Hebrew held the key to anything worth knowing. She found his flippant dismissal of scripture thoroughly repugnant and turned her back completely on the philosopher who had once fascinated her.

She started to regard her previous attachment to learning as a wrong turn, a distraction from the real requirements of life. As she would later explain, "I do not deny that I had all my life placed much weight on bourgeois proprieties, customary manners, and a good name, as if true virtues: but in this case [her conversion to pietism in the 1660s] I paid no attention to them, I considered them transient in comparison with heavenly matters or as a heavenly gift and entrusted good which I could give back to God, just as everything that is mine belongs to God and has been given to me by God."

Her quick intellect, her massive learning, were surrendered as sacrifices to the dictates of religious conscience. A decade after her meeting with Christina, she met Jean de Labadie, a charismatic pietistic preacher who convinced her to completely renounce her former life and follow him in creating a new religious sect. She died, still sacrificing herself to Labadie's vision, in 1678.

And yet, if Anna Maria van Schurman was a Scared Straight example of what can happen when a great mind begins to doubt itself under the manically benevolent pressure of religious rectitude, Christina's subsequent career is one of the dangers of naïve and unchecked ambition. She was received in triumph by

Rome, but her extravagant generosity had rendered her penniless, and her status as a titular Queen without a country made her more often than not an embarrassment wherever she went. She burned decades of her life chasing phantoms of power, writing letters to the monarchs of Europe proposing grandiloquent plans that she no longer had the political or financial clout to make real. (My favorite of her schemes called for Cromwell becoming Catholic, giving England to the Pope, who would then give it back on condition of religious liberty being granted, at which point Cromwell would become King Oliver.) She would show up uninvited at the court of Louis XIV or back in her native Sweden, and was always entirely unaware of just how deeply unwanted she was.

And yet, the beautiful thing about Christina is that, no matter how many times she was put off by the crowned heads of Europe, no matter the volume of polite requests to Never Come Back, her self-confidence was so vigorous, her sense of worth so unbounded, that she was never broken by the insistently grinding machinery of European diplomacy. An entire continent brought all of its diplomatic wiles to bear on this one lone woman and she, through sheer force of will and character, always picked herself up unscathed to follow a new star.

And, in fact, it was Christina who lived to laugh last. Her finances eventually straightened out, she rented a modest estate near Rome where she spent her last years creating a small artistic garden of paradise amidst the stringencies of Pope Innocent XI's reign. He meant to crack down hard on what he perceived as the decline in women's virtue, ordering it illegal for any woman to take a music lesson from a male teacher, and strongly indicating it as preferable that women not learn music at all. Christina's small estate, which as the dwelling of a titular queen was outside of the Pope's jurisdiction, thus became a sanctuary for female performers and artists of all types, the instrumentalist Angelica Quadrelli actually living with Christina to escape Innocent's plan of throwing her into a nunnery, while female composers were able to continue their work thanks to her patronage, including the great Barbara

Strozzi (and if you haven't tasted some of Strozzi's compositions yet, might I suggest here

http://www.youtube.com/watch?v=y49oqANUSus

as a good place to start?). Surrounded by paintings and music, friendship and intellectual stimulation, she finally succeeded in finding a life entirely to her temperament. When she died, Rome would throw itself into convulsions to pay her tribute. Gripe as the clerics might, the people really did rather love the odd Swedish former monarch who kept alive in their city a bit of the spirit of their ancient greatness, and who was entirely and always, herself.

We do not know what happened at Christina's meeting with Schurman. They did not resume their connection, so presumably they didn't hit it off. Christina doubtlessly struck Schurman as focused too much on matters of the mind and the world, while Christina's brain was swirling too much with things of the future to be held back by the grim example of a once great mind voluntarily sacrificed at the altar of religious fervor. It's tempting to see the moment as a passing of the torch, Christina continuing the work that Schurman was no longer willing to do, keeping the light of unchecked scholarship flickering even through the myriad defeats she experienced at the hands of an indifferent continent, preserving its promise for the coming century, one that would know its worth, and act on it.

Further Reading: Veronica Buckley's *Christina: Queen of Sweden* is one of my favorite history books ever. Margaret Goldsmith's earlier biography is also quite good, but Buckley crackles with a relentless, Christinian energy. For Anna Maria van Schurman, Joyce Irwin's intellectual portrait that precedes her translation of *Whether a Christian Woman Should Be Educated* is rich with not only bits of Schurman's life, but many other female intellectuals and artists of the time whose works are definitely worth the revisiting.

THOSE WE LEFT BEHIND:
THE "FORMER ATHEIST MEMOIR" FAD
AND WHAT WE CAN LEARN FROM IT

(Originally published as "The Turncoats" in *The New Humanist*, June 2013)

2006 was the Year of New Atheism, and it brought in its wake a flood of anti-atheist sentiment, the most interesting manifestation of which was a steady trickle of memoirs by former atheists and secularists repenting of their ways and proclaiming their new belief in God. The reaction of the atheist community to these works was largely dismissive, and indeed there is much in them that doesn't bear close scrutiny. However, they have something crucially important and often disturbing to say about how we secularists treat our own that we can't afford to ignore as non-belief comes into fruition not only as an intellectual position, but as a lifestyle and source of community.

The most common type of story that we see is that of the atheist turning desperately towards theism as a way to improve his or her self-image. In this vein are Alicia Chole's *Finding an Unseen God* (2009) and Dave Schmelzer's *Not the Religious Type* (2008). These are, by and large, the same book, and there is much we can learn from that very identity of life story. In both memoirs, the authors start off with an over-inflated sense of their own creative and intellectual gifts. Chole describes herself as a "disciplined" student always looking for a good debate, a girl who locks herself in the bathroom with books so that she can be alone within (and this is her phrase) The Sanctuary of Her Mind. Schmelzer grows his hair long and wears oversized sunglasses to ape his favorite authors as he dreams of becoming a great and monetarily successful writer.

Then things start going wrong as the world shows itself less dazzled by their gifts than they expected. Chole's prose positively *seethes* with resentment at the lack of recognition from her teachers. They never quite give her what she thinks she deserves, and her attempts to translate her despair into poetry similarly founder, driving her into the arms of a community with slightly lower expectations - the partiers and drinkers. But then an encounter with a drink that proves too delicious (she won't say what, I and my cocktail shaker are disappointed to report) scares her into a life of tee-totaling, and so she must search for a group with even lower expectations, finding just that in a pair of hyper-Christians who see her as every bit as brilliant and creative as she considers herself to be. Since her atheism previously consisted, as far as she reports it to us, of the usual Why Does God Let Bad Things Happen... argument, it doesn't take much to toss it aside in favor of a community that allows her to keep her exaggerated self-conception with a promise of divine love to boot.

Similarly, when Schmelzer reaches college, he sees his grades plummet in a story familiar to many who were tops in their high school only to find that college brings an entirely different level of expectation. In subsequent years, his attempts to make a living at being a playwright continually run aground. In the midst of his despair, he begins praying and is able to convince himself that his internal monologues during these prayer sessions are actually dialogues with the divine. Not only that, but God is telling him that he is the hero in a grand adventure about to unfold - that he is the Frodo (his analogy) of what is to come. The idea makes him Feel Good where the few arguments (and again, they don't go much beyond the "atheism" of Chole if he's laid them all before us) that hold up his notion of atheism don't, and soon he constructs a life philosophy based around the validity of these conversations.

And there they both stay - rationalizing their choices in similar ways that exude that particular form of double-think unique to the fragile and frustrated psyches of third tier intellectuals. Chole, almost immediately after a section bemoaning those who substitute "truth" with "feelings" when choosing a life philosophy, offers her own four point system of why she believes in Christianity, two of which amount to "It makes me feel good and makes other

272

people feel good." Schmelzer gives himself over entirely to the feeling of security he gets from his unending personal conversations with God, culminating in one of the book's most ghoulish sections.

He tells of standing by the bed of his daughter who is suffering from a potentially fatal heart problem, and describes Joy as the core of the entire experience because, in the midst of it all, he had some top-notch God conversations. Again and again in his memoir, he comes back to how deeply satisfying that experience was, and how grateful he is to those who prayed for his daughter's recovery.

Not once does he thank the doctors or the nurses who worked for a year to save his daughter's life. We never even hear their names. This is telling - to salvage his own sense of identity he constructed a divinity of impeccable solidity who had him and his concerns always at heart. From that moment on, maintaining that relation became the alpha and omega of his life to the point that *actual people* disappear, their efforts accounted as nothing next to those prayers that he believes help him on his journey towards Better God Chats.

There is much to be learned here about how we treat our own. In no sense were either of these people profound atheists - charitably, we can say that they left their versions of atheism at an early age, so we shouldn't expect too much depth from their recollections of it. But they were people willing to take a risk on something that only offers sober reality as a shield against the realities of death and suffering, and we somehow let them down. How do we stop this from happening to the new generations of non-believers now tentatively pushing themselves forward?

A good deal of the work has already been done. Thirty years ago, when Chole and Schmelzer were struggling with their identity, there was no such thing as an Atheist Community. Isolated individuals, perhaps, but nothing to compare with the current internet presence of humanists or the string of student alliances dotting the country. That craving for community and acceptance that drove both of these people into the arms of Christianity is now something that can be satisfied within the bounds of non-belief. It is heartening to see these student alliances not merely resting content with their role as stand alone philosophical clubs, but engaging in charitable work in their communities, offering the chance to help others without having to join a primarily religious organization to do it. It falls on us to do everything we can to foster and encourage this public spiritedness, to give the coming humanists not only a place to gather and people to talk to, but something to do beyond arguing. For my generation and those before me, the choice was Be Christian or Be Alone, and that is somewhat wonderfully no longer the case, nor will it ever be again.

But.

Atheism is a harsh mistress. For centuries, being horrendously outnumbered and fundamentally powerless in society, atheists had only one thing to sustain them - the rigid rigor of their argumentation, the pure force of their ideas and minds. Anything less than perfection in logic and consistency couldn't be tolerated, because it was the only thing we had going for us. So, our most pointed invective was often aimed at each other, and anybody who wasn't quite up to snuff tended to get cast overboard as hindering the fragile ship of non-belief. When the Choles and Schmelzers came our way, we could be cruel and dismissive, and their writings show that they felt it.

Is the answer, then, simply to chill out a bit, to relax the rigor of our mutual analysis and let everybody believe what they will? Not quite, but to see why we need to take a look at another memoir by a former atheist who took a distinctly different path.

While Schmelzer and Chole left atheism for reasons of self-image and happiness, Francis Collins departed for reasons of what he felt to be intellectual consistency. His *The Language of God* (2006), while not strictly a memoir, does begin by laying out his reasons for leaving the atheism that had been with him up through college. A successful student of biology and medicine, raised in a family that encouraged open thought and personal growth, Collins could afford to approach the question of atheism from the point of view of argumentation without being weighed down or influenced by overriding psychological considerations. He read around, came to a copy of C.S. Lewis's *Mere Christianity*, and was converted. The persuasiveness of Lewis's rather pedestrian Moral Law argument entirely won him over to the idea that God manifests himself through humanity in ways that exist outside of natural space and time.

After Lewis, each argument which made a leap from "We don't know yet" to "It's the Judaeo-Christian God who did it!" became increasingly easy to swallow, and his dedication to fishing out alternate explanations increasingly less pronounced. We see this in his treatment of Freud, where he claims that Freud's idea of God as a paternal substitute can't be true, because the Biblical God is often harsh, and not a being of "benevolent coddling and indulgence." I don't know about you, but Coddling and Indulgent are pretty close to the last two things I think of when I consider Freud's portrait of paternal constructs, and I wonder just how deeply Collins must have thought about Freud and his arguments to have come to this conclusion.

Similarly, when evaluating Lewis's claim that *agape*, or selfless altruism, is a uniquely human trait that makes no sense evolutionarily and must be therefore of divine origin, Collins allows himself to skip merrily over three decades of primatology that speak overwhelmingly to the contrary (by the by, for a charming account of this body of work check out Frans de Waal's recent *The Bonobo and the Atheist*, though it's probably best to jump ahead when he starts going on about his unfortunate theories about what atheism is and where it comes from). And what a fateful skipping that becomes - because once you too blithely admit a qualitative difference between animal and human morality that can only be bridged by God's plan, it becomes very easy to believe that life itself *had* to have a divine source, that there is a yawning chasm between life and non-life that can't be spanned scientifically. And once Collins was willing to place God in that particular gap, it was easy to start using God as the universal answer for *anything* that hasn't been completely explained at this particular moment in human history. Since science hasn't yet come up with a conclusive answer to what happened before the Big Bang, why not put God in there too?

Had he started with considering the Big Bang instead of taking a morality-first perspective, I think even Collins would recognize that the God answer is the positing of an overly specific solution to a problem of unknown dimension. I think of it like two friends walking along and suddenly coming upon a hole a hundred feet deep and three hundred feet wide.

"What do you think is supposed to go in there?" the first says.

"It's for a 1982 vintage Boba Fett action figure," the other assures him.

"Well, that's *one* thing that could go there," the first begins.

"No, that's what goes there," the other interrupts. "It's my favorite thing, so that's what goes in the hole."

There is a hole in our data of what happened before the Big Bang - we're working on it, but it'll probably take a while. But that doesn't mean we get to just plug in our favorite answer and call it a day. The data that we have prior to the event is nonexistent - there is literally zero of it in our hands. Choosing a definitive answer, particularly one as specific as the concept of God, with that amount of data to go on is reckless bordering on maniacal. I think Collins would have recognized it as such had he not come to this argument after having already made so many concessions to the moral law argument he decided *must* be true. Ignoring well-known studies of primate morality for no good philosophical reason allowed God a wedge into humanity and thence cosmology. After all of those forced moves, Collins had no choice but to declare himself a theist.

As much as it would help us nurture and support the psyches of people like Chole and Schmelzer, then, I have to say that the damage done by foregoing rigor is far worse than the benefit gained. I think we could stand to be a good deal more pleasant about it - and once we realize and honestly believe that the world is not going to imminently destroy us for our heresy anymore, we should be able to unclench a bit and take steps towards making ourselves generally less assy on the world stage and with each other. Guided by the cautionary tales of Chole and Schmelzer, Collins and Flew (whose memoir shares many of the faults of the others, but which I decided not to include in the light of Richard Carrier's persuasive argument that he didn't, in fact, write it himself <link: http://richardcarrier.blogspot.com/2007/11/antony-flew-bogus-book.html>), we can build a community of humanists who support each other and contribute substantially to the life and well-being of the world while still engaged in the meticulous intellectual work that will keep us from falling for an emotional argument in philosophical clothing.

GIORDANO BRUNO
AND THE SECRET ORIGINS
OF MODERN PHILOSOPHY

(Originally published in *Philosophy Now*, September 2013)

Philosophically, the sixteenth century was a mess. The rise of Protestantism knocked a millennium's worth of self-assured theological development for a loop, opening the gates to all manner of new philosophical disciplines and roving intellectual cutpurses. Everything was up for grabs, and in the chaos some found freedom, many reaped profit, and the most daring often ended their improbable lives in tragedy. Giordano Bruno (1548-1600) was one of the latter, now known more for being burned alive at the hands of the Inquisition than for the actual content of his thought and life. For anybody interested in how modern philosophy cobbled itself together from the swirling mass of occult mysticism and scholastic rigor that preceded it, Bruno's work, composed while wandering through every major intellectual center of sixteenth century Europe, makes an ideal starting point.

In a mere fifty two years of life, nine of which were spent rotting in an Inquisitorial jail cell, Bruno traveled to and lectured in Venice, Rome, Naples, London, Wittenberg, Frankfurt, Paris, Toulouse, Prague, and Zurich. His intellectual deftness allowed him to fit in with Calvinists, Lutherans, Catholics, hermetic magicians, and Jews with equal felicity. His belief in an infinite universe dominated by the ideas of love and forgiveness let him listen to and learn from each of these vibrant communities, and so his works brilliantly (if somewhat over-verbosely) encapsulate the contradictions and enthusiasms of his supremely contradictory and enthusiastic century.

When Giordano Bruno was born, the Council of Trent, which had started three years before as a grand attempt to honestly address the complaints and concerns of the Protestants, was already sliding into the harshly reactionary attitude that would spark a century of war and end the life of thousands of "heretics", Bruno included. But that would be in the future – the young Giordano (or Filippo as he was known at the time -early modern academics had a charming and infuriating habit of changing their name every fifteen damn minutes) started off his theological career most promisingly. Arriving at Naples in 1562, his astounding memory and rich language made an impression on his higher ups, and he was shipped off to Rome to perform memory tricks for the Pope.

The importance of memory is an increasingly foreign concept to a generation that, as a matter of course, carries access to the entire collected wisdom of mankind in its pocket, but in the sixteenth century, lawyers, clerics, and kings were all keenly interested in ways to boost their powers of recall as a means of bypassing the laborious process of accessing archives and their dependence on shifty librarians. A lawyer wasn't worth hiring unless he could deliver a six hour speech from memory, and for a king or pontiff who had dozens of disparate items brought before him each day for judgment and action, a keen head was indispensable.

It should come as little surprise, then, that Bruno, after getting excommunicated for picking theological fights with the wrong friars, earned most of his bread by teaching his memory system to the rulers of whatever country his wanderings landed him in. His usual pattern was to enter a city, find a way to display his gifts of memory and fluency in mathematics for the academic elite, and then parlay that display into a teaching position or private tutorship that would last the two or three years it took him to inevitably clash with the academic establishment, call them all asses (his favorite word), write inflamed philosophical dialogues that belittled them in a manner more reminiscent of an 8 Mile rap battle than an academic paper, and flee to greener pastures just a step ahead of the lynch mob.

What started as a sure means of survival, however, proved to be the doorway to an entire philosophical system that would synthesize a century's worth of confusion and progress into a hopeful whole before being prematurely terminated by the executioner's flames. For Bruno's memory system revolved around the construction of elaborate wheels of association that brought mathematics, language, mythology, and philosophy all together in one interrelated whole. As he refined his methods, it became clearer and clearer to him that the universe could not be as Aristotle had laid it out millennia before. If everything is connected, then there can't be unbridgeable qualitative differences between objects in the observable world. The sun, he hypothesized, must be made of the same things as the Earth, and the stars as well, all part of an interconnected atomic system whose reactions push forward the ticking of the universe. The universe, he came to realize, is an infinite construct which must be broken down to the level of the infinitesimal to be understood.

Keep in mind, he wrote these observations a full thirty years before Galileo published his observations of the sun and Jupiter, and a century before Newton and Leibniz discovered calculus by playing with those very quantities of the infinite and infinitesimal that Bruno guessed must lie at the heart of a proper mathematical analysis of the cosmos. But what is truly remarkable is that Bruno's prescience was not at all remarkable for his time. His infinite universe was already hypothesized a century before by Nicholas of Cusa, his atomism was there in the ancient works of Democritus, and his mathematical tinkering with the infinitely small can not only be found in a nascent form in the works of Archimedes, but also in his exposure to Fabrizio Mordente, a geometer whose invention of the adjustable compass so impressed Bruno that it took him a whole *five months* to steal Mordente's ideas and then stab him in the back in a series of wickedly funny but entirely unfair pamphlets.

Bruno's was not the gift of originality, but that of synthesis. By taking all of these insights and combining them with his love of Platonic emotionality and hermetic uniformity, he created an astounding whole, the swan song of Early Modernity in its most rapturous and hopeful form. In surveying the spectrum of the cosmos through his profoundly ordered memory, Bruno saw it stretching out forever into the past, with always the same messages asserting themselves. Not Catholicism, nor even Christianity, had a unique claim to the truths of existence, but rather everyone from the Egyptian priest to the skeptical Greek made their crucial contributions, all connecting to the unity of the universe in their own ways and by their own lights. To discount their ideas because of the lack of Jesus in them Bruno found foolish and short-sighted. He had no patience with the concept of Hell as being entirely foreign to his love-bound universe, and rarely spoke of the Paradise of angels outside of how we experience it on Earth through our contemplation of the infinities of existence. For Bruno, interconnection meant that all of the stuff of divinity is within each human, and so any notion of original sin or fearful gods judging our unworthy world is the foundation of political control, not genuine philosophy.

What I find astounding is that all of this borrowing and stitching together produced a conception of the universe that closely mirrors that of Spinoza's revolutionary *Ethics*, written nearly a century later, with its focus on the perfection of the infinitely complex universe and man's highest calling to contemplate it and find our own natures written therein. Perhaps, had Bruno been a bit more staid in presentation or less combative in personality, and if he had not lived in an era when Catholicism was desperately thrashing about to find its feet again, we would be looking to him rather than Spinoza as the true link between medieval and modern philosophy.

In principle, he looked forward to a religion that accepted all approaches to self-enlightenment. In fact, he wasn't above exploiting religious prejudice to get what he needed. In delivering a funeral oration to a collection of influential Lutherans, he spoke of the Pope as a gorgon whose "blasphemous tongues, more numerous than the hairs of his head, assist and administer, every one of them, against God, Nature, and humanity, who infect the world for the worst with their poison of ignorance and depravity." Two years later, in the clutches of the Inquisition, he was denying the authority of his Dominican jailers to judge him, saying that he only acknowledged such authority in the person of the Pope, that erstwhile world-consuming gorgon.

After nearly two decades of wandering and writing, Bruno had put enough heretical notions to paper to convict him a hundred times over. He centered an entire lecture series around 120 Errors of Aristotle at a time when Aristotelian philosophy formed the core of Catholic theology. He quoted obscure Egyptian texts and pre-Socratic Greek philosophers with the same frequency as Thomas Aquinas or Peter Lombard. He hypothesized a heliocentric infinite universe made of the same fundamental elements as the Earth, all in constant flux, capable of generating its own compounds and even life when the celestial spheres of Ptolemy were still the dogmatically accepted building blocks of the Christian universe. He wrote his philosophy as Italian dialogues and sprawling verse poems when Latin was the accepted language of academic discourse. He denied Hell and railed against religious persecution as contrary to the unified, love-permeated cosmos that he felt must be the true font of existence. Further, since we are all made of the same stuff, and are constantly evolving into other things, then equality must be the nature of man (even if some of them are asses), and this was against not only every reigning theological notion, but every political one as well.

In the end, it wasn't his writings that landed him in the clutches of the Inquisition, but his own quarrelsome nature. After moving to Venice to take up a potentially lucrative position as a private tutor, he soon felt the itch to return to Frankfurt, the center of the publishing world at the time, to continue his writing career. His patron insisted that Bruno stay and finish teaching him the memory system he had promised. Bruno refused and started packing his bags, only to find a half dozen gondoliers grabbing him in the middle of the night and locking him in an attic. (I don't know if this is something you can still hire gondoliers to do, but I certainly hope it is.) His patron fired off a letter to the local Inquisition detailing all of Bruno's departures from Orthodoxy listed above, and more besides, and thence began Bruno's nine year legal dance with first the Venetian, then Roman, Inquisition.

This trial ought to be an object lesson for anybody wanting to know how the Inquisition actually worked outside of its Spanish variant. Popularly considered the kangaroo court of early Modernity, the Italian branches of the Inquisition had strict procedural protocols, rules of the game that had to be obeyed. Bruno knew these rules all too well, and was able to nimbly dance around them for the better part of a decade until he made the fatal mistake of attempting to go over the Inquisition's head, straight to the Pope, for acquittal. If Bruno's life of perpetual fleeing taught him anything, it should have been that his political instincts weren't precisely the most finely honed, and yet he finally threw away his strength, theological quibbling and rules monkeying, in favor of a political gambit that was doomed to fail. The Inquisition could put up with much in the name of protocol, but a challenge to its own authority coming from within its own prison was too much. Giordano Bruno was burned to death on February 17, 1600.

FURTHER READING:

Bruno's writings encompass a number of different styles, from his mammoth satirical play *The Candlemaker* to the Platonically inspired Italian Dialogues of which *The Heroic Frenzies* is the most readily available in English to his verse epic *de Rerum Natura* clone, *On the Immense and the Numberless.* The language is what you would expect from a sixteenth century Italian – florid and emotional and never content to use one word where a list of ten synonyms is at hand. Be prepared for long sections praising himself, and longer, but much funnier ones, decrying the asininity of everybody who disagrees with him. I'd start with *Frenzies* and see how you like it – some find the mixture of poetry and dialogue enchanting, others distracting, but it certainly is a literary experience Of Its Time, and that's worth treating yourself to now and then. Also, the Cambridge Edition of *Cause, Principle, and Unity* is not only valuable for the main text, but has a nice introduction to what made Bruno's philosophy so revolutionary in its time. For biographies on Bruno, the classic is by Frances B. Yates, though it definitely has an axe to grind. More recently, Ingrid Rowland's *Giordano Bruno: Philosopher/Heretic* (2008) is beautifully written and also pretty fun!

THE INSUFFICIENT SELF:
THE CULT OF MEDITATION AND ITS SPIRITUAL OFFSPRING

(Originally Published in *The Freethinker*, July 2013)

If you were to ask a stormtrooper how the Death Star works, he'd probably say, "Well, it's big and round and I keep my blaster in a cabinet over there." The part is rarely a reliable expositor of the whole. And yet, so much religious practice which styles itself as Enlightened is based on an unshakeable faith in the potential omnipotence of the part. From the over-confident musings of meditation-driven philosophy to the crude reliance of New Age Spirituality on *feelings* for determining questions of existence, we're given to understand that, by turning inward, we can discover everything about ourselves there is to know.

It's hard to fault this approach to knowledge of the self. For millennia, such techniques were all we had. If you wanted to figure out where the border between consciousness and unconsciousness lay, or why sometimes you felt compelled to do things that were so entirely against your self-interest, there was nothing to do except sit on a rock and Think Hard about it. We came up with a lot of promising guesses that way – notions about what constitutes identity and volition that are very okay, one might even say outstandingly passable. Granted, there was also a lot of metaphysical phantom conjuring that consisted of little more than elegantly garbed wishful thinking, a sort of necromancy of childhood hopes rendered weighty by being in Greek or German. But, on the whole, something like progress was being made.

And then a few people got the genuinely wonderful idea that, instead of continually running aground by pinning one's hopes entirely on the ability of the conscious self to describe the content of the complete self, maybe one could investigate the parts of that entity from without, determine the mechanisms of each manifestation of selfhood and see what commonalities might be found between them. The romantic lone man sitting on the rock was replaced by small teams of dedicated but effectively anonymous men and women shocking slugs and getting mice drunk while making countless tallies of the results.

The lone men were made understandably uncomfortable by all of this. They dug their heels in and tried to pass off incompleteness as profundity. "What need for the mere mechanics of neurons when you can go on a deep voyage of inner discovery and find out your TRUE nature?" they whispered in hushed tones and mocked the slug shockers for their mechanistic accountancy. Never mind that their methods still hadn't moved on from a reliance on the part being able to account for the whole that had made the methods of the slug shockers so necessary in the first place. "Inner Voyage" SOUNDS like it should get you somewhere impressive, right?

Unfortunately, giving something an awesome name doesn't guarantee its greatness, otherwise I'd be watching "Snakes On a Plane" right now instead of writing this article. The techniques of meditative inquiry have natural boundaries, and on the other side of those boundaries lie vast plains and continents of self-knowledge that those techniques simply cannot access. Attempts to do so come off as little more than educated guesses draped in metaphor. When consciousness comes face to face with a mental process, it necessarily interprets it through a conscious filter and vocabulary which is qualitatively unequal to the task of sensibly reporting what it's witnessing.

Consciousness in this instance is like a rhinoceros seeing a giraffe for the first time – it might try very gamely to describe the giraffe in rhinoceros terms, and even construct some very neat extended metaphors that try and twist rhino words to fit giraffe attributes. But the fact remains that that brave fellow isn't, nor will he ever be, our best source for figuring out what that giraffe is all about. And to put your foot down and insist in spite of all evidence to the contrary that his grasping metaphors are the result of deep insight instead of a fundamental failure to Interpret The Other is to invite philosophical stagnation.

This is what's happened to those religions that took the bold move in eschewing theology in favor of a focus on developing the potential of introspection, Buddhism and its spiritual cousins being the most notable. The great irony is that what started in freedom from dogma has become itself so dogmatic in the face of alternate approaches to investigating the conscious self. Buddhist apologists insist that their methods have privileged insight into the mind, and when it is pointed out that Necessarily Limited is a more apt word than Privileged, they seek the sure security of, "It's an Eastern thing, you wouldn't understand." That response served them in good stead a century ago, when it was still an open question whether the conscious mind didn't after all have access to the full self. Since then we've come to see that it doesn't, and that so much of the self and construction is beyond any possibility of even being witnessed by conscious self-reflection, let alone interpreted thereby, that the Eastern Defense has more of the tinny crinkle of denial and desperation about it than the authoritative heft of just rebuke.

"But I like meditating – I find it a good and centering practice," you might say. Great. I like flailing around like an idiot to "Jump For My Love" on Just Dance 3. I find it a good and centering practice, and every once in a while have a good idea while doing it. But I'm not going to recommend that it replace neurological research as a truth-seeking method. To make the extreme claim that meditation and its variants are the only source of profoundly true ideas about the self is, at this stage in history, merely an obstructive act born of reactive fear and dogmatic zealotry. Even the relatively benign claim that meditative insight and scientific research ought to work together to plumb the depths of the self strikes me as a proposal on the order of Eh. It's when you wanted to go to a PG-13 rated movie as a kid but you couldn't because you had to bring your five year old brother with you, and so you ended up having to watch The Care Bears Movie instead so he wouldn't get scared. It's a nice thing to do, but it also means you're going to have to wait YEARS for him to grow up before you can get where you wanted to go. The difference being that kids, given time, *will* grow up, while religions, given time, are not guaranteed to grow wise.

Really, though, it's not the methodological orthodoxy of Buddhism that troubles me over much. Every once in a while you'll see an until-then promising neuroscientist tumble into its grasp and flop about vaguely (but oh how financially profitably) therein for the rest of his career, and it's sad to watch, but we're hardly *hemorrhaging* scientists this way. What I find rather more insidious, or if not insidious at least tedious, are the pop culture descendants of this stubbornness about the priority of introspective insights.

"It's true because I *feel* it's true."

For Christians, this way of solving ontological dilemmas reared its head in the sixteenth century, established itself as a standard theological approach in the nineteenth, and really hasn't looked back since. The proof of Jesus's divinity wasn't in the logical conjurations of Aquinas, but in the heart and what it seemed to tell you was true. What's amazing is how much this evaluative mode has penetrated the non-Christian community. People who were immune to its crass subjectivity when coming from Christian mouths and pens somehow found it entirely persuasive when coming from the more *philosophical* religions, or perhaps one should say religious philosophies.

If, as some Buddhist practice would have it, the real deep truths about existence are available exclusively through properly performed meditative practice, then it's but a small (though irresponsible) step to the notion that how we *feel* about something determines how it is. If our conscious mind is uniquely capable of grasping reality that can't be determined through merely scientific methods, why shouldn't our subjective feelings about something inform what possibly exists and what doesn't?

One feels that death just can't be the end, so it isn't. One feels that there's a grand something out there looking out for us, so there is. One feels so good performing certain rituals, so those rituals must be connected somehow to the truths of the universe. Again, there are entirely good reasons for having started down this line of evaluation.

Feelings are great things – they push us towards stuff that is generally good for us and away from things that stand a chance of hurting us. They are the chemical reins by which our DNA orients us towards self preservation. But again, it's a question of spheres of influence.

Just as the conscious self isn't guaranteed exclusive insight into unconscious matters of the self (or indeed into the mechanisms behind its own conscious acts), so do feelings naturally have their limits. They are a control mechanism directed survivalwards, not a matchless arbiter of truth. When they are working properly, they are tools employed to compel us to move in the direction that our internal neural calculus has determined is best. That calculus is based on genetic predisposition and experience, and the further from experience it is asked to render judgment, the more suspect its decisions. We feel fear at the sight of a massive snarling dog. Well and good. We feel that our spirit is incorporeal and will survive death to rejoin the universe's energy. Little bit dodgy.

Meditation can be a good practice. Feelings are fine things. Obviously. But to claim for them the universal power of insight into anything they happen to touch is obtuse and frankly insulting to the people who are giving their lives over, one slug neuron at a time, to figuring out how the self is actually constituted. To denigrate that work because the oracular proclamations of hilltop monks and inner voices are easier to grasp and sexier is an act of petulant adolescence. They have their place, and that place is severely limited. For the rest, we must rely on the glorious but sure footed blandness of scientific rigor married to boundless curiosity. And it will take time but, after all, God didn't create the universe in a day...

MARIA MONTESSORI: WHEN GENIUS DEVOURS ITSELF.

(Originally published at *MadArtLab*, May 2014)

There are some people who lack the splendid good sense of dying at the right time. Geniuses who flared with an early fire and then ground out their latter days in petty feuds and stifling orthodoxy. That line of demarcation between early brilliance and later brutality is always fascinating – what happens to genius when it turns against its own best interests – and there are few examples of it so marked as that of the great educational innovator of the twentieth century, Dr. Maria Montessori.

Had Montessori died in 1913 at age 43, at the height of her fame and insight, this would be a pretty straightforward little article about somebody seeing a problem, and using her own profound scientific instinct to make the world incalculably better. But she didn't – she lived on to 1952, and in that time manifested a resistance to innovation and adaptation that all but destroyed the Montessori Method.

That decline is a wonderful, awful tale, but preceding it is a series of triumphs unprecedented in the history of public education. Montessori was born in 1870 in an Italy only recently united by the singular diplomatic genius of Cavour. Her native country was, and I'm being charitable here, a sloppy sloppy mess at the time. A conjured amalgam of former papal states, Habsburg possessions, and dirt poor southern territories, there was little uniting these regions except for the vague feeling that once, a while ago, all of them had something to do with the Renaissance. What was needed was a universal education system to raise the shockingly low standards that abounded throughout Italy – a new, united and educated generation to steer the ship of state into the future.

Maria Montessori was a product of that intense sense of the future and its possibilities. Her mother actively encouraged her in every bold and unorthodox step of her early career, and her father, while not always happy with her startling life choices, nevertheless refrained from getting in her way. At the time, students out of elementary school had a choice between taking either a classical or a practical track for high school. Most girls, if they continued their education at all, went for the classical track, with its training in ancient languages and literature. Maria, however, opted for the practical, with its modern languages, science, and math. Initially, she wanted to be an engineer, but once she submerged herself in the sciences, she found herself beckoned by medicine.

This was, of course, madness. No woman had ever been accepted at the University of Rome to study medicine. The idea of a lady doctor was clearly absurd, and Maria's father was concerned lest their family become the farcical cautionary tale of Rome. Somehow (possibly through the intercession of the Pope!) Maria was accepted to study, and proved herself one of the greatest students in the history of the college.

Which wasn't hard, as Italian universities of the late 19th century were famously amongst the most slovenly run and ill respected institutions of Europe. Students showed up, or more often didn't, heard a couple of lectures, took some tests, and got their degrees. Most were in it for the social standing a degree conferred, and so made the absolute minimum of effort in attendance and study. Expectations were crushingly low, but Maria, to the shock of everybody, seemed to actually *want* to learn, showed up for every lecture, and filled every moment with books and questions. She was easily made a doctor with the overwhelming recommendation of the faculty and thereupon began her practice.

Initially, she had no thought of specializing in the science of education. Her field was a biological anthropology which sought to use scientific measurements to determine psychological types. Her early writings focus on such matters as the relation of nose ratios to secretiveness or madness, a line of inquiry which was to have disturbing consequences in the early twentieth century in the hands of eugenics-leaning governments. Fortunately, an experience at the University's psychiatric clinic deflected her attention onto her true path.

Common practice at the time dictated that the mentally challenged all be lumped together in barren rooms to prevent overstimulation of their imbalanced minds. Maria noticed that, after meals, the children would fling themselves down on the floor looking for crumbs and food scraps. The other doctors looked with disgust on the practice as an example of their mental deficiency, but Montessori saw it differently. What she saw were children so starved for mental stimulation that they were turning to scraps and crumbs to get it. These children didn't need less sense training, they needed more.

She was soon given the chance to put her ideas into practice at the Orthophrenic School, observing and developing methods to teach and develop the senses of such children, and then tethering that sense development eventually to intellectual learning. In doing this, she was working in the tradition of Itard and Seguin, whose research in the early nineteenth century had demonstrated the potential of using a sense-based approach to help foster learning in the mentally disadvantaged. By working with blocks and feeling the shape of cut out letters, they were able to eventually teach abstract concepts to children who were given up as lost by the rest of the medical world. Montessori felt she could extend and systematize their work, and was soon pulling off minor miracles at the Orthophrenic School, teaching the children to first distinguish the crude sensory differences of objects, and then through a process of refinement, bringing them to more abstract understanding of the world and their function in it.

It was a culminating moment in the history of education for the mentally challenged, but she soon realized, with a clear instinct for the psychology of children, that the methods she was using with the patients at the Orthophrenic School could also be used to improve education for all children. But before she could apply that knowledge, Montessori had a personal struggle to overcome. She had fallen in love with another doctor at the school, and had a child by him. Of course, it would destroy her fragile reputation to publically acknowledge having born a child out of wedlock, and so she was faced with keeping the child but losing her career or continuing her work but remaining a stranger to her own son.

She chose the latter. For the first fifteen years of his life, Mario Montessori's mother was a passing acquaintance in his life, and until her death she continued to refer to him publically as her nephew, a role he understood and came to accept. She left the child behind to be raised by her family and returned to her work.

That work led to the establishment in 1907 of the revolutionary *Casa dei Bambini*, an experimental school that was the original idea of some low-rent landlords seeking a way to keep the children of their buildings from running wild, defacing property, during the day. They decided to create a small school in the building, and called upon the world-famous Dr. Montessori to design the program and oversee its implementation. Given free reign, she developed the system that continues to be used in Montessori schools the world over.

Traditionally, children were held to be incapable of learning reading before the age of six, and were expected to sit still and be lectured at over the course of a day by way of education. Montessori, by observing children at play, discerned a thirst for understanding their environment and mastering new skills. So, she organized her school around that sense of independent mastery. The children would have a choice of activities in a large cupboard that they could take out and play with for as long as they wanted. The teacher would show them how each activity worked, and then leave them to figure the rest out on their own. The children naturally worked their way from the simple challenges (placing cylinders in the right shaped holes) to the more fine-tuned motor applications, and demanded more.

So, Montessori decided to try teaching them to write and read through a senses-first approach, crafting letters for their hands to trace and letting them hear the noise of the letter as they felt its contours. And, very soon, those children began putting their letters together to make words, writing everything they could think of anywhere that they could find (a task made easier in Italian by the fact that things are actually written as they sound, unlike the "knight" and "through" bestrewn wrecks of English spelling). Once they had that down, reading was a comparative snap. While the national schools had children just starting to struggle with their first copybooks at age six, Montessori's children were writing full sentences at age four.

Not only that, but visitors to the *Casa* noted how orderly and attentive the children were, how they took turns serving each other at lunch, and how engaged they were in their own learning processes. Reports of the school's miraculous results flew over Europe and across the sea to the United States, while Montessori found herself besieged with letters from teachers curious to learn the method. On a tour through the United States in 1913, she was treated like an A-List celebrity, her lectures instant sell-outs wherever she went.

And that's where the story should stop. She gets on the boat in 1913, sails back to Italy. Oh no, iceberg. Terrible loss. Much weeping. But at least we still have her work. But no, the boat arrived fine, and Montessori settled in to a decades long struggle to preserve the purity of her method. She resigned her official positions, making herself financially dependent on sales of her learning apparatus and teacher training course fees. She steadfastly refused to let anybody but herself train teachers in the Montessori Method. Worse, she insisted that her system was absolutely complete, that any of her disciples who spoke of merging it with other educational theories or altering the order of the apparatus was a traitor to the movement. As a result, she cut the Montessori technique completely off from other developments in the field of education, and particularly from the important ideas of Dewey and Kilpatrick in the social education of children.

She did important work in her later years, especially in overseeing the development of Montessori schools in India, but her refusal to update her methods, to scientifically test her assertions, or to allow the training of teachers outside of her immediate control all crippled the development of her educational philosophy and practice. When she died, the Montessori method was a phantom of an idea in the United States, where it once seemed poised to take over the educational system entirely. It would take a new generation with fresh concerns to revive her concepts and restart the Montessori movement we know today.

However lamentable the end, there is no doubt about the ultimate impact. Take a walk down the toddler aisle at your local Target, and what you'll find is device after device aimed at the sensory training that Montessori made famous. Those techniques, and the underlying idea of the importance of agency in education, have, when combined with Dewey's principles of school as a social and creative space, formed the core of our modern educational system. And, in an age when More Testing is the answer to every educational problem, perhaps it's time to step back and consider Montessori's fundamental wisdom again, about how children, through learning, become themselves.

Further Reading: Rida Kramer's *Maria Montessori: A Biography* is fantastic. It features a forward by Anna Freud, and engaging insights into the history of education theory. More than that, it doesn't attempt to exaggerate Montessori's importance or cover up her faults, but tells the engrossing story of what happens to genius when it refuses intellectual cooperation.

FIVE THOR COMICS MY ATHEIST HEART HOLDS DEAR

(Originally published at *The Twilight of Nearly Everything*)

For nearly fifty years now, Thor has been the comic book writers have seized on to ponder the complexity of mankind's relation to the deities we have created. And amidst all of the skull-cracking and "I Say Thee NAY!" they have managed to craft in that time some of the medium's most stirring representations of religion awry, and the humanity at the heart of it all. With the release of the second Thor movie tomorrow, it seems a good time to look back at five Thor comics that challenged our notions of the greatness of the gods.

5. THOR 294 (Writer: Roy Thomas. Art: Keith Pollard and Chic Stone)

When Roy Thomas took over Thor, he brought with him a desire to do justice to the deep tradition of Norse mythology and a sensitivity to the subtlety of man's mythological craftsmanship. In this issue, we are treated to the secret origin of Odin, and not only that, but the story of how the gods fashioned their own identities from bits and pieces of the world they found both buried in the memories of shared experience and in the world around them.

Caught in a cycle of destruction and rebirth, the young gods must answer the question of why they are here and how they came to be, and in doing so act out the origins of our own creation myths. In a move that has a certain whiff of Feuerbach about it, Thomas shows Odin fashioning his pantheon, and the universe about it, from those things he most admires and fears about himself and the departed universe that gave him birth, only to watch that true and personal origin get buried in the myths spun by his children.

And isn't that always the way? You find something astounding and great about yourself, and you feel the need for it to be more than just personal, to be a manifestation of a great and eternal truth, and so you cut it out of yourself and make a god of it. Humans are *always* doing crazy stuff like that, and Thomas captures it beautifully in this issue.

But my favorite part about this comic is the Letters page, which I'm pretty sure isn't reproduced in collections, so you'll have to shell out the big $5 to get an original copy, but it's worth it because Thomas devotes two whole pages to an essay about the tilting of the Earth's axis, Ragnarok, and how all of that ties into Marvel continuity, which is the sort of thing you just don't see anymore. PLUS, if you're a Wagner fan, this issue has all sorts of little call-outs to the *Ring*'s conception of Norse myth, and that's always fun.

4. JOURNEY INTO MYSTERY 87 (Writer: Stan Lee, Art: Jack Kirby)

Okay, this issue has nothing whatsoever to do with Humanism, or Atheism, or Theology, or really anything, and everything to do with the Ritual of the Stan, which is something everybody ought to do at one point, regardless of what you believe about the heavens above. The Ritual of the Stan is where you grab a bunch of Stan Lee comics and read through them until you get one which doesn't *quite* hold together when read quietly to yourself. Then, you get up, flip back to the beginning, and read it aloud, *in the manner of Stan Lee*, and behold as it all starts coming perfectly together!

Some comics are just meant to be read aloud.

This is a pretty good one for it (though Loki's second appearance is a great one too, if for nothing else than the culminating moment where Thor throws a bunch of bread crumbs at a group of pigeons and thereby saves the world). Thor spent a lot of time in the early issues fighting Commies. Issue 84, which was his second appearance ever, was one such and here, just three issues later, they're back! Really, the cover says it all (again, read it quietly to yourself, and then read it *as Stan Lee!* and suddenly "electronically treated chains" makes total sense).

Is it one of the best issues of Thor ever written? No, but it's one of the best times you'll have reading a Thor comic, and even atheists deserve a bit of fun now and again.

3. THOR 493 (Writer: Warren Ellis, Artist: Mike Deodato, Jr.)

Before writing the heaven-shaking *Supergod,* Ellis wrote the World Engine story arc for Thor in the middle of the comic book Dark Ages, better known as the mid-90s. It was not an environment friendly for the crafting of complex mainstream comic book tales, but there were gems among the fist fights and flexed pecs, and World Engine was one of them. This is the third issue in the arc, and what makes it so remarkable is how directly it engages with the various explanations that exist in the Marvel Universe for the existence of the Asgardians, even while Thor finds himself grappling with the consequences of a mortality thrust upon him by his harsh father.

We see the Asgardians as they exist in the mythology of their human observers, and at the same time as laughing creatures of a science evolved beyond any merely human understanding. As beings who began with a purpose, perhaps, but who have squandered it and now burn themselves out in the fire of their own scorn and retribution. It is a grim story with the only relief coming when Thor and The Enchantress, long the bitterest of enemies, set aside the immensity of their godly past and decide to be, if only for a short time, a couple of mortals with nothing to lose.

2. Thor 577 (Writer: Dan Jurgens, Artist: Scot Eaton)

This is a single issue from one of the greatest arcs in Thor history. I've written about the arc as a whole elsewhere, but this issue is a pretty good stand-alone representation of everything that is challenging and exciting about the larger story. The humans have brought Asgard crashing down to Earth, and in the rubble and disaster of the moment, Thor has declared that the Asgardians will now take charge of the planet.

In the crucial moment of decision, Jurgens is at his best, showing us how, once a binary religious mindset kicks in, it runs roughshod over the humans it is meant to help. Lady Sif, Thor's longtime friend and a potent warrior of Asgard, argues passionately that what the disaster betokens is that humans are now past the stage of needing gods, that their cohabitation of the planet will only bring suffering to both, but Thor, mad with frustration and egged on by Loki (of course), will have none of it, and so sets humankind in the teeth of benevolent tyranny, curing it of all its ills if only it will obey.

The whole series, from the *Spiral* arc through *The Reigning* and into this, the first issue of *Gods and Men*, investigates the consequences of charity unchecked by wisdom, and the compromises that power makes with itself in its perpetuation, and is, I think, not merely one of the best Thor experiences to be had in comics, but one of the greatest experiences, period.

1. Thor: God of Thunder 8 (Writer: Jason Aaron, Artist: Esad Ribic)

The Thor comic has gone through some exciting and unsteady times as of late, dying and being resurrected, and then dying AGAIN and being resurrected AGAIN, each time with a change of numbering that was entirely traumatic to all of us who love seeing those numbers in the longbox march magisterially forward. Jason Aaron rescued the situation last year with *Thor: God of Thunder*, bringing the world of comics a tale of stark and uncompromising honesty that catapulted Thor back into the consciousness of a resurrection-weary reading public.

He also brought us our first true atheist anti-hero in the form of Gorr, the God Butcher, a character whose modest goal is to eliminate all gods from the universe and thereby free mortal existence from its self-abasing subservience and the destructive violence that comes with it. You could pick anything from the first ten issues and it will be golden, but my favorite is issue 8, if for no other reason than the conversation between Gorr's son and a young version of Thor:

Thor: You think this is a good thing, the killing of gods?

Gorr's Son: It will be a better world without gods. No more fear of eternal damnation or lust for eternal reward. No more hatred between believers of rival faiths. Without the lie of eternity to serve as our crutch, we will have no choice but to finally cherish what precious little time we have. And to put our faith in only ourselves and one another.

It is a beautiful moment, tucked away in a little side-panel, but it says everything that needs saying about the tensions at the heart of Thor's place in the Marvel universe, and about religion's continued place in the hearts of a humanity that is starting to find its way back to itself again.

AND BEFORE YOU ERUPT IN INDIGNATION:

I am aware that Walter Simonson is not represented on the above list, and that his absence is an act of sheer madness. He is the man who defined how Thor looks and sounds, and how his universe hangs together, and anybody looking for a good Thor story will find it written upon each page of Simonson's time at the helm. This list is the intersection of my personal favorite Thor stories (which include many, many Simonson issues) with my favorite humanist comics, with Stan Lee thrown in to add a bit of jolliness to the mix. The time when I just talk for pages and pages about my fifty favorite Thor comics is still far off, we can hope.

GETTING STARTED:

Marvel is good about making back issues available in trade format. The whole Warren Ellis story arc is available in *Marvel Visionaries: The Mighty Thor: Mike Deodato Jr. Journey Into Mystery* 87 and *Thor* 294 are both available at a great price in the *Marvel Essentials* series (each contains a ton of issues, though just in black and white). And there are complete trades of *Thor: Gods and Men* and *Thor: Godbomb*, available at your friendly Local Comic Shop! So get reading! Verily!

Giovanni Boccaccio:
Master of Mythology
And Soft Core 14ᵗʰ Century Erotica

(Originally Published at *The Humanist*, October 2014)

For six hundred years, before, "Did somebody here call a plumber?" and, "Did somebody here call a second, hunkier plumber?" the lifeblood of Western erotica was drawn from a series of stories improbably written during the depths of the Black Plague. As two out of three Florentines died in the course of a single year, one man wrote a book that formed the basis not only of Europe's erotic imagination, but the foundation of narrative fiction itself, for the next half-millennium. That book was the *Decameron*, and the rotund mass of excitable contradictions that penned it stands at the very threshold of modern humanist fiction.

Giovanni Boccaccio (1313-1375) was, like Leonardo da Vinci, an illegitimate child. Unlike Leonardo, however, his father was quick to bring him into his new family and business, entrusting him with the most important of tasks, and generally making illegitimacy seem so light a burden that Boccaccio passed the favor forward by siring five illegitimate children of his own later.

His father was a businessman invested deeply in fostering economic relations between Florence and Naples, and it was the vivacious world of the marketplace that stamped Boccaccio's early life. While the clerics and academics scribbled away in towers, agonizing over the twists and turns of Scholasticism, Boccaccio was doing business with traders from all parts of the world, grappling with the unique humanity of each, and the many ways by which people seek purpose and pleasure. His early books, including the *Decameron*, were celebrations of this hectic merchant-class spirit, of love and duplicity, compassion and lust, all jostling against each other to produce People, As They Are.

With that background, Boccaccio could have led a thoroughly robust, eminently enjoyable, and entirely forgotten life as one of the thousands of merchants working their way valiantly, if not always quite honestly, to the heart of the post-feudal world. But it so happened that he also was allowed to pursue an entirely unique course of education as well. While he was supposed to be studying law, he was actually learning at the feet of some of the most eclectic minds of fourteenth century Italy. Their interest was in learning Everything, in gathering all of human knowledge up and using it to create works of imposing referential erudition but little psychological insight. Under their spell, Boccaccio wrote his early works, imitations of his favorite authors spattered with references to antiquity and given to explosive bouts of whimsical autobiographical ecstasy and bottomless grief. In the *Filocolo* (1336), he veers wildly between styles, a tour de force pastiche of everything available in the literary air at the time, driven forward by his unrestrained emotionalism.

He was trying everything that literary life had to offer, digesting it, and reproducing it at first as a gifted mimic, and ultimately fusing the voices of a continent together into the narrative pulse that would drive Europe away from the grandeur of the epic, towards the psychological complexity of the domestic and mercantile spheres. He mixed the elegance of the Latin classics with the simple emotionality of French balladry, and at the end of the day, he had forged the modern secular Storytelling Voice, which would inspire Chaucer some decades later to summon English literature forth from the ether.

In 1341 and 1342, returning to Florence after his formative years at Naples, he wrote the *Comedia delle Ninfe* and the *Amorosa Visione*, which accelerated the turn towards the middle-class as the subject of fiction, and of the qualities and needs of the heart as superior to all other concerns. He was finding his voice, but it was still hemmed in by the need to Dazzle With Erudition. He wanted to put all that he knew on the page, while at the same time staying true to a realistic portrayal of humanity and its foibles, a tension that was only decided in favor of reality at last when that reality came barreling grimly down upon him and everyone he loved.

For 1348 was a Plague year. For Florence, it was *the* Plague year. When it ended, only one out of every three citizens remained. In the midst of omnipresent death, half the survivors threw themselves into religious extremism, while the others lost themselves in chasing pleasure while they could, ripping to tatters the web of traditional wisdom that had driven society automatically on, and making room for something new. It is that sense of reworking the boundaries of humanity's potential in the midst of absolute tragedy that gives the *Decameron* a fearless radiance that excites still.

That, and all the sex.

Because, let's face it, the *Decameron* is as much a masterpiece of new narrative style as it is a shameless erotic smorgasbord. The entire third chapter is composed almost exclusively of stories that center around elaborate schemes that culminate in serial humping. A convent gardener is used as an object of sexual pleasure by every nun on the premises until he gets too worn out to work and pleads for a more sensible love schedule. An abbot tricks a man into believing he is dead, and keeps him in a dark room, convincing him it is Purgatory, to cure the man of his jealousy, all while flagrantly carrying on a hot affair with his wife. Two lovers use a monk as their unwitting go-between to pass messages about likely times to meet for mutual carnal knowledge. A woman gets fed up with her husband, who will only have sex on days that aren't religious holidays, and runs off with a pirate king to make mad unrestrained love multiple times a day. A woman cheats on her husband in the husband's full view and somehow manages to convince him that it was a vision induced by a magic pear tree. A holy hermit, overcome by the beauty of a visitor, convinces her that his penis is the devil, and her vagina is hell, and that, as good Christians, they must find a way to put the devil back in Hell, mustn't they?

The heroes are cunning tricksters, impelled by love or something slightly less pure to twist the social system to their advantage. One of the earliest stories features a greedy and utterly profane merchant who, by dint of a cunning and entirely insincere deathbed confession, manages not only to get his hosts out of a sticky situation, but also to get himself canonized in the process! Rapscallions become saints. Saints become horny lechers like the rest of us. And the most consistent heroes are not brave Christian knights, but honorable Muslim rulers, impassioned lovers, and poor but clever scamps of every flavor.

It's a Great Book that also happens to be a great book. In those one hundred stories lies the seed of everything we consider now to be a good yarn. The scoundrels whom you can't help but root for, the teenagers risking everything to outwit the system in order to enjoy a perfect day, the women who are frank about their desires and rather fed up with being treated as incorruptible marble objects. Han Solo. Ferris Bueller. Carrie Bradshaw. Boccaccio gave us leave to care seriously about characters like these and their stories, and we haven't stopped caring since.

After the Plague, Boccaccio was absorbed equally in tasks diplomatic and literary. His status as the great writer of Florence meant that, whenever a diplomatic mission needed that extra savor of distinction, he was put in charge of it and packed off to some corner of Italy for a while. That might have given him yet more material for a second *Decameron*, but he was decisively re-routed to other pursuits by the advice and friendship of the man he looked up to as the greatest poet and mind of his age, Petrarch.

Petrarch was the great influence in the second half of Boccaccio's life, and it's hard to say whether that was for good or for ill. The two shared a beautifully nerdy love of the works of antiquity, bubbling over with glee whenever one or the other unearthed a rare Latin manuscript in their travels. Together, they pushed Leontius Pilatus to translate Homer's works into Latin and so to add another shade altogether to European literary life (incidentally, after a troubled life, Leontius died when struck by lightning, a rather fitting end, when you think about it). Petrarch encouraged Boccaccio to continue work on the great compilations of Boccaccio's later life, including the massive and authoritative collection of ancient mythology, the *Genealogica*, which reigned for centuries as the standard text on the study of mythology and contained a stirring defense of the study of pagan beliefs. He also buttressed Boccaccio's belief in the project of vernacular poetry, and together their amassed prestige pushed poetry into a place of prominence in Western intellectual life. And, on the human side, he was a friend, somebody who understood the younger man's bursts of temper, and who always had a room available whenever fortune took a downturn, which it often did.

However.

He was also a Christian moralist who drove Boccaccio to a life of contemplative solitude, to ponderous moral reflection, and to an increasing cynicism about the world and the pleasure to be had in it. The boy who ran through the marketplace and university, absorbing everything he heard and turning it into a new sense of narrative promise had become the scholarly hermit, obsessing over politics and whether the last letter he wrote to Petrarch had been quite flattering enough. From having written a startling collection of the lives of famous women, he fell to authoring a nasty and misogynist rant, the *Corbaccio* (1365). He felt ashamed of the impulses that had made him such an intoxicating writer, and retreated as an independent artist. He was looking backwards, to Dante and the works of Rome and Greece, and sideways, to Petrarch, but no longer forward.

Not that he needed to. The *Decameron* was such a complete Europe-wide success that he could have rested on its merits the rest of his career. Instead, he produced a definitive accounting of ancient mythology, saved countless precious manuscripts from destruction, brought us the *Iliad* and the *Odyssey*, wrote the first work devoted exclusively to giving full credit to woman's place in history, and played an important role in organizing a new generation of writers to create poetry and narratives in their country's native tongue about the everyday people they knew. He found a new self which, if less sexy than Boccaccio Mark 1, was as useful in the grand project of collecting and appreciating the vastness of human belief.

In 1374, Petrarch died, and bequeathed to his friend Boccaccio his fur mantel, knowing how bitterly the cold of his often poor lodgings bit at the younger poet's bones. One year later, Boccaccio passed away while wrapped in that very mantel, and if the case can be made that the real Boccaccio died twenty years earlier, suffocated by the moral mantel of Petrarch, at least both kept him warm.

FURTHER READING: The *Decameron* can be found anywhere. It is one of those books you need to have on hand at all times in order to be called a bookshop. *On Famous Women*, his collection of a hundred plus biographies of famous women, is also readily available in English translation. *Amorosa VIsione* was finally translated into English for the first time in 1986, and will run you about $100 for a used copy, so best of luck with that. A first volume of Boccaccio's massive *Genealogica* was finally released in English in 2011, and runs to a modest 928 pages if you want to get *really* into the roots of European mythological studies. For biographies of Boccaccio, Branca's 1976 *Boccaccio: The Man and his Works* gives you a good sense of Boccaccio's literary importance, though if you don't know Latin the extensive untranslated quotes might be a bit bothersome.

WILL IMMORTALITY SPELL
THE END OF RELIGION?

(Previously Unpublished)

"Mom, what was it like, back when people died?"

I shall not live forever. My children probably won't either, though they'll live a good deal longer than I. But there is a very real chance that my grandchildren will, and it gets one to wondering about the social consequences of immortality, and in particular the fate of religion in a world that has stepped out from beneath the shadow of death.

The easy answer is, of course, that if religion has not evaporated on its own by then, immortality will certainly provide the final blow. Without the fear of personal dissolution, the enticements of religion become purely social, and if there's anything we've learned in the past two decades, it's that religion hardly holds a monopoly on meaningful communal experiences. And its touted moral role has been anything but positive in a world based increasingly on inclusion rather than hierarchy.

It is hard to point to anything that religion does uniquely well besides providing a sort of leitmotivic assurance that our souls are eternal, and once eternity becomes a terrestrial matter, that game will be up as well. But that's only if you look at the things that religion *says* it does well. Let's not forget that power which religion wields but only rarely discusses: The power of differentiation.

What religion lets you do, with no prerequisites, is differentiate yourself, make yourself not only unique and special when the dreary commonplaces of life scream otherwise, but also a bit existentially higher than those around you. You have a secret that they will never know, the poor bastards, and even if you don't have to worry about death, that little bit of a boost to your workaday esteem is a heady thing. Yes, there's an equivalent to be had within the confines of humanism, a way to recognize the overwhelming uniqueness of each individual, but it takes study and patience and a willingness to be, at the end of that whole process, another human among humans.

Now, what one hopes is that the very same processes which extend human life indefinitely will also be busy at work improving that life, giving us collective goals we can hardly imagine now, and providing ways for every member of society to contribute positively towards those goals. In such a world, the need for a desperate collapse into the embrace of a self-defining religion would not be terribly keen. Why thrash about for a pseudo-identity when life is giving you a challenging and fulfilling one on a regular basis?

It's entirely possible, though, that instead of getting better at meaningfully incorporating individuals into the larger human project, we shall merely get better at sating them. Soma and avatars for all. And while that's the worry that most dystopian accounts of the future engage with, I'm not overly concerned about it. Look around today and you see everywhere an eruption of interest in how we work mentally, and how truly intersubjective our own capacity for satisfaction is. The world that will grow out of now can only be more aware of the need for substantial, whole-brain-satisfying inclusivity and connection. It will build schools and public areas, projects and games, based on all of that knowledge, and the humans that will come out of that background cannot help, I think, but have a sense of self that will not need a rough spackling of religious affiliation in order to feel of worth.

No, what concerns me more is the Bouvard and Pecuchet Effect. Flaubert created these two clerks in 1863 and wrote a novel detailing their various attempts to keep each other intellectually engaged in life. They splash about in every area of human endeavor, only to find each wanting, their increasingly encyclopedic grasp of nature and culture tending to depress rather than elevate them. It's a brilliant, if thoroughly demoralizing, book that did not catch on in its own time, perhaps because it was really meant for an age that hasn't happened yet. How do you sustain interest in your development if you have all of time in which to achieve your goals? Where will the panicked thrill of urgency come from that we all need as the crucial spice of existence?

I personally can't imagine anything better than an effective eternity with the book of the universe for company – rather like Henry Bemis in *Time Enough at Last*, with all of his tomes stacked neatly about him. But I admit to being an overly excitable nerd with no filter for distinguishing what I find interesting from what is actually important (whatever *that* means). For many humans, Bouvard might be more the standard, and to them the call of religion and its random imperatives might be just the thing, if only for a while. They might well need a place to go that makes no sense, is contrary to everything they know, and somewhat noxious to boot, precisely because it is so opposed to the constructive predictabilities of a life eternal.

So it falls to us, a generation or two removed from those humans we can't possibly guess at, to put down our hopes as best and often as we can, so that when the future looks back for guidance as to what to do with themselves, they'll have a chorus of elder advice and impossible dreams waiting for them, pushing them on with our unique gift of mortality-born earnestness and purpose whenever their own compass fails to point true.

"You're not answering my questions, mom. What were they like?"

"Well, son, they made a lot of guesses about what life might be like for us. And you know what? They were all totally, lusciously, beautifully wrong. But we'll forgive them. After all, they were only mortals."

www.ingramcontent.com/pod-product-compliance
Lightning Source LLC
Chambersburg PA
CBHW051815090426
42736CB00011B/1487